REAL
IRISH
NEW
YORK

A ROGUE'S GALLERY OF FENIANS, TOUGH WOMEN, HOLY MEN, BLASPHEMERS, JESTERS, AND A GANG OF COLORFUL CHARACTERS

DERMOT McEVOY

Skyhorse Publishing

Skyhorse Publishing books may be purchased in bulk at special discounts for sales promotion, corporate gifts, fund-raising, or educational purposes. Special editions can also be created to specifications. For details, contact the Special Sales Department, Skyhorse Publishing, 307 West 36th Street, 11th Floor, New York, NY 10018 or info@skyhorsepublishing.com.

Skyhorse® and Skyhorse Publishing® are registered trademarks of Skyhorse Publishing, Inc.®, a Delaware corporation.

Visit our website at www.skyhorsepublishing.com.

10 9 8 7 6 5 4 3 2 1

Library of Congress Cataloging-in-Publication Data is available on file.

Cover design by Kai Texel

Print ISBN: 978-1-5107-3648-1
Ebook ISBN: 978-1-5107-3649-8

Printed in the United States of America

This book is dedicated to Judith Volkmann and her husband Neil Granger. No man has ever had better friends.

IN MEMORIAM

While writing this book three people very close to me died. Two nephews born two years apart died two years apart.

My nephew, William McEvoy, was a very spiritually gifted young man and he left us too soon.

Another nephew, Eugene (Geno) Cella, also left us. He was very proud of being half-Irish and was in the process of trying to get his Irish passport when he passed. Hopefully, there's a place for him in Fenian Heaven.

God love both of them.

And then there's my first cousin, Monsignor Vincent Bartley. Vince and I had a great relationship and whenever we were together there was nothing but laughter. He was the son of my Aunt Kathleen McEvoy Bartley—the matriarch of the McEvoy family—and a brave Irish revolutionary in her own right, a hostage and survivor of the North King Street Massacre in 1916 and later a member of the women's IRA's auxiliary, Cumann na mBan. When I was writing a book, Vincent was always the one I went to when I was writing about the Church. No one can imagine how much I miss him.

CONTENTS

INTRODUCTION

When I was a kid, my father's Italian friends used to brag about how Columbus discovered America. "But how about the Irish longshoreman who threw him the rope when he docked?" the old man would retort. He was going for the laugh, but he was also sending a message—the Irish were here in New York before you guys and they sure as hell weren't leaving now.

William Faulkner once wrote, "The past is never dead. It's not even past."

Especially when it comes to the Irish.

Those two statements, from my father and Faulkner, say a lot about the Irish and their relationship to New York City. Driven out of their homeland by the British, especially during the Great Famine of the 1840s, the Irish arrived in New York City with a bang. They were feared, hated, reviled, and told to go back from where they came by the WASP establishment. But that was impossible. They were stuck. And they were in America—and New York—to stay.

The first thing they had to overcome, just like in Ireland, was Protestant hegemony. They did not fit into the proper, orderly little Protestant pigeonhole that was designated for them. Let's face it, they were rambunctious Catholics. And out of Ireland, they would not do what the Protestants, the same Protestants who had stolen their land and tried to starve them to death back in the old country, wanted them to do.

This time they had someone on their side—the archbishop of New York, John Joseph Hughes. "Dagger John," as he was called, would take his feral countrymen and, like a good bishop, shepherd them. In the time of the Know-Nothings—nativists who mirrored the Make America Great Again gang of today who want to keep other ethnic groups out of *their* America—Hughes knew how to fight fear with fear. Bullies don't really like a fight, and if there is one thing about the Irish, they will fight. Check out the lyrics to their national anthem. In New York City, at least, the Know-Nothings would not be putting match to Catholic churches for sport. They knew better.

Every decade would bring a new challenge. The 1860s brought the Civil War. The Irish were ambivalent. They did not like the abolitionist Republican party because of their anti-Irish bias. But they saw an opportunity in war, and, as the Know-Nothings found out, they would fight for their new country, the United States of America. Without them, the Union would have been lost.

After the Civil War was over, many Union soldiers went back to Ireland to fight in the Rebellion of 1867, an unmitigated disaster for these "Fenians." A few years later, out of jail and forced out of their own country again, the Fenians would find refuge in—where else?—New York City. The two most prominent, John Devoy and Jeremiah O'Donovan Rossa, would stay in New York and fight for an independent Ireland with great success.

The Irish began to rise. Archbishop Hughes had set up his own Catholic infrastructure—schools, hospitals, orphanages, universities—and the Irish did not have to depend on Protestant hegemony anymore. Their system was just as good, if not better, than the services rendered to the rest of the citizens of New York.

After the Civil War, most of the ships in Manhattan, as my father had hinted, were loaded and unloaded by Irish longshoremen. And these stevedores, many Irish speakers, put their imprint on their backbreaking profession. They called their job "*Loingseoir.*" ("Lung" is the Irish word for "boat.") It became corrupted by English speakers, and that's how anyone who works with ships became what we know today as "longshoremen." The Irish were already putting their own unique stamp on their city.

Soon they were more than longshoremen. They were teachers, priests, nuns, lawyers, doctors, and, through the magic of Tammany Hall, politicians. They were cops and judges, and their politicians, like Al Smith and Jimmy Walker, were running the city and the state.

But they did not forget Ireland. John Devoy, a Fenian felon refugee, was an extraordinary mentor of revolution. Under his guidance, prominent men—and martyrs—of the 1916 Easter Rising were nurtured, like Tom Clarke and Sir Roger Casement. Jeremiah O'Donovan Rossa engineered his dynamite campaign from Staten Island and, in his final salute to Ireland, was returned home after death to light the match in August 1915 to the blaze that would become the Easter Rebellion. Without the guidance and money from New York, there would have been no War of Independence. Eamon de Valera found refuge in New York as Michael Collins wiped out the British Secret Service, making way for the Anglo-Irish Treaty of 1921. When the North ignited again in the 1960s, New York once again became a focal point for gunrunning, money, and political agitation. And the Good Friday Agreement that finally brought peace to Northern Ireland had its genesis in the Big Apple.

Some of the Irish became Cardinals, others gangsters. Margaret Sanger took another direction and created Planned Parenthood. A man like Mike Quill, in the tradition of Jim Larkin and James Connolly, ran the transport union. Elizabeth Gurley Flynn agitated from the left. Dorothy Day inspired with the Catholic Worker Movement, and acolytes such as Michael Harrington went on to pique the soul of America and the Kennedy brothers with *The Other America*. W. R. Grace became the first Irish Catholic mayor of New York City while guys like George M. Cohan and James Cagney paved the way for wise guys like George Carlin from White Harlem. There were writers like Jimmy Breslin, Pete Hamill, Joe Flaherty, and Frank McCourt. Fighters for the liberal cause included Paul O'Dwyer from County Mayo and a millionaire from Boston named Bobby Kennedy who tried to save a Brooklyn ghetto called Bedford-Stuyvesant. There were Westies and bank robbers like Willie Sutton and cold-stone killers like "Mad Dog" Coll, born Uinseann Ó Colla in County Donegal. They were all part of Irish New York.

Another Irishman, journalist Peter Finley Dunne, who also made New York his home, famously said, "Comfort the afflicted and afflict the comfortable." Most of the Irishmen and women I've mentioned agreed with that sentiment—to the extreme. Irish New York's imprint would be worldwide, but it all started at the mouth of the Hudson River in the greatest city in the world—the *Real* Irish New York.

PART ONE

FENIAN NEW YORK

WHEN IRISH EXILES NEEDED A HOME THEY LOOKED TO THE BIG APPLE

Fenian—A member of an Irish revolutionary movement organization that advocated an independent republic.
—THE RANDOM HOUSE COLLEGE DICTIONARY

Fenian—an elite—albeit usually unsuccessful—Irish Revolutionary
—DERMOT MCEVOY

There is no doubt in my mind that without New York City there would be no Republic of Ireland today. Without the money, political influence, and hospitality New York—the original sanctuary city—provided for Ireland's failed revolutionaries, independence would have been impossible.

New York has always been a refuge for Irish rebels, going back to the United Irishmen, who led the Risings of 1798 and 1803. Thomas Addis Emmet was banished after the 1798 insurrection and imprisoned. In 1803 his brother, Robert Emmet, was apprehended in the abortive 1803 scuffle and sentenced to death. From the dock before his execution he left behind a legacy in words that would beat in Irish hearts for the next century:

Let no man write my epitaph; for as no man who knows my motives dare now vindicate them, let not prejudice or ignorance, asperse them. Let them and me rest in obscurity and peace, and my tomb remain uninscribed, and my memory in oblivion, until other times and other men can do justice to my character. When my country takes her place among the nations of the earth, *then and not till then*, let my epitaph be written. I have done.[1]

Thomas Emmet, who was living in Paris and acting as an agent to Napoleon for his brother, fled to New York and joined the bar. He was attorney general of New York state from August 1812 until February 1813, when he was removed by the Federalist Party. He became one of the most prominent jurists in the city and was called by United States Supreme Court Justice Joseph Story to be "the favourite counsellor of New York." Emmet died in 1827 and was buried in the churchyard attached to St. Mark's-in-the-Bowery.

Even William Theobald Wolfe Tone, son of Wolfe Tone, martyr of the 1798 Rebellion, found refuge in New York after the Battle of Waterloo. He died there in 1828 and is buried in Green-Wood Cemetery in Brooklyn.

Perhaps the most prominent Irish refugee before the Civil War was Thomas Francis Meagher. Meagher, one of the leaders of the Young Ireland movement along with the likes of Thomas Davis, William Smith O'Brien, John Mitchel, and Lady Jane Wilde, Oscar's mother, found himself deported to Australia after the skirmish called the Rising of 1848. By 1852 he had escaped to New York and by the time of the Civil War he had President Lincoln's ear as he personally raised the Irish Brigade, the famous "Fighting 69th" Regiment, which shed its blood at such battles as Antietam, Fredericksburg, and Chancellorsville.

The Great Famine in the 1840s forced millions of Irish out of Ireland, initially flooding the big cities of the East Coast of America, especially New York and Boston. New York became a popular target for settlement because it already had an Irish population and a strong leader in the aforementioned Archbishop "Dagger" John Hughes. These refugees came for food and jobs, but they never forgot Ireland. In fact, pushing the Irish out of Ireland would, in less than seventy-five years, help push the British out of what is now the Republic of Ireland.

THE FENIAN BROTHERHOOD

In 1858 James Stephens established the Irish Republican Brotherhood in Ireland. It was a secret organization pledged to freeing Ireland from Britain by physical force. The following year in New York City, John O'Mahony, a veteran of the Young Ireland movement who had been exiled as a Fenian felon, opened a sister organization, the Fenian Brotherhood. This was to be the beginning of New York as a hotbed of anti-British activity, which would last through the establishment of the Irish Free State in 1922.

Many New York Irish fought for the Union in the Civil War. O'Mahony, like Meagher with the "Fighting 69th," organized a regiment of the New York National Guard (the 99th) composed entirely of Fenians. The Civil War proved a tough training ground for many Fenians, and after the war they put their training to use, returning to Ireland to fight in the Rising of 1867. They were betrayed by informers, and many of them were arrested as they got off the boat in Ireland, revealed by their Union Army–issued boots, of all things.

JOHN DEVOY, FENIAN PIED PIPER, RULES FROM NEW YORK

The failure of the '67 Rising would see many Fenians imprisoned by the British. One of those felons was John Devoy, who after jail time, finally made his way to New York in 1871 (along with Jeremiah O'Donovan Rossa). He soon became active in Clan na Gael, the successor to the Fenian Brotherhood.

It was from this base in New York that Devoy organized the voyage of the *Catalpa* in 1876, which freed imprisoned Fenians from an Australian penal colony. The story of the *Catalpa* is one fraught with drama and high-seas adventure. Devoy called on the expertise of former Clan na Gael member John Boyle O'Reilly, then a newspaper editor and poet residing in Boston. O'Reilly was an old friend of Devoy's and a former Fenian felon himself who had escaped from a penal colony in Australia via whaler ship. O'Reilly, according to Devoy, offered "invaluable co-operation" as he put Devoy in touch with the proper people to implement the audacious procedure and offered key insider advice. In a thrilling ending worthy of an Errol Flynn swashbuckler, the freed Fenians escaped a British warship by hoisting the Stars and Stripes: "My flag protects me," said the *Catalpa*'s captain, "if you fire on this ship you fire on the American flag!" Devoy called the mission a success because of "a combination of Irish skill and pluck and Yankee grit." O'Reilly congratulated Devoy, declaring: "All credit belongs to you, old man. Soon the world will know what you have brought about." With this daring Michael Collins–esque escape, Devoy began to attract prominent Irish rebels to New York.

Probably the most important rebel to arrive in New York during this time was Thomas Clarke. Clarke emigrated in the early 1880s. He became an American citizen in Brooklyn in 1883. (He would become the only American citizen executed by the British in 1916. His citizenship certificate can be viewed at the National Library at Collins Barracks in Dublin.) He left New York to take part in Rossa's ill-conceived "Dynamite Campaign" and subsequently spent fifteen years in British dungeons. Upon his release, he returned to New York and struck up a strong, lifelong friendship with Devoy. In 1901 he married Kathleen Daly in New York. John MacBride— another 1916 martyr—was best man and Devoy was also a member of the wedding party. The newlyweds were true New Yorkers, living in Manhattan, the Bronx, and Brooklyn. "New York was as new and interesting to me as anywhere else in America," Kathleen wrote in her autobiography, *Revolutionary Woman*. Tom was instrumental in the start-up of Devoy's newspaper, the *Gaelic American*. Eventually the Clarkes moved to Long Island to run a farm. But the thought of an impending war between the British and Germany moved them back to Dublin in 1907. He opened a tobacconist shop on the corner of Parnell and Sackville (O'Connell) Streets, under the shadow of the Parnell Monument, where every young Irish revolutionary—such as Seán MacDiarmada, Patrick Pearse, Joseph Mary Plunkett, and even Michael Collins—would journey to discuss treason. The strong bond that Clarke and Devoy had forged in New York would play a vital part in the coming rebellion.

Another Irish expatriate who was under Devoy's sphere of influence was John Kenny from County Kildare. Kenny was a brilliant businessman and a member of Clan na Gael, for which he served as president on several occasions. He was instrumental in the rescue of the Fenian felons from Australia during the *Catalpa* adventure and kept his maritime interests alive with the financing of one of the first attack submarine prototypes, John Holland's *Fenian Ram*. (The *Fenian Ram* survives and can be viewed at the Patterson Museum in New Jersey. It is probably the only nonyellow submarine to have a song written about it—"The Great Fenian Ram" by the Wolfe Tones.) Kenny was also active in the Land League, which was organized in the late nineteenth century to help impoverished Irish landowners and was headed by Charles Stewart Parnell.

He swore Tom Clarke into the Clan na Gael and was responsible for choosing Clarke for a "special mission" in England, which turned out to be a bombing attempt on London Bridge, for which Clarke did hard time. Years later, when Clarke resigned his position on the *Gaelic American*, Kenny took over as business manager. With the outbreak of the Great War, Kenny traveled to Europe, hoping to involve Germany in Ireland's fight for freedom. (The intelligence he gathered was passed on to Sir Roger Casement back in New York.) In the two years leading up to 1916, he served as a courier of money between New York and Dublin, knowing all the key players involved. He died in New York in 1924.

O'DONOVAN ROSSA: "SEND HIS BODY HOME"

On June 29, 1915, Jeremiah O'Donovan Rossa, the old Fenian, died on Staten Island. Legend has it that Devoy wired Clarke in Dublin, "Rossa dead. What should I do?"

Clarke replied: "Send his body home at once!" Thus began the long, final, and heroic journey of Jeremiah O'Donovan Rossa.

Like a lot of the Fenians, Rossa was a very tough character. His family in West Cork was fairly comfortable until the time of the famine, which destroyed it. It was the trigger that set him afire with nationalism. The odd thing about Rossa is that he never got to fight in any of Ireland's battles. As plans were being made for a rising in 1865—it was postponed until 1867—he was arrested in Dublin and sent to British prisons, where, under brutal conditions, he would live for the next five years. He was freed in an amnesty and sailed for America, arriving in 1871 with Devoy, who he had met in prison.

Rossa's personal life was as complicated as his political one. He was married three times, with his first two wives dying at a young age. In all, he fathered eighteen children. In America he was famous for the dynamite campaign, which tried to blow up prominent British landmarks during the 1880s. Ironically, one of his bombers was Tom Clarke, who would be a central character in his final sendoff. During his time in New York he challenged the Fenian John Daly to a duel which never took place. He was also shot by a deranged British woman named Dudley because of his dynamite campaign but survived to live another thirty years.

When Rossa died, Clarke said, "If Rossa had planned to die at the most opportune time for serving his country, he could not have done better."

In one of the great shows of nationalistic theater, Clarke paraded the body around Dublin as if he had found the Fenian Lazarus. (Devoy once said: "No matter how the Irish treat a leader when living—and the treatment is often very bad—they never fail to give him decent burial.") This idea of using the honored dead as props might have led the British to bury the executed 1916 leaders in a quicklime mass grave to avoid propaganda. Rossa laid in state at the City Hall and was given a funeral mass at the Pro Cathedral. Thousands followed his coffin to Glasnevin Cemetery on August 1, when Patrick Pearse gave his famous speech: "the fools, the fools, the fools!—They have left us our Fenian dead, and while Ireland holds these graves, Ireland unfree shall never be at peace." Rossa's funeral was the unofficial launch to what would become the Easter Rising eight months later.

EAMON DE VALERA HITS NEW YORK—AGAIN

In one of the most bizarre moves in Irish revolutionary history, Eamon de Valera left Dublin in May 1919 for a twenty-month stay in America. (In a parallel historical situation, this would be like George Washington saying in 1776: "I'll see you guys in two years!") It was the first time he had visited the city of his birth in nearly forty years. He arrived in New York in June and was feted by Devoy and company at the old Waldorf Astoria hotel on 34th Street (on what is now the site of the Empire State Building). De Valera's rationale for leaving his country in a time of revolution was to bring Ireland's cause to the attention of the world and to raise money for the emerging nation. (He left the dirty work of revolution back home to the minister for finance, one Michael Collins, who quickly learned how to terrorize the British terrorists.)

At first, Devoy and de Valera got on famously. Devoy even went so far as to comment that Dev was "the best leader that Ireland has had for a century." But things began to sour when philosophical questions arose between the Irish Americans and de Valera, particularly during the American presidential race of 1920. Also, questions about how the national loan should be solicited had the two sides butting heads. The National Loan was a bond organized by finance minister Michael Collins to raise money in Ireland and America for the nascent revolution in Ireland. If de Valera thought he was going to come to New York, act like a dilettante, and order John Devoy around, he had another think coming. By August 1920 Devoy was calling de Valera "the most malignant man in all Irish history!" The Fenian honeymoon was definitely over.

Relations between Devoy and de Valera became so toxic that Devoy started referring to Michael Collins in the *Gaelic American* as "the recognized leader of the fighting men of Ireland" (inferring that de Valera was sitting on his arse, living it up at the Waldorf—which, to a great extent, he was!). Terry Golway wrote in his Devoy biography *Irish Rebel* that "Devoy would later write that had it been up to him, he'd have had de Valera shot rather than waste the government's time and money with a mere prison sentence." Coincidentally, one month and two days after Collins's Squad shot up the British Secret Service in Dublin, de Valera returned to Dublin, perhaps thinking that the tide of the war had turned on the side of the rebels—and they would need him to make peace. Once again, Dev's narcissistic timing was impeccable.

DEVOY: PRO-TREATY TO THE END

John Devoy, perhaps because of his great admiration for Michael Collins (and antipathy toward de Valera), was strongly pro-treaty. He returned home to Ireland for a hero's welcome in 1924, feted by the government of William T. Cosgrave. He would die while on vacation in Atlantic City, New Jersey, on September 29, 1928. He was given a state funeral in Dublin and buried in the appropriately named "Republican Plot" of Glasnevin Cemetery, just two graves from his old friend and antagonist, Jeremiah O'Donovan Rossa.

The road to Irish independence—which seemed to wind its way through New York—was a long and tenuous one, stretching from the 1867 Fenian Rising to the establishment of the Irish Free State in 1922. It can be safely said that without the help of America—and in particular John Devoy and his New York allies—Ireland, today, would still be part of the United Kingdom. America and New York not only gave shelter to innumerable Fenian felons, but also raised millions in funds that brought everything for the nationalistic movement, from propaganda to guns and bullets. New Yorker—and he was a real dyed-in-the-wool New Yorker—John Devoy devoted his life to Ireland, albeit in exile three thousand miles from home. In the annals of Irish history, he is ranked at the top of the Fenian hierarchy and as Patrick Pearse noted in 1915, he was, without a doubt, "The greatest of the Fenians."

CHAPTER ONE

FENIAN ODD COUPLE

THE UNLIKELY FRIENDSHIP OF JOHN DEVOY AND SIR ROGER CASEMENT

They say that politics makes for strange bedfellows. Well, two of the oddest ducks to share the same Fenian bed were Sir Roger Casement—executed for his part in the Easter Rising—and John Devoy. If you read Irish history, you would be led to believe that Devoy, the leader of Fenianism in the United States at the time of the Rising, probably loathed Casement.

You could not find two men more different in background: Casement—Protestant, knighted for his work in the British Foreign Service, and a latecomer to the nationalist movement—and Devoy—Catholic, imprisoned before the Rising of 1867, and banished to America.

Devoy became the driving force behind the new militant nationalism that spread throughout Ireland through the Gaelic League and the eventual establishment of the Irish Volunteers. Devoy supplied money and ideas to keep the movement afloat. He also nurtured and groomed rebels in exile in New York—like 1916 martyr Tom Clarke—for their return to Ireland.

Devoy did not meet Casement until 1914 when he was seventy-four. By that time Devoy had failing hearing and eyesight

Based on comments from those on the Irish side of the Atlantic, you would think that Devoy and Casement shared no common ground. "Casement had come into things national," Kathleen Clarke, Tom's widow, recalled in her autobiography, *Revolutionary Woman*, "and Tom knew very little about him. Naturally, he had no cause to place much confidence in him; and the fact that he had been knighted by England in recognition of services rendered made Tom suspicious of him. Casement was not long enough in nationalist things in this country to prove his genuineness."

Joseph Plunkett's sister Geraldine's opinion was brutally stark: "John Devoy simply hated him," she wrote in her autobiography, *All in the Blood*.

With the outbreak of the Great War, Casement landed in New York, living at the St. George Hotel in Brooklyn Heights. Devoy was suspicious of Casement because he sided with John Redmond, the leader of the Irish Parliamentary Party, in Redmond's takeover of the Irish Volunteers in 1914. This may have also been the reason why Tom Clarke didn't trust Casement and it wouldn't be a shock if Clarke relayed this opinion to his old friend, Devoy, in New York.

Oddly enough, Devoy's autobiography, *Recollections of an Irish Rebel*, shows an affection for Casement that one would not expect from the tough old Fenian jailbird. The book was not published until a year after Devoy's death in 1928. (The interesting thing about the book is that it basically stops after the Easter Rising. There is not one mention of Eamon de Valera, Michael Collins, or the Treaty.)

Although he was suspicious of Casement because of the John Redmond/Irish Volunteers fiasco and highly skeptical of his plan to seek German help for the coming uprising, Devoy introduced Casement to his German contacts (Franz von Papen—future stooge of Adolf Hitler—was a prime New York contact for Devoy), gave him an immense amount of money (probably in excess of $10,000), and packed him off to Europe.

Devoy did so with reservations because he did not trust Casement's traveling companion, one Adler Christensen. "[I] missed the fact," wrote Devoy in his autobiography, "that the acquaintance between the two was only of a few weeks' duration. Had I understood that, I would have objected strongly to Christensen's going as Sir Roger's companion."

It is thought that Christensen might have been a British agent, maybe a German agent, or even a double agent playing both sides. He may also have been Casement's lover. "Christiansen . . . double-crossed us," said Devoy, "[and] proved himself a trickster and a fraud."

Devoy is blunt in his assessment of Casement and his work in Germany.:

Casement's mission to Germany had three main objects: First, to secure German military help for Ireland when the opportunity offered. Second, to educate German public opinion on the Irish situation, so that the people would stand behind their Government when it took action in favor of Ireland. Third, to organize, if possible, Irish prisoners of war into a military unit to take part in the fight for Irish freedom. Casement did his best in all these things, but did the first ineffectively, succeeded admirably in the second, and failed badly in the third.

Devoy may have been old, frail and crotchety, but he was an excellent judge of character. While Tom Clarke may have been suspicious of Casement's motives—he probably thought him a British agent—Devoy took Casement for what he was—a true patriot—with a strong shake of salt:

> While a highly intellectual man, Casement was very emotional and as trustful as a child. He was also obsessed with the idea that he was a better judge than any of us, at either side of the Atlantic, of what ought to be done (though he was too polite and good natured to say so), and he never hesitated to act on his own responsibility, fully believing that his decisions were in the best interests of Ireland's Cause. This created many difficulties and embarrassments for us.

"Practical politics he did not understand," wrote Devoy, "but the end to which the practical politician, the statesman and the soldier should devote their efforts he understood most thoroughly. He was an idealist, absolutely without personal ambition, ready to sacrifice his interests and his life for the cause he had at heart, but was too sensitive about the consequences to others of his actions."

When Casement was in London awaiting trial, Devoy selflessly donated $5,000 he had just inherited from his brother's estate in New Mexico to Casement's defense. In his autobiography he slammed the British for their whispering campaign about the "Black Diaries," Casement's supposedly notoriously graphic descriptions of his homosexual romps on two continents—which may or may not have been a fabrication of the British Secret Service—as "foul and slanderous propaganda to arouse public opinion in America against him."

He wrote of Casement's demise at the end of a rope on August 3, 1916: "Thus ended the career of one of Ireland's noblest sons. . . . [H]e was withal one of the most sincere and single-minded of Ireland's patriot sons with whom it was my great privilege to be associated. His name will ever have a revered place on the long roll of martyrs who gave their lives that Ireland might be free."

CHAPTER TWO

FENIAN LETTERS FROM NEW YORK

THE LETTERS OF NORA CONNOLLY AND LIAM MELLOWS HIGHLIGHT REBELS IN EXILE

I rish American writer Rosemary Mahoney's (*For the Benefit of Whose Who See, Down the Nile,* and *Whoredom in Kimmage,* among others) family was highly politicized at the time of the Easter Rising. "My maternal grandmother, Julia Fraher," Mahoney told me, "and her five sisters, who had recently emigrated from County Limerick to Boston, were serious Sinn Féiners, my grandmother most of all. She was a member of Cumann na mBan. She donated money to the Irish Republican Brotherhood to help them buy arms and campaigned at all the Boston meetings for a free Ireland. She knew everybody in the cause. Many involved in the Easter Rising, in one way or another, stayed at their house in Dorchester, Massachusetts. Julia must have been in her mid-twenties at this time. Not married yet."

Not only did they stay at Julia Fraher's house, but they also wrote her letters from their bases in New York. Some of the letter writers included Nora Connolly and Liam Mellows. The letters are filled with the mundane, but also the poignancies of the time.

NORA CONNOLLY, the daughter of 1916 martyr James Connolly, wrote in July 1917 from her apartment on Vanderbilt Avenue in Brooklyn, and her homesickness is obvious: "It was just a year ago that I left Mama and got away. It seems years now." Maybe her homesickness had something to do with her opinion of New York: "New York is an ugly horrible place. Anyone who prefers New York to Boston must be mad." She goes on to gloat over Eamon de Valera's victory in the Clare by-election and mentions a mutual friend: "I saw Liam Mellows on Monday. He is looking well but horribly Yankeefied."

In August she wrote again, voicing a common summer lament from Irish immigrants: "I cannot write to you now as much as I would wish because I am simply dying with the heat." On a more serious note she laments the death of Muriel MacDonagh, wife of 1916 patriot Thomas, who was drowned in a tragic swimming accident: "Wasn't that dreadful news about Mrs. MacDonagh? Just think of the two little ones left without father or mother." In June 1918 Connolly was heading for home and obviously worried about German U-boats: "Dear folks won't you pray that we reach home safely," and she adds a bit of Fenian gossip also: "Mrs. [Hanna Sheehy-] Skeffington is sailing on the same boat."

LIAM MELLOWS led men in the west during the Rising and escaped to New York, where he was jailed for his support of Germany during the Great War. He would return to Ireland and act as director of supplies during the War of Independence. He went against the Treaty and was captured when the Four Courts in Dublin fell to Pro-Treaty forces. Jailed, he was murdered by the Free State in retaliation for the murder of Seán Hales, TD, Teachta Dála, a member of the Irish parliament.

In April 1918 he wrote to Julia and is delighted about the news from home: "Everything at home looks well. It's laughable to see the hierarchy advocating strikes & John Dillon embracing Sinn Féin." He celebrated a special anniversary: "Do you know that today is the anniversary of the beginning of that week in 1916? I see by a paper from home that Galway was ablaze with bonfires on Easter Saturday night. That's grand."

In June Mellows (who signed his letters in the Irish: "O'Maeliosa") offers his condolences to Julia on the death of her mother, but the discussion soon turns to brutal politics: "Well, God rest her soul. Who knows but that it is all for the best. She would feel so bad if she lived long enough to witness the trying—indeed terrible times—that are coming. God help us all & give *us* the courage & faith to endure & the people at home the strength to suffer, for we are on the verge of impending & terrible events. But we can win. That I do not doubt. To doubt it is to lose & we cannot lose for the hand of God is with us & He can triumph over the poor efforts of mortal men."

By August there is a familiar Irish lament in the letter: "It must be the heat, and sure that is enough to drive anyone—like the cows in summer with the gadflys—mad." But the talk soon turns to politics and the dreaded threat of conscription: "The people at home are sticking [or striking] out well, but they expect Conscription the end of October, then—God help us all."

By January 1919 Mellows was living on West 96th Street in Manhattan and worried about cases of influenza and pneumonia that were striking family and friends on both sides of the Atlantic. But politics was always in the forefront as he mentions being elected a TD to the first *Dáil*: "Everything goes well in Ireland—the spirit is wonderful, as the results of the election has shown. . . . You will see by it that your humble servant has been elected to two seats [Galway East and North Meath]. The whole thing came as a surprise to me; unsought and unwanted. God give us all the strength, wisdom, & principle to do what is right."

He speaks of his adventures at the White House: "Diarmuid [Lynch] and myself paid a visit to Washington six weeks or so go and called at the White House to see the President [Woodrow Wilson] to present a demand from the people of Ireland for representation at the 'Peace' Conference. His Lordship was not home, but we left the 'scrap of paper' and bowed ourselves out of the august presence of his secretary's secretary. Some style, eh!" His spirits remain high: "As the Yanks in New York say— 'Safety foist' "

In August 1919 Mellows was living at 220 East 31st Street in Manhattan and was congratulating Julia on her marriage to Michael Rohan: "I hope you are happy in your new home and that Michael is as kind and loving a husband he was before the great event in Boston." But the talk quickly turned political: "The President [Eamon de Valera] will speak in Baltimore but I don't know exactly when as his tour is not yet mapped out completely. He returned from California yesterday delighted with the result of his trip."

CHAPTER THREE
NIALL O'DOWD

FENIAN NEW YORK—HOPEFULLY— ENDS WITH THE MAN WHO ORCHESTRATED THE GOOD FRIDAY AGREEMENT

John Devoy arrived on American shores in 1871, and Niall O'Dowd arrived in 1978. Although a hundred years apart, their similarities don't end there. Both chose the same professional—journalism—to help their people.

Devoy had the *Gaelic American* to promote his Fenian ideas. O'Dowd, first stationed in San Francisco, started by launching the *Irishman* newspaper with $952 he put together with the help of his friend Tom McDonagh. When O'Dowd moved to New York he started *Irish America*, the first Irish American glossy magazine. He followed this by creating the *Irish Voice*, which was aimed mostly at young Irish immigrants. In the age of the Internet he founded IrishCentral.com, which today commands four million plus monthly readers. One thinks that Devoy would be impressed by O'Dowd's entrepreneurial workmanship.

Without Devoy, there would be no Republic of Ireland today. Without O'Dowd, there still might be a raging war in Northern Ireland and the possible eventual reunification of both North and South would be impossible. O'Dowd's actions on the Good Friday Agreement, now threatened by Brexit, made the peace that is Ireland today possible.

I asked O'Dowd how he feels about being compared to the old Fenian? "Devoy is a personal hero," O'Dowd told me in an interview, "a man who gave his whole life to Irish freedom. There would have been no Easter Rising without him and he understood the American role like no other before him. He was a rebel in the truest sense. He was a key figure in the Fenian rising, the 1916 Rising, and the War of

Independence. He refused to buckle to de Valera and understood his evil machinations in America. Most importantly, Devoy met Charles Stewart Parnell and encouraged a 'New Departure,' the attempt to solidify and align constitutional and physical force nationalism aided by America. It was the exact same template that Hume-Adams-Clinton created over a century later. I long believed that the modern New Departure based on the Devoy model was the key to creating the Irish peace process."

The key to the Good Friday Agreement was President Bill Clinton. O'Dowd was early in his recognition of Clinton as someone who would be sympathetic to the nationalist cause in Ireland. "What attracted me most was he wasn't George Herbert Walker Bush who had shown no interest during his time in office in Ireland," said O'Dowd bluntly. "We knew Clinton had been to Oxford during the Irish Civil Rights movement and was interested in the issue. He was also a clean slate, a new face with little to fear from taking on the issue. I was frankly amazed about how much he knew when I first met him. What people miss is his incredible mind and ability to see the next move on the chessboard before anyone else."

Clinton, the master politician, also knew that the Irish peace process was a winning political issue for him. "He was keenly aware of the importance of the issue to Irish Americans in key states such as Pennsylvania and Ohio," said O'Dowd. "He understood there wasn't an Irish vote per se but a huge fount of goodwill for any American who took on what seemed a thankless task in Northern Ireland. It was post the Cold War, the alleged end of history, the South Africa and Israeli peace processes were underway, and Ireland was about to have its moment. It could never have happened during the Cold War or after 9/11, but there was a critical decade when there were relatively speaking, no huge pressing foreign policy problems. It was an inspired choice by an uber politician."

CLINTON SUFFERS "IRISH ALZHEIMER'S"

Probably the most accurate joke about the Irish ever is "Irish Alzheimer's—they forget everything except the grudges!" It seems Bill Clinton has also inherited this gene. British Prime Minister John Major tried to help President Bush in the 1992 election by probing what Clinton was doing in Britain when he was a Rhodes Scholar there. (Current US Attorney General William Barr, then Bush's AG—obviously boning up for his Trump tricks of the future—was behind the Clinton probe.) Clinton never forgave Bush. How important did O'Dowd think this factored in Clinton's taking on the Irish issue? "I think it was a factor but not a huge one," replied O'Dowd. "Clinton was already ready to act, and Major's foolishness just added some fuel to the fire."

The fingerprints of the Kennedy family are all over Clinton's Irish policy. One of the first important things was the appointment of Senator Ted Kennedy's sister, Jean Kennedy Smith, to be Clinton's new ambassador to Ireland. "Incredibly important," said O'Dowd. "For decades the job had mostly been the retirement home for rich old farts utterly uninterested in getting involved up North. Kennedy Smith took on the State Department and the British government and finally ensured that the Irish voice was heard. She took risks for peace, traveled North, met Adams, pushed for a visa and special envoy, got Joe Cahill a visa against all the odds. Could not have happened without her."

Conversely, even with Kennedy Smith in place, not every Irish American politician, regardless of party affiliation, was behind the program to break the deadlock on Northern Ireland. One such important person was House Speaker Tom Foley who, according to Conor O'Clery in his exciting book on the peace process, *Daring Diplomacy*, was an "Anglophile."

"Foley was so busy kissing British butt that he completely failed to read the signs even though folks like Ted Kennedy warned him change was coming," O'Dowd candidly put it. "He was the worst kind of Irishman, England's favorite pet. I hold him in complete contempt. I mean even Daniel Patrick Moynihan came around." Foley soon lost his seat in the 1994 Republican takeover of the House. So, Newt Gingrich gets some undue credit here too.

One of the least appreciated men involved in the Good Friday Agreement was Taoiseach [the name for the Irish Prime Minister] Albert Reynolds. I asked O'Dowd why he gets such short shrift for his efforts in pursuit of peace. "You are completely right," O'Dowd replied. "I think it was the ignominious way he was forced out of office just a few months later that tarred him. He was a clear example of the right man at the right time first and foremost a pragmatic businessman ready to do a deal on a transactional basis and to hell with ideology. He saw it as a problem to solve not to admire its difficulty as so many mainstream politicians did. He deserves better from history."

Several men put their reputations on the line to move the peace process forward. Without these men—Senator Teddy Kennedy, former Congressman Bruce Morrison, businessmen Bill Flynn and Chuck Feeney—there would have been no Good Friday

Agreement. "Kennedy was the gatekeeper to the Irish issue on Capitol Hill," said O'Dowd. "Nothing moved without his say so. He was a loyal decent man who stepped back and let Clinton have all the glory but his call on approving the Adams visa was the key, allowing Clinton to grant it. That was the singular moment when the pendulum swung from centuries of acquiescence to British policy on Northern Ireland to taking up an approved Irish position. The British never knew what hit them.

"Bruce Morrison was always the smartest politician in the room," continued O'Dowd. "He understood the nuances of Northern Irish politics which is a minefield and never made a mistake as spokesman for the Irish American delegation. He was a rock star in Ireland because of the Morrison Visas which allowed forty thousand Irish to immigrate legally.

"Bill Flynn provided a powerful legitimacy as a leading business figure," said O'Dowd. "He was the exact opposite of the stereotypical drunken plastic Paddy putting dollars in the tin can. In addition, he forged a powerful link with the Loyalists and got them included in every major delegation to America. He was chairman of the National Committee on American Foreign Policy which allowed the perfect platform to invite Adams to speak to. He and his successor Tom Moran at Mutual of America were vital figures in presenting a new and different face of Irish America.

"Chuck Feeney," said O'Dowd, "is an incredible character: a multi-billionaire who gave it all away. His presence made it much easier to bring other business leaders on board as he was a legendary figure, and everyone wanted to know him. He was the best reader of intentions I ever met, knew instinctively what people were planning and thinking. I began to believe he could see around corners. I came to rely heavily on that insight before major meetings. When push came to shove, and Sinn Féin wanted one million dollars to set up a DC office as part of the deal he immediately said 'yes.' I think I picked the only businessman in the world who would have so answered. His philanthropic donations to Ireland North and South runs into the billions. He transformed the educational system North and South at university level, and he played a key role in achieving peace."

O'DOWD GOES CLOAK & DAGGER

Soon after Clinton's election, O'Dowd became the point man between the IRA and the White House. I asked how he got drafted into the cloak and dagger world of espionage that led to the Good Friday Agreement? "I drafted myself as no one else seemed to be doing anything," he told me. "I had created Irish Americans for Clinton after a meeting with the candidate. I was aware from my sources that there were major discussions going on within the IRA about future strategy in the wake of the election of Bobby Sands and the political support that engendered. I thought it was time to put a new strategy together."

Soon O'Dowd found himself having surreptitious meetings with IRA contacts. One of the first was with "Ted" at Wynn's Hotel on Lower Abbey Street in Dublin. "Ted Howell was the Quiet Man behind much of the Sinn Féin/IRA strategy and responsible for America," O'Dowd remembered. "He was at the level of Adams and [Martin] McGuinness, but incredibly low key. I had been told that convincing him was vital. I quickly learned that was true. We met in Wynn's Hotel off O'Connell Street, a highly unlikely place to be spotted, frequented mainly by up-from-the-country shoppers. I put it to him that Clinton's election opened up a huge new vista for them, but they needed to show they were serious. I suggested an American delegation I would put together and an outreach to them with the blessing of the new White House. In return, the IRA should show their good intentions with a ten-day ceasefire. Long term I told them I thought I could deliver a US visa for Gerry Adams."

Being the intermediary between the IRA and the White House resulted in some harrowing experiences. "[I was] picked up in my hotel once by a driver to go to a clandestine meeting," O'Dowd recalled. "He never uttered a word, just drove at speed, dodging up side streets doubling back, constantly checking his mirror. We drove through a loyalist area and for a terrible ten minutes I thought he was from the UDA or UVF and I had been kidnapped. I almost wept with relief when we hurtled back into a nationalist area. On another occasion I was followed late at night from Belfast to the Irish border by a car with its headlights full on right behind me the entire way, slowing when I slowed, accelerating when I did. At the Ballygawley Roundabout, close to the border, I signaled I was exiting, but drove around again and drove to the village and lost them."

WINNING TRUST

Both sides, the IRA and the White House, were suspicious of each other. One of O'Dowd's jobs was winning the trust and confidence of both. O'Dowd found that being totally truthful was the best policy. He succeeded "by always telling the truth about what I thought I could do, about what the true situation was, and about what I thought they both needed to do. I tried to be as honest as possible, you learned quick the Provos did not do exaggeration or BS. Likewise, the White House wanted solutions, not more problems. The hardest part with them was IRA activity on the run-up to the ceasefire, especially dummy bombs at Heathrow. I had to explain this was good news in that it meant they were signaling strength not weakness before the ceasefire. It was not easy. A huge problem was language. The IRA talked and thought like an army, clear concise, objectives known. Clinton was a jazz singer, improvising brilliantly as he went along. I had to interpret one side for the other, often for hours."

The biggest obstacle to getting a visa for Gerry Adams was the State Department, which was staunchly against it. "The British had had it their own way for centuries when it came to Ireland and their 'special relationship' with the U.S. seemed eternal. They had long dismissed Irish Americans as rabble-rousers, so I was happy about that—we sneaked up on them."

According to *Daring Diplomacy* by Conor O'Clery, one of the most interesting things O'Dowd ever said about the British, Clinton and the peace process is that "there were no votes in the British position." In other words, there were no votes in supporting the British position on Ireland. "There is no British American ethnic constituency while in key election states like Ohio, Pennsylvania, Michigan, and New Hampshire there are huge numbers of Reagan Democrats and Irish ethnics. That was a no brainer to point out."[2]

RAY FLYNN'S MONKEY-WRENCH

As part of the quid pro quo for getting Adams a visa, O'Dowd had to get a cease-fire out of the IRA. Boston Mayor Ray Flynn spectacularly blew that up and got O'Dowd into trouble with the IRA. "One of the worst moments of my life was when Flynn pulled out," O'Dowd recalls. "I literally had the ceasefire letter from the IRA in hand and history on the horizon when Flynn screwed me over and went on a solo effort and decided to bail out. I should have known, but he was a high-profile political figure at the time and a valuable name. I flew over to Ireland to explain and just admitted I had picked the wrong guy. It was a tense meeting at first, but [the IRA] believed me."

The one big issue to break the deadlock was to get a visa for Gerry Adams so he could visit the United States. Under tremendous pressure from the British, the State Department, and everyone else, Clinton went with his gut and granted the visa. Looking back, how important was that one single act that four years later would result in the Good Friday Agreement? "Incredibly important because there wouldn't be a ceasefire without it—and Adams will tell you that," O'Dowd said. "Breaking the international isolation, joining Irish America and Irish Republicanism at a different level than ever before. My favorite moment was the Larry King interview with Gerry Adams and the broadcast was banned in Britain. It shows you the insanity of it."

O'Dowd's relationship with Adams goes back to 1983. The two of them have a solid, trusting friendship. "[Our relationship is] incredibly important and mine in him," said O'Dowd. "He never lied or varnished the truth. After the London dockland bombings and the end of the first IRA ceasefire, the Taoiseach and the White House were waiting on definitive word from me. I asked Adams straight, was it the end, and he said no, he could get it back. That conversation shaped all future U.S. and Irish policy and he kept his word. I have great admiration for him. He's very different as a private person—a lot of biting Northern humor, great to be around. I've seen him hold a room like very few others as well."

One of the most important—and overlooked—ingredients in the Good Friday Agreement was the contribution of the North's Loyalist Protestants. How important was the work of people like Gary McMichael, David Ervine and David Trimble? "The Loyalist leaders were a revelation to me, and I got to know them well, especially Gary McMichael and David Ervine. They were street smart savvy guys who understood just how much they had been used by 'respectable' unionism. They were the great surprise of the peace process to me and I learned an awful lot about how bad things were for their people too. David Trimble clicked his heels the first time I was with him and it went downhill from there. But he stood up when it most counted and I give him full credit for that."

Was the Good Friday Agreement maybe President Clinton's most crucial foreign policy achievement? "He thinks so himself," said O'Dowd. "Maureen Dowd has written that the first visit to Belfast and Derry in 1995 were the best days of his presidency."

NIALL O'DOWD—ILLEGAL IMMIGRANT

O'Dowd first came to the United States in 1978 on a student visa and overstayed it, making him an illegal resident. "I did not consider it a big deal at the time," he recalled, "as there was nowhere as much focus on it as now. You just went about your business and kept your slate clean. I had a very fatalistic attitude that whatever would be would be; that I'd get legal someday and there was not much point stewing over it."

It was through *Irish Press* editor Tim Pat Coogan, the prominent biographer of both Michael Collins and Eamon de Valera, that O'Dowd got his visa. "Tim Pat did indeed furnish me an I-Visa so I could report for the *Irish Press* from the U.S. Later there was a scheme known as the Donnelly Visas set up to allow some Irish undocumented an opportunity to become legal as the 1965 Act had barred immigration essentially from Ireland. I got one of those."

In this time of Trump and Immigration and Customs Enforcement (ICE) being on the rampage against illegal immigrants, O'Dowd reflected on how it could have changed his situation back then: "I would not have come to America."

His experiences as an undocumented alien have influenced how he views the new American immigrants, no matter what their background: "Very much so. It was once the Irish who were demonized. Irish Americans sometimes fail to grasp that."

Luckily for both Ireland and America, Niall O'Dowd—like John Devoy, Tom Clarke, and Jeremiah O'Donovan Rossa—made it to New York and made the world a better place for Irishmen and women on both sides of the Atlantic.

PART TWO

IRISH NEW YORK AND THE ARTS

NEW YORK HAS ALWAYS BEEN THE ARTS CENTER OF THE WORLD AND THE IRISH IMMIGRATION EXPERIENCE HAS ONLY ENHANCED IT

America has long been entertained—and educated—by Irish New York. I think the New York Irish of the baby boom generation, as well as the rest of the country, may have learned more about Irish history by listening to the Clancy Brothers and Tommy Makem then reading any history book. There they were one Sunday night singing on the *Ed Sullivan Show* about Brennan on the Moor and his deadly blunderbuss. Thirty years later, there was Larry Kirwan and Black 47 extending the history lesson with his songs about Michael Collins, James Connolly, and Bobby Sands. Different sounds, but the same message.

Boomers grew up on the old Warner Brothers movies of the 1940s on TV, and who was more popular than James Cagney and his brilliant New York swagger? Not only did he play Rocky Sullivan in *Angels with Dirty Faces*, he *was* Rocky Sullivan—a New York Irish wise guy to the bone. A half-century later the top-notch entertainment continues with John Keating's wonderful work at the Irish Rep, where he delights in all sorts of roles, a kind of Barry Fitzgerald for the twenty-first century.

And speaking of Irish wise guys, how can we ever forget George Carlin, a kid from white Harlem who first made us laugh at his wacky weatherman, then made us think about the serious issues of the day like war and hate? He was the antithesis of Cagney, but they also had a lot of Irish New York in common. Both demonstrate the great diversity that New York breeds.

As you walk around Irish New York you walk by them every day, the statues of Admiral Farragut in Madison Square Park and General Sherman at the corner of Central Park opposite the Plaza Hotel on Fifth Avenue. You just take these great sculptures for granted, not thinking that they were done by the Dublin-born, New York–raised and–educated Augustus Saint-Gaudens. When you visit Dublin you are struck by the vision of Charles Stewart Parnell sitting atop his monument on Upper O'Connell Street and suddenly you realize how prolific Saint-Gaudens was and what a great educator he was with his statues, not only in New York and Dublin but also in Boston and Chicago. President Teddy Roosevelt's favorite sculptor made his mark on both sides of the Atlantic.

All these artists came out of *Real* Irish New York and America—and the world—are better off because of them.

CHAPTER ONE

IRISH NEW YORK'S SHOWBIZ EVOLUTION

HOW JIMMY CAGNEY MORPHED INTO GEORGE CARLIN

It's the attitude that always got me.

In the 1935 Warner Bros. movie *G Men*, Robert Armstrong, an FBI supervisor, says of his New York recruit, James Cagney: "Mr. James Davis, Doctor of Law, Doctor of Philosophy, Phi Beta Kappa. Now, isn't that sweet? Phi Beta Kappa."

Cagney, standing behind him, cuts in, "What's yours? Flatfooted Copper?"

It was the perfect wise guy retort, delivered with lots of relish, red onions, and mustard by the quintessential New York Irish of his time, Jimmy Cagney.

And who can forget Cagney in *Public Enemy* in one of the most classic misogynistic scenes in movie history when poor Mae Clarke keeps saying, "You know what I wish?"

Cagney has had enough: "There you go again with that wishin' stuff again. I wish you was a wishing well. So that I could tie a bucket to ya and sink ya!" Then pow! The grapefruit right into Mae Clarke's kisser.

I grew up with Jimmy Cagney and guys like Pat O'Brien and Spencer Tracy. O'Brien was Father Jerry Connolly from *Angels with Dirty Faces* who gives counsel to Cagney's splendidly rotten Rocky Sullivan, who is quick with the quip: "Whadda ya hear? Whadda say?" Then there was Tracy as "Fadder" Flanagan, the priest ahead of his time—in a good way—with an interest in the rancid youths of Boys Town. They were the priests of my youth, just like the priests at St. Bernard's Church over on West 14th Street. They were too good to be true.

But I didn't like them. I liked Cagney, the Irish wise guy, the guy with the quick retort, the guy with the New York Irish guts. The guy who laughs at death as the OSS agent in *13 Rue Madeleine*. The seriously demented, mommy-loving psychopath Cody Jarrettt in *White Heat*, who, almost comically, asks a hostage locked up in the trunk of a car how he is. The hostage says, "Hot," so Cody, with typical Cagney joie de vivre gives him a little ventilation by shooting him right through the trunk. And he even dies in hellfire with great élan: "Made it, Ma! Top of the World!"

Ten years later the nuttiness of Cody Jarrett was reincarnated in *Shake Hands with the Devil*, in my opinion, the best movie ever made about the Irish revolution and the one that Cagney called "The best movie I made overseas." He is Dr. Sean Lenihan, an instructor at the Royal College of Surgeons on St. Stephen's Green in Dublin by day but who, by night, is really an IRA Commandant, reporting to General Michael Collins. Like Cody, Lenihan is a ruthless misogynist and sociopath who will go against Collins and peace in the end and be senselessly gunned down.

"MALICE"

And everyone knows where Cagney got those moves—the gutters of New York City. He once was asked to describe the Irish in one word and his response was: "Malice." Thus, a great Hollywood career was born.

According to his autobiography, *Cagney by Cagney*, he was born on July 17, 1899, in what is today known as Alphabet City, Avenue D and 8th Street. When he was an infant his family moved to Yorkville on the Upper East Side. At the turn of the twentieth century, Yorkville was, in Cagney's words, "almost exclusively first-generation German, Irish, Jewish, Italian, Hungarian and Czech." It was the home of the immense Jacob Ruppert & Company brewery, which ran from 90th to 95th Streets between Second and Third Avenues, and its flagship brand, Knickerbocker Beer.

Colonel Jacob Ruppert Jr. went on to own the great Yankee teams of the 1920s and '30s. Ironically, and luckily, this same Yorkville neighborhood gave Ruppert his Hall of Fame first baseman, Lou Gehrig, who was born at 309 East 94th Street in 1903.

Cagney was three-quarters Irish, with his maternal grandfather being Norwegian. "My mother's mother was Irish," he stated, "born in County Leitrim around 1846. . . . My dad's people I never knew."

But he remembers his father as a bit of a good-time dandy: "From early on he had been rather well acquainted with saloons. He knew how to serve the product, and he knew how to consume it. . . . Pop's gentle waywardness was thoroughly engrained. He had the charm of an Irish minstrel, he did everything to the tune of laughter—but he was totally deficient in a sense of responsibility to his family." He died in the flu epidemic of 1918, and the burden of supporting the family was shifted to Jimmy's mother, who was pregnant with her daughter, Jeannie, at the time—a full twenty years after the birth of her son Jimmy.

"My childhood," Cagney remembered, "was surrounded by trouble, illness, and my dad's alcoholism, but as I said, we just didn't have time to be impressed by all those misfortunes. I have an idea that the Irish possess a built-in don't-give-a-damn that helps them through all stress. Moreover, we had the advantage of an awful lot of love in our family, and wherever I lived when I was a kid—East Seventy-ninth Street, East Ninety-sixth Street, Ridgewood out on Long Island, and back again to Manhattan—we had each other, and that was enough. We went to church every Sunday and instructions every Tuesday to become good Catholics. We all made our First Holy Communion and received Confirmation at the proper time."

The rock in the family was his mother, she of the Leitrim blood. "A question people have asked me through the years," recalled Cagney, "is why the Cagney boys didn't get involved with guns and crime the way my old Sing Sing pals did. The answer is simple: there wasn't a chance. We had a mother to answer to. If any of us got out of line, she just belted us, and belted us emphatically. We loved her profoundly, and our driving force was to do what she wanted because we knew how much it meant to her. . . . We loved the great staunchness of her, and at times we four brothers together would impulsively put our arms around her, hold her, and hug her. She'd look at us, her nose would get red, and she'd start to cry. She just couldn't take all that love."

Next to a brainy family—two of his brothers went on to become physicians—the thing that impressed Cagney the most were his neighbors, who were made up of every ethnic and religious background imaginable. His youth was a living New York City melting pot: "We kids picked up all kinds of phrases from the Italians, the Czechs, the Germans, and the Jews, and in school I was a rather good German student. At least 90 percent of my classmates were Jewish, mostly up from the Lower East Side, and as I studied German, I learned the Yiddish equivalent from my Jewish pals. I still speak some German but a lot more Yiddish. . . . I enjoy speaking Yiddish. It's a wonderful tongue for storytelling, and on occasion I've inserted a few bits of Yiddish dialogue in the pictures for the sure-fire comedy effect. We realized when we did it that there would be very little small-town reaction, but in the big towns where there was a substantial Jewish population the effect was pretty stimulating."

The biggest sport in the neighborhood was not baseball, but bare-knuckled fist-fighting: "About all this street fighting I've discussed, it's important to remember that the Cagney kids conformed to the well-established neighborhood pattern. We weren't exceptional. We weren't battling phenomena or hyper-aggressive. We weren't anything more than normal kids reacting to our environment—an environment in which street fighting was an accepted way of life. And in reacting to the environment we had what I suppose could be called colorful young lives."

And it was a rough neighborhood too. Cagney remembers a visit his local baseball team—he was the catcher—made to the Ossining Correctional Facility—Sing Sing on the Hudson: "Everybody on our team knew *somebody* there. That is proof, if proof be wanted, that our neighborhood produced something more than ex-vaudevillians."

His personality soon took him to the vaudeville stage as a song-and-dance man. Eventually the dyed-in-the-wool New Yorker found himself in Hollywood, and a picture named *Public Enemy* made him a star. His favorite? "Many people assume that one of those knock-down-drag-'em-outs would be my choice. A discerning critic like Peter Bogdanovich can't understand why I choose *Yankee Doodle Dandy* over *White Heat* and *Public Enemy*. The answer is simple, and it derives from George M. Cohan's comment about himself: once a song-and-dance man, always a song-and-dance man. In that brief statement, you have my life story; those few words tell as much about me professionally as there is to tell."

YANKEE DOODLE DANDY REMOVES "THE TAINT"

Cagney arrived in Hollywood at the depth of the Depression and described himself "as a decidedly Rooseveltian Democrat."

He backed many liberal causes during the '30s and was getting that "commie" tag right-wingers liked so much back then. So, after Pearl Harbor, he went looking for a "vehicle." Then the George M. Cohan story, *Yankee Doodle Dandy*, dropped into his lap.

"[Cagney's brother, agent, and business advisor] Bill wanted to do the Cohan story as a 100 percent American experience," wrote Cagney, "principally to remove the taint that apparently still attached itself to my reputation—a reputation now scarred by my so-called radical activities in the thirties when I was a strong Roosevelt liberal. Anyone of that background was usually colored pinko in hue at the very least. Bill chose *Yankee Doodle Dandy* with deliberations."

But when the screenplay that Warner Bros. had commissioned came in, it was a disaster. "It's no good, I won't touch it," Cagney told the studio. "But I tell you what I'll do. I'll give it a blanket OK now if you put the Epstein boys on it to liven it up and inject humor. Julius and Phil Epstein were two very bright lads. They had invigorated the scripts of *Strawberry Blonde* and *The Bride Came C.O.D.*, and I knew and liked them both. The minute Phil and Julie went to work, I made the deal to do *Yankee Doodle Dandy.*"

Warner Bros. was very lucky in 1942 to be employing the Epstein brothers. Not only did they straighten out *Yankee Doodle Dandy*, but they also wrote the screenplay ("Round up the usual suspects") on the run for *Casablanca*. *Yankee Doodle Dandy* in 1943 won the Best Actor Award for Cagney, plus two other Oscars for Best Sound Mixing and Best Original Musical. *Casablanca* would win the Epsteins the Oscar for Best Writing, Screenplay, in 1944, plus the Academy Award for Best Picture and Best Director for Michael Curtiz.

SUCCESS BREEDS CONSERVATISM

Cagney voted for a third term for FDR in 1940 and in '44, but after that—some would say cynically his money safely made—he considered himself "an archconservative."

"My move to conservatism," he explained, "was precipitated by my lack of admiration for Mr. Truman's performance after he took over from FDR, and so I cast my first non-Democratic vote, for Tom Dewey." Cagney's assessment of Truman is interesting, considering most historians consider him one of the greatest American presidents of the twentieth century.

"In any case," he considered, "I believe in my bones that my going from the liberal stance to the conservative was a totally natural reaction once I began to see the undisciplined elements in our country stimulating a breakdown of our system. From what I've seen of the liberal attitudes toward the young and the permissive attitudes in the schools, and everybody pulling every which way from center, I consider these all inimical to the health of our nation. Those functionless creatures, the hippies, for example, just didn't appear out of a vacuum."

So, by 1976, when *Cagney by Cagney* was published, Jimmy was in the camp of other Irish Americans like Ronald Reagan, the former governor of California getting ready to embark on a presidential bid, and George Murphy, his fellow song-and-dance man, who was elected as a GOP senator from California despite the LBJ landside of

1964. (Murphy left us with one of the greatest faux pas of all time when he said that Mexican migrant farm workers were better than American workers because they were "built close to the ground.")

There was something unusual about the "archconservative" in that he considered himself an environmentalist. "For fifty years now," he wrote, "I've been trying to do my own broadcasting about ecology in my own way, never hesitating to let people know exactly what I think about this hideous wasting of resources."

He said the "senseless destruction of the land has infuriated me for years." Cagney lamented the American highway system—the concreting of America—a civil defense initiative of the Republican and conservative Eisenhower administration. He also worried about the wasting of our "precious clean water."

Yet, his friend and fellow Warner's contract player, Ronald Reagan, when he became president, cavalierly misconstrued scientific fact and stated, "Trees cause more pollution than automobiles do."

Reagan was also the president who appointed James G. Watt to be the most reactionary secretary of the interior in history—up to that time. He not only hated the land but also the Beach Boys! One wonders what Cagney thought of his fellow archconservative Reagan at that time.

So Cagney had his farm, his place on Nantucket, and his yacht, from which to pontificate about "the undisciplined elements" of American society. One of these "undisciplined elements," one George Carlin, was about to blow Jimmy Cagney and everything he stood for out of the water.

CAGNEY & CARLIN—SO MUCH ALIKE, SO DIFFERENT

As James Cagney was morphing into an archconservative, George Carlin was going the other way. Let's face it, George Carlin was the anti-Yankee-Doodle-Dandy.

George Denis Patrick Carlin. You can tell by the spelling of "Denis"—only one "n"—that Carlin came from real Irish Catholics. Born in 1937, Carlin was separated from Cagney by forty years and twenty-five blocks to the west. He grew up on West 121st Street between Broadway and Amsterdam. "Uptown, down the hill, on the Broadway which Jesus tell us 'leads to destruction,' lay a mostly Irish neighborhood beginning around 123rd Street, known back then as White Harlem," he recalled in his posthumous memoir, *Last Words*. "White Harlem was tougher and more crowded than the streets around Columbia. Its buildings were older and many didn't have elevators. The whole area had a decidedly working-class flavor and, of course, was a lot more fun."[3]

And the Irish, known for their tribalism, were just as tribal in Morningside Heights. "We hated the Columbia students. It was our neighborhood—Irish Catholic with a lot of hostility on every corner. Out of every twenty Irish kids there were probably thirteen or fourteen getting their asses kicked regularly back home. They felt the need to pass that along."

While Cagney adored his mother, Carlin took a slightly more cynical view: "She [Carlin's mother Mary] was a woman with decidedly aristocratic pretensions, indoctrinated with the idea that she was 'lace-curtain Irish,' as opposed to the shanty kind with its stereotypes of drinking, lawlessness, laziness, rowdiness, all the things which—to the degree that ethic generalities have any meaning—come from that side of their national character that makes the Irish fun."

And like Cagney's father, Carlin's was also a ne'er-do-well, with a fondness for the drink. He recalls the old man's version of the Pledge of Allegiance: "'I pledge allegiance to the people of the United States of America and all the political crap for which they stand. Big dough shall be divisible with union dues for all.'"

"As conclusive evidence it's scanty," Carlin wrote, "but suggests to me that my father saw through the bullshit that is the glue of America. That makes me proud. If he transmitted it to me genetically, it was the greatest gift he could have given."

THE GIFT OF NEW YORK

Like Cagney, Carlin was blessed with the gift of New York and its amazing diversity. He waxed poetic about street games: "When we got tired of being little pests, there were games: Chinese and American handball, boxball, ring-a-levio (called ring-a-leary-o in my neighborhood), blacksmith, Johnny-ride-a-pony, kick the can, roller hockey and a strange game called three steps to Germany. Plus all the city-street variations of baseball: stickball, punchball, stoopball, curb ball and baseball-off-the-wall."

While fistfighting was Cagney's street sport of choice, by Carlin's time street fighting was phasing out in favor of stealing—showing a strong American progression among the lower-class Irish in only forty years. "[B]eing a big-city kid, I was good at stealing," Carlin recalled. "Being white, I was less likely to be scrutinized while browsing the racks."

"Now we'd be called 'delinquent,' 'troubled,' 'alienated' or worse," he recalled. "Certainly some of the guys from the neighborhood later did time. But there was something innocent about running wild on the streets back then. For one thing the streets were pretty safe. There were no weapons and no one ever got hurt."

And like Cagney, New York became Carlin's oyster. "By the time I was seven," he wrote, "I was slipping into the subway to head downtown to Central Park, Times Square, Rockefeller Center, Wall Street, Chinatown, the waterfront—great tracts of unexplored territory, an urban El Dorado, just sitting there waiting for an adventurous child. Afternoons of collecting autographs, sneaking into movies, browsing in department stores, walking up the stairs to the observation decks of the RCA and Empire State Buildings, stealing stuff from novelty stores, climbing trees in Central Park, riding elevators on Wall Street or simply walking around taking in the big show—the greatest entertainment on earth. It gave me the feeling I belonged, I was entirely at home in the vast city I was growing up in."

GEORGE CARLIN, CATHOLIC, LIKE IT OR NOT

One also gets the impression that Catholicism had a bigger impact on Carlin than on Cagney because he kept coming back to it. "New York City was a great education," he said, "but first grade with Sister Richardine in Room 202 also meant other awesome new experiences: sex, music and the roar of the crowd."

One would think that Carlin had terrible things to say about Catholic education, à la Frank McCourt, but it wasn't so: "Corpus Christi School, revolutionary for its time, had no report cards or grades. There was none of that cutthroat competition spirit which so improves our American way of life. We were encouraged to study and excel simply for the joy of discovery. If we were inculcated with anything it was the simple idea that the future would take care of itself if you did right by yourself today."

But like most Catholics, Carlin had ambivalences about his religion, particularly about abortion. He starts his memoir out about how his mother nearly aborted him at an underground clinic near Gramercy Park but changed her mind. From his own personal near miss, he frankly spoke about an abortion his wife had when they were under severe financial strain.

He could be the Irish wise guy about abortion: "Why is it that the people who are against abortion are people you wouldn't want to fuck in the first place?"

But he could also be dead serious when calling out how spurious pro-lifers can be: "The satirical method was to focus on the meaning of the term 'pro-life.' What's pro-life about being obsessed with the unborn and then, once it's a child, refusing it health education and welfare? What's pro-life about sending the child off in a uniform at age eighteen to die? Or killing doctors who perform legal abortions? If all life is sacred, why is it an abortion for us but if it's a chicken it's an omelet?

"Consistency matters. If life begins at conception, why isn't there a funeral for a miscarriage? If life begins at fertilization and most of a woman's fertilized eggs are flushed out of her body once a month, doesn't that make her a mass murderer? Could it be that 'pro-life' is actually a code for hating women—the source of life?"

He tipped his hat to the Catholics again when he mentioned one of his numerous heart attacks: "Catholic hospitals have always been good luck for me."

RACE, THE RADIO, AND A POLITICAL AWAKENING

Like Cagney, Carlin was impressed with New York's wonderful diversity. Cagney learned a lot from other white ethnics, be they German, Czech, or Jewish. Carlin's education came from his fellow residents of Harlem, the blacks. And it continued when he went into the Air Force. "Socializing with black airmen came very naturally to me," he said. "On the Harlem streets I grew up on as a kid, we were cheek by jowl with blacks and Latinos of all kinds: Dominicans, Puerto Ricans, Cubans, and we all got along pretty well. We had to."

"I gravitated to the black airmen," he continued, "some of whom were from around my neighborhood in Harlem. Others came from the South Side of Chicago or the Hough neighborhood in Cleveland. I had more in common with them—jazz, R&B, stuff I could talk about. The white kids were mostly farm kids from upstate New York, Ohio and points west. No 'bonding' with them."

It was while in the service that Carlin first got into radio, his path into show business. He ended up after the service working at a radio station in Boston where he got in trouble when he cut Richard Cardinal Cushing off in the middle of the Third Sorrowful Mystery. There was hell to pay because you don't cut Cardinal Cushing off in the middle of the rosary. Cushing's show ran between 6:45 and 7 p.m. every evening. Cushing was still going on about the Third Sorrowful Mystery ("'The Crowning of Our Lord with Thorns,' for those of you who care," said Carlin in his autobiography) at 7 p.m. when, following network rules, he pulled the plug on Cushing. There was outrage from the Catholic community, but the network backed him up. Carlin, apparently, learned something from *following* the rules—and it was not good.

It was in Boston that he hooked up with his comedy partner Jack Burns, who turned him into a liberal. "I began to realize," he wrote, "the error of what had been handed to me through the Catholics, the Irish, my mother, through the Hearst legacy in our family. It didn't take much reasoning. It immediately struck a chord. Of course that's how I feel! Of course I'm for the underdog! Of course it's right-wing business assholes who've been keeping me down! The first time those doors opened for me was thanks to Jack."

JFK was an eye-opener for Carlin: "When Kennedy came on the scene, I identified closely with the youthful Irish Catholic man of ideas. He wasn't my class but he was my tribe. A politician, yes; but like a lot of my contemporaries, I wasn't old enough yet to have been disappointed. With him a new beginning seemed possible, a chance for ideas to be advanced that took into account how people felt and lived, how the world treated them. A slow but sure march toward more concern about people and less about property. The black struggle was the most visible and emotional example of it, but Kennedy's promise included much else, explicitly and implicitly, about people who had been ignored or marginalized in the rush to the fifties' consumer paradise."

THERE'S NO BUSINESS LIKE SHOW BUSINESS—AND "HE'S A CATHOLIC!"

Carlin's radio jobs took him and his partner Jack Burns all over the country. Lenny Bruce took him under his wing and Carlin saw the political side of the business, how censorship worked, and how his religion also played into the picture.

"By now it was becoming pretty clear that Lenny wasn't being arrested for obscenity," Carlin wrote. "He was being arrested for being funny about religion and in particular Catholicism. A lot of big city cops—not just in New York but in Philly, San Fran, Chicago—tend to be Irish Catholic. In addition Lenny's persecutors had names like Ryan (the judge who tried him in absentia in Chicago), Hogan the DA who went after him in New York) and Murtagh (the trial judge in New York). Lenny's Chicago trial began on Ash Wednesday, 1963. In court judge and jury having just come from Mass everyone had ash crosses on their foreheads." It was eye-opening for Carlin. "It was the most dramatic evidence I'd had to date that these lines were sharply drawn, the legacy of that Catholic upbringing, that clannish Irish working-class neighborhood ethic was a rigid demarcation. Just because you grew up with a guy and shared A, B, C, D and E with him didn't mean that on F through Z you wouldn't be diametrically opposed to each other."

Finally, he was getting on TV and making a name for himself. He was a regular on the talk-show circuit of the time—Johnny Carson, Mike Douglas, and Merv Griffin. He wasn't crazy about the circuit, but it helped him ascend to the next showbiz level which eventually got him on Ed Sullivan, the apex for a comedian in the 1960s. He recalls his experiences on Sullivan in hilarious detail:

> Then there was *The Ed Sullivan Show*. The horrible, horrible *Sullivan Show*, torture chamber of comedians. . . . *The Ed Sullivan Show*'s worst weapon of torture was that it was live. There were no second takes on *Sullivan*. If you fucked up, all America saw it. If Mr. Pastry dropped his plates or Jackie Mason gave Ed the finger there were no do-overs, no cutaways, no edits. No apologies were accepted. . . . The final turn of the screw: Sullivan himself. During your set, Ed would stand onstage over to stage right. Out of camera range but *onstage*. So the entire audience never watched the comic. They were watching Sullivan to see if he would laugh. And he never did. . . . Add all this up and you have the graveyard of laughter. Playing comedy to the *Sullivan* audience was agony. You'd get more laughs in a mausoleum.
>
> There was one tiny ray of sunlight. Ed found out that I was an Irish Catholic from New York. . . . One show he called me over after my set to where he stood, stage right. This was supposed to be a big honor. We had some inane exchange and then he said out of the blue, 'You're a Catholic!' and then gestured to the audience with that weird insect thing he did with his arms: "Give him a big hand! He's a Catholic!"

THE INFAMOUS SEVEN WORDS

After Sullivan and before the time of Reagan, Carlin started pushing the envelope, becoming more edgy. His album, *Class Clown*, hit the nail on the head. There's not a better example than "The Heavy Seven" Words Carlin declared you can never say on television: shit, piss, fuck, cunt, cocksucker, motherfucker, and tits. He said them on WBAI Radio in New York—where else?—and the shock rose all the way up to the Supreme Court.

The case, *FCC v. Pacifica Foundation*, was decided in 1978 in a 5-4 decision that the FCC ruling did not violate the First or Fifth Amendment rights of Carlin but limited the scope of the ruling to Carlin's appearance on WBAI.

In 2004 Carlin explained what he was trying to do: "These words have no power. We give them this power by refusing to be free and easy with them. We give them great power over us. They really, in themselves, have no power. It's the thrust of the sentence that makes them either good or bad."

And, as he continuously reminded us, "There are, however, some two-way words. Like prick," he wrote in his memoir. "It's okay to prick your finger. But don't FINGER YOUR PRICK!"

GOING RADICAL WITH RONALD REAGAN

With the coming of Jimmy Cagney's hero, Ronald Reagan, as president, Carlin's humor turned darker—and louder. "Throughout the eighties," he wrote, "I had outbursts of anger. It kept building up and festering. . . . But good stuff came from that anger. Gradually, I learned to channel it where it really belonged—fueling the new voice that had made those brief appearances at Carnegie. A voice that slowly grew sharper, stronger, populating my whole personality; more authentically me, more authoritative."

"But the election of Ronald Reagan might've been the beginning of my giving up on my species," he went on. "Because it was absurd. To this day it remains absurd. More than absurd, it was frightening: it represented the rise to supremacy of darkness, the ascendancy of ignorance."

It was at that time that some of his standard characters like the hippie-dippy weatherman took a backseat to his humor aimed at the political establishment: "The noisier the culture becomes, the stronger your voice has to be to be heard above the din. . . . But smarter. Be louder. Be on my fucking toes. . . . My overall reaction to the Reagan years was one of storing up ammunition. Arming myself and storing the armaments away for use later on."

SEX AND THE 1991 GULF WAR

"The reason I prefer the sledgehammer to the rapier and the reason I believe in blunt, violent, confrontational forms for the presentation of my ideas is because I see that what's happening to the lives of people is rapierlike, it is not gentle, it is not subtle. It is direct, hard and violent."

The Gulf War in 1991—not to be confused with the newer, better, and more disastrous Iraq War a decade later—brought out a new, almost vicious Carlin, a man who would not put up with the government lying and the bullshit any longer. His HBO Special *Jammin' in New York* marked a new beginning to his humor. It was more scorched earth than humor, his anger filling the performance. Looking back on it, Carlin said that "there was less an unpatriotic ring to it than a loud dissenting one. America loved war, I said. In our history we've had a major war every ten years. We suck at everything else but we could bomb the shit out of any country full of brown people. Only brown people. The last white people we bombed were the Germans. Because they were trying to dominate the world, and that's our job!"

And like a comedic Sigmund Freud, he found war to be all about male genitalia— and its limitations. "I shifted to my theory that war is just men waving their pricks at one another. We bomb anyone we think has a bigger dick than us. That's why rockets, planes, shells and bullets are all shaped like dicks. America has an overpowering need to thrust the national dick deep into other nations."

OUT OF CAGNEY AND INTO CARLIN

It's amazing to see the differences in the aging Cagney and the aging Carlin. The two came from almost identical New York Irish backgrounds, albeit separated by forty years, yet their outlooks on life collided as they grew older.

Cagney was still waving his Yankee-Doodle-Dandy American flag and was worried about hippies smoking dope while Carlin was challenging the very fabric of America with statements like "Bullshit is the glue of our society" and "It's called the American Dream because to believe it, you have to be ASLEEP!"

The difference might have been financial—Cagney was secure while Carlin had a lot of financial and IRS problems—but their divergent views are radical on both the left and the right.

How much did their Irishness play into their views? It's hard to say. Cagney was proud to call himself an "archconservative," while Carlin declared, "I love anarchy. Anarchy and comedy are a team."

Cagney and Carlin, Irish kids from the gutters of New York, who went their separate ways and no matter their politics, gave us great entertainment for nearly a hundred years.

CHAPTER TWO

AUGUSTUS SAINT-GAUDENS

THE DUBLIN-BORN, NEW YORK RAISED SCULPTOR IMMORTALIZED LINCOLN, FARRAGUT, SHERMAN, COOPER, AND PARNELL

The name Augustus Saint-Gaudens means nothing to most Americans. This is surprising, because Americans view and admire his works across the United States daily.

If you're staying at the Plaza Hotel in New York you are amazed at the golden prominence General William Tecumseh Sherman and his horse, led by allegorical Victory, has over that part of swanky Fifth Avenue. If you live in Chicago, you thrill to his portrait of Abraham Lincoln in Lincoln Park. In Boston, his Shaw Memorial at the edge of Boston Common celebrates the black soldiers of the Union Army and their leader, Robert Shaw. In Washington, DC the poignant grief of the Adams Memorial is sure to provoke the most stoic of hearts. New Yorkers walk by Admiral Farragut in Madison Square every day without even thinking that this was the man who said, "Damn the torpedoes, full steam ahead!" during the Civil War.

And most people don't know that the man with the strange name of Saint-Gaudens was born in Dublin to an Irish mother, Mary McGuiness, and a French father, Bernard, in the great famine year of 1848. At six months, Augustus—known to one and all as "Gus"—was swept away to New York in steerage to avoid the Great Hunger. The family first landed in Boston, but soon settled in New York. Young Gus grew up in the city of the Irish "Gangs of New York," and worshipped at Old St. Patrick's Cathedral on Mulberry Street, the home of Archbishop "Dagger" John Hughes, who shepherded his Irish flock against the nativists who wanted to ship all of them back to Ireland. It is also the New York of the Civil War riots of 1863, not one of the better moments for the Irish.

Gus's father opened a shoe repair shop and kept a sharp eye on his son. At thirteen, young Gus was apprenticed to a cameo maker, where he soon showed he had exceptional artistic talent. This led him to studies at Cooper Union and the National Academy of Design. Years later, he would thank Cooper Union with a sculpture of its founder, Peter Cooper. In 1867, with one hundred dollars in his pocket, his father shipped him off to friends in Paris for further study. In 1870, he found himself in Rome where he met his wife, Augusta (her nickname was Gussie).

FARRAGUT, LINCOLN, GRIEF, AND SHERMAN

Gus and Gussie returned to New York, where, in 1876, he received his first great commission—the statue of Civil War naval hero Admiral David Farragut in Madison Square Park. His friend Stanford White designed the pedestal. Saint-Gaudens and White also hooked up again in 1894 with Saint-Gaudens's controversial nude statue of Diana, which was mounted at the top of the original Madison Square Garden.

With studios in New York, Paris, and Cornish, New Hampshire, Saint-Gaudens became the most prolific American sculptor of the late nineteenth century. *Standing Lincoln* in Lincoln Park, Chicago, was unveiled in 1887 with Stanford White designing the base. Lincoln was followed in 1891 by the Adams Memorial (commonly known as *Grief*) in Rock Creek Cemetery in Washington, D.C. Once again, White contributed the base upon which the statue rests.

The year 1897 saw the unveiling of perhaps his greatest work, the Robert Gould Shaw Memorial in Boston, which commemorates the black Union soldiers of the Massachusetts 54th and their leader, Colonel Shaw. Another black soldier, former Secretary of State Colin Powell, had this to say about it on PBS's *American Masters*: "I think the Shaw Memorial is a very moving experience when you first see it. And what I always notice first are the black soldiers, who are leaning forward slightly as they march south out of Boston, heading to destiny. And what moves me is this look of determination on their face—they're leaning into the future. Once a black man put on that blue uniform with the gold buttons—and U.S.—and carrying a rifle, a weapon, and performing a mission for the nation then ultimately no power on the earth can persuade that individual that he is not the equal to his white brother. And there in the middle of it on a horse, sitting up tall, is Colonel Shaw."[4]

The year 1903 saw the dedication of Union General William Tecumseh Sherman outside Central Park at the intersection of 59th Street and Fifth Avenue. The massive gilded statue of Sherman on horse, led by Victory, is one of most august, eye-catching, and dominating figures on the entire island of Manhattan.

THE PARNELL MONUMENT, THE LAST GREAT WORK

A monument to Charles Stewart Parnell was the idea of John Redmond, the leader of the Irish Parliamentary Party (IPP). Redmond had stood by Parnell in his time of scandal and thought a monument might be a way to reunite the IPP. The Parnell Committee was formed in 1898 with the purpose of raising money by public subscription to build the statue. Saint-Gaudens took on the project, and the cornerstone was laid in 1899 at Sackville and Great Britain Streets, now O'Connell and Parnell Streets. It was the last great project Saint-Gaudens was to undertake.

The project was marked by tragedy from the start. After the Paris Exhibition of 1900, Saint-Gaudens was struck with intestinal cancer. Although weakened, he continued to work. The work on the statue took place at his Cornish, New Hampshire, studio. But a fire in 1904 destroyed the almost completed statue with only the head surviving. "More than all the rest of my losses in the fire," Saint-Gaudens said, "I regret, as an Irishman, the loss of the Parnell statue."

Although ill, Saint-Gaudens went back to work to fulfill his promise to the people of Ireland. The final version of the monument has Parnell in a frock coat with one hand resting on a table and the other pointing in the direction of the Rotunda Maternity Hospital. The obelisk behind him is made from ashlar granite, and the four Irish provinces and the thirty-two counties adorn the base. The quote behind Parnell declares: "No man has a right to fix the boundary to the march of a nation. No man has a right to say to his country: 'Thus far shalt thou go and no further.' We have never attempted to fix the ne plus ultra to the progress of Ireland's nationhood and we never shall."[5] In Irish on the base of the statue is the inscription: "Go soirbhigidh Dia Éire dá clainn" (May God make Ireland flourish for her people).

DEATH

Saint-Gaudens died in 1907, four years before the unveiling of the Parnell Monument. In the year of his death, President Theodore Roosevelt said of him: "There is no greater artistic genius living in this or any other country."

When he was late in delivering his Shaw Memorial, according to the *American Masters* documentary, Saint-Gaudens defended himself, saying: "It's the way a thing's done that makes it right or wrong. That's the only create I have in art. After all statues are plastered up before the world for centuries while man and nations pass away."

It was a wise perspective. Parnell's statue was dedicated in 1911, and within seven years John Redmond would be dead and his Irish Parliamentary Party would be extinct because of revolution. Eleven years later, the British would be gone from Dublin forever. But Parnell is still there, hoisted on his monument by a Dubliner born into the Great Famine, who came of age in New York, and who survives in his monuments to greatness.

CHAPTER THREE

THE CLANCY BROTHERS AND TOMMY MAKEM FOREVER CHANGE IRISH AMERICA

FOUR LADS FROM IRELAND TEACH THE IRISH THEIR HISTORY IN SONG

In the New York of my youth, the idea of an Irish song was Bing Crosby crooning "Galway Bay" or "Too-Ra-Loo-Ra-Loo-Ral" from *Going My Way*. It was pure schmaltz, not to mention not very Irish. You just knew "Mother Machree" was waiting in the wings.

Then, like a bomb, three guys from Carrick-on-Suir, County Tipperary, and one from Keady, County Armagh, went on *The Ed Sullivan Show* one Sunday night and forever changed how Irish America viewed their lost culture. They were the Clancy Brothers—Paddy, Tom, and young Liam—and Tommy Makem from the North. They not only sang with energy but became teachers to several generations who forgot—or never knew—what being Irish meant. They sang of revolution, the atrocities that the British had inflicted on Ireland, drink, lost love, and, of course, Catholicism and its many limitations. They did it with élan and laughter. And they did it all from their base in—where else?—New York City.

THE LONG JOURNEY TO IRISH NEW YORK

Like many an Irishman, their journey to New York was a circuitous one. For an Irishman, it seems, the direct route between two points is not a straight line.

"When World War II broke out in 1939," Pete Hamill wrote in his foreword to the group's *Irish Songbook*, "Tom and Pat joined the RAF, like so many of the 'wild geese' before them, and were gone for years. By 1950, after various adventures which had included Pat's expedition to Venezuela to search for emeralds, they had emigrated to Canada. They worked for a while in Canada, and then made their way to Cleveland, Ohio, where they had relatives. They spent most of their time working days in an auto body plant, while Tom continued his acting in the evenings with the Cleveland Repertory Theater."[6]

Their next stop was the Big Apple. "In New York," Hamill continued, "they found a splendid tavern called the White Horse, filled with old wood and much noise and a variety of painters, writers and poets (it was the favorite saloon of Dylan Thomas), and also found a way to live to the fullest in America. Tom and Pat became actors, taking part in one of the early O'Casey revivals at the Cherry Lane Theater of *The Plough and the Stars* and acting all over the off-Broadway scene; they also discovered folk singing."

The two were joined in 1955 by their brother Liam and Tommy Makem. Soon, they cut their first album, "The Rising of the Moon," about—what else?—rebel songs. A second album of drinking songs followed. Hamill continued their story: "'One fine morning three of us were out of work,' Liam remembers, 'and we decided, what the hell. Several people had been bugging us to form a group and play together. We talked Pat into closing the Tradition Records' office for a while, and we went out to Chicago for a six-week engagement at the Gate of Horn." They were an instant, rousing success.

A short time later they were sent Aran sweaters by their mother and they not only were a roaring singing success, but they singlehandedly revived the sweater industry in Ireland—even today Aran sweaters are often called Clancy Brothers sweaters.

LIAM CLANCY, ROGUE

My father loved them and made me listen to all their albums. Soon I was hooked too. I took a liking to the youngest of the group, Liam, who was born in 1935.

When I was growing up in the Irish-heavy north Greenwich Village of the 1960s, most of my pals wanted to be Mickey Mantle or Willie Mays. I was different. I wanted to be Liam Clancy.

Why?

Because he was a rebel. And a rogue. He taught me about the audacious Brennan on the Moor and the deadly fate of young Roddy McCorley. He sang sad love songs in that beautiful voice that would bring you to tears—then tore into the English with something like "God Bless England" or "Mr. Moses-Ri-Tooral-i-ay."

I first learned of the pleasures and evils of drink because of "Whiskey, You're the Devil" and a metaphorical young girl named "Nancy Whiskey" who'd grab you "by the knees." And he didn't let the all-powerful clergy off the hook either, poking gentle, but pointed, fun at the priests and nuns in the audience.

There was another reason he was my hero—I knew Liam *always* got the girl. And, boy, knowing what I know now, did he ever!

I got to know Liam casually in the 1970s and '80s when he drank at the Lion's Head saloon on Christopher Street in the Village. I would tease him about why he always wore a cap—the worse show business sin, baldness!—and he would go right back at me, commenting about my sparse red beard.

At the Head, he was a regular and a regular guy and, because of his albums, part of the family. He was loved and admired on both sides of the Atlantic and, as soon as his death was announced on Raidió Teilifís Éireann on December 4, 2009, my phone started ringing with calls from cousins and friends in Dublin. His loss was profoundly felt not as a celebrity, but as a friend.

A SUPERB PERFORMER AND SHOWMAN

The Clancy Brothers and Tommy Makem famously burst on the scene with an appearance on *The Ed Sullivan Show* in January 1961.

"We weren't that impressed," wrote Liam in his autobiography. "We were arrogant. Young and arrogant. As they say in Ireland, we didn't give a tinker's damn."[7]

At the last minute, Pearl Bailey was forced to cancel and the Clancys and Makem filled in, getting fifteen minutes of uninterrupted publicity. Fifteen minutes—the longest performance block in the history of the Sullivan show—and eighty million viewers later, they were, as Tom Clancy succinctly said, "Fuckin' famous!" After working at their craft in the back room of the White Horse saloon on Hudson Street in the Village for years, instantly, because of the power of television, they were celebrities.

Greenwich Village contributed a lot to the group. Back then, in the early '60s, it was a hotbed of poets and folksingers. Odetta at one joint, Tom Paxton at another, Peter, Paul & Mary around the corner. And a young future Nobel Laureate, Bob

Dylan, hobnobbing with them all, especially one Liam Clancy. Liam was Dylan's hero too.

"People," the *New York Times* quoted Liam in his obituary, "who were trying to escape repressed backgrounds, like mine and Bob Dylan's, were congregating in Greenwich Village. It was a place you could be yourself, where you could get away from the directives of the people who went before you, people who you loved but who you knew had blinkers on."[8]

Blinkers off, Clancy, in Dylan's eyes, attained new artistic heights. "I never heard a singer as good as Liam, ever," said Dylan. "He was just the best ballad singer I ever heard in my life."

A MAN OF HIS TIME THROUGH HIS SONGS

In 1969 Tommy Makem left the group and was replaced by another Clancy Brother, Bobby. Bobby, in turn, was replaced for a number of years by Louis Killen, from New-castle-on-Tyne. By the middle of the '70s, the group stopped performing together (until a reunion in 1986) as Paddy returned to his farm in Ireland and Tom was acting on Broadway in Eugene O'Neill's *A Moon for the Misbegotten*.

In 1976, Liam and Tommy Makem became a musical team after the latter appeared on Liam's Canadian television show and subsequently became a co-per-former. They then hooked up as a team and performed together for thirteen years.

Liam could sing about anything—the sea, apple orchards, traveling people—but he also had a social conscience. He sang poignantly about homelessness in "Streets of London." He sang about our delicate ecological balance on Mother Earth in "The Garden Song."

He did not avoid the hot issues of the Northern Ireland Troubles either. In the 1970s, when RTE banned the voices of protest in the North—one of the dumbest political decisions ever conceived by the minister for Posts and Telegraphs, the highly overrated Conor Cruise O'Brien—Liam did not forget the struggle. It was almost impossible, even in the United States, to get a recording of "The Men Behind the Wire," but Liam sang it—and was criticized for it—when others would not even touch the incendiary rebel song, one of the best songs to come out of the recent Troubles.

Liam's nationalism ran deep. His family owned a pub in Tipperary during the War of Independence, and the Black and Tans often paid unwelcomed visits.

He could as easily recite Robert Emmet's "Speech from the Dock" as belt out Padraic Pearse's "Oro Se Do Bheatha" in Irish.

But he was also a showman in the best sense of the word. He could robustly recite the degenerate French poet Charles Baudelaire's "Get Drunk," then launch into a rendition of "Ar Fol Lol O," a song about the innate beauty of mankind.

His signature song, of course, was "The Band Played Waltzing Matilda," maybe the most beautiful anti-war song ever written. At concerts when he sang this song you could hear a pin drop and when he was finished there was no applause because the audience was stunned. It was not unusual to hear sobbing from man and woman alike.

THE *ALMOST* CLANCYS & MAKEM SITCOM: "BIGGER THAN THE BEATLES"

A couple of years ago, I came across one of the great oddities about the Clancys and Makem. On TV, there was an old rerun of Danny Thomas's show *Make Room for Daddy* from 1963 called "Oh, the Clancys." They sang "Brennan on the Moor" and "Portláirge."

I was so surprised by this show I emailed the late Jerry Campbell, who was their manager for most of the 1960s. Back in the '60s, Danny Thomas not only had his own show, but with Sheldon Leonard also successfully packaged two other hit sitcoms: *The Andy Griffith Show* and *The Dick Van Dyke Show* and the groundbreaking *I Spy* which featured Bill Cosby, the first African American star of a TV series. Campbell's email response shocked me:

I had a deal with Danny Thomas & Sheldon Leonard. What you saw was basically the "pilot." It went well and I got a firm offer for CB&TM to star in their own weekly show on NBC, produced by Danny Thomas & Sheldon Leonard & I was to be the associate producer. Lot of money involved. Firm 13 weeks on NBC, plus 13-week options on & on and rerun right going on for years.

Then the "fun" began!! When the "folkies" found out about it, they hit Liam hard—He was 'selling out,' etc. Heavy duty pressure from a number of people. Basically, these people were very jealous that they hadn't been offered the "deal." They all backed Liam into a corner & I kept explaining to him what was going on, so did the William Morris Agency who represented Thomas &

Leonard and so did NBC. Then, a number of people got onto Tommy Makem & he caved in saying he didn't want to play an Irishman on TV. I told him point blank that I would be hard put to see him playing an Italian on the show. Crazy Shit!! All the "Irish" who got into the "discussion" were basically afraid CB&TM would be very successful and they didn't want that to happen & CB&TM. I didn't, couldn't understand this. When these same people who talked Liam & Tommy out of "selling out" got their own deal with the networks, they jumped right on the "bandwagon." They turned down the entire deal—left big time $$Millions on the table.

They did the same thing on a movie deal I had with Peter Bogdanovich for them to star in a Western that he & Larry McMurtry wrote. CB&TM made some big-time dumb career decisions, but there was nothing I could do about it. If they had accepted the deals I got for them they would have been bigger then the Beatles.

There is some controversy connected to the whole project. James McCormick, a longtime student of Irish history and traditional music, also saw the pilot and he has a different version than Campbell. "I asked Tommy Makem," McCormick told me, "about it one evening during intermission when he was playing at the Irish Pavilion in NYC. He told me that they turned down the offer of a TV series because they were serious actors and it would have been a stage-Irish version of the Beverly Hillbillies—i.e., green Irish boyos bedazzled by the intricacies of NYC. [For example, in the TV pilot, Tommy says to Danny Thomas, 'I didn't know there were so many mines in NYC. Every block there's miners coming up to the street.' To which Danny clues in the ignorant culchie about subways.] They probably could have made out quite well financially if they had taken up the offer, but as the old adage goes: 'What's the price of your soul?'"

McCormick also had some interesting observations about the movie that wasn't. "As for the Peter Bogdanovich movie, Liam told me about it the first time I met him at Mooney's Pub in Ring, County Waterford, in August 1970. It was supposed to be a Western with John Wayne, in which the boys were a gang of horse thieves (Liam was named Aloysius). I asked him about it some years later and he told me that things didn't work out, but he did learn how to ride a horse as a consequence."

"OUR REVELS NOW ARE ENDED"

One of my proudest possessions is a copy of *The Mountain of the Women* that Liam sent me. It is a brutally honest look at the rise, the tragic fall, and the heroic resurrection of Liam Clancy. I gave Liam a cameo in my Michael Collins fantasy novel, *Terrible Angel*, sent him a copy in Ireland, and invited him to my book party at the old Lion's Head, now the Kettle of Fish. In response, he sent his autobiography to me with this inscription: "For Dermot McEvoy, January 17th, 2003. One good book deserves another. Thanks for thinking of me. I'd love to have been at the launch in the Head/Kettle of Fish. Let's have a glass there sometime. Give my best to any of the old gang you may come across and—great good luck with the book.—Liam Clancy."

Toward the end of his life he added a documentary that went beyond *The Mountain of Women*. *The Yellow Bittern: The Life and Times of Liam Clancy* is a naked look at Liam's career and loves. In it he discusses his newborn sexual freedom in America and his several illegitimate children. At times the honesty makes the viewer uneasy.

He once famously said to Bob Dylan: "No fear, no jealousy, no meanness" which is about the best philosophy a man can have in this tough life. Liam ended every concert with "The Parting Glass." It's as if Liam was trying to give his life philosophy—be true to yourself and do no harm to others.

Of all the money that ere I had, I spent it in good company.
And of all the harm that ere I've done, alas was done to none but me.
And all I've done for want of wit, to memory now I cannot recall.
So fill me to the parting glass. Goodnight and joy be with you all.
Of all the comrades that ere I had, they're sorry for my going away,
And of all the sweethearts that ere I had, they wish me one more day to stay,
But since it falls unto my lot that I should rise while you should not,
I will gently rise and I'll softly call, "Goodnight and joy be with you all!"

They're all gone now. Liam, Tom, Paddy, and Tommy Makem. But they live on in their recordings as alive as they ever were. So alive that you'll always have the feeling in your heart that Willie Brennan and his horse are still riding high on the moor and his blunderbuss is still in search of English landlords. Let's always hope so.

CHAPTER FOUR

JOHN KEATING OF THE IRISH REP

AN IRISH-BORN NEW YORK ACTOR WORKS HIS CRAFT AT THE IRISH REP

The *New York Times* called John Keating "the Irish Rep's great clown . . . an exuberant string bean with a shock of curly hair." They could have added that they were talking about one of New York's great imported acting talents. He could also be called "the natural." Most actors have been educated in a system: "the Method" or the "Stanislavski's System" or the "Meisner Technique," etc., etc.

Keating is more from the Spencer Tracy school of acting: "Know your lines and don't bump into the furniture."

He was born in Waterford in 1968 and raised in Anacarty, Co. Tipperary. "I went to boarding school growing up, Rockwell College, also in Tipperary," he told me. "That's where I first became interested in acting. It was an all-boys school, and the school play each fall was a large event in the school calendar. I played female roles three years in a row! The highlight was probably Gwendolyn in *The Importance of Being Earnest*, we still have a photo in Tipperary of me sitting quite elegantly in repose, but with my tights having lost their elastic and draped entirely around my ankles!"

And like many fine Irish actors—Barry Fitzgerald, Arthur Shields, Cyril Cusack, and Jack MacGowran, just to name a few—Dublin made a great impression on him.

"My dad is from Dublin," said Keating, "and is a retired large animal vet. I worked with him as his assistant every summer for six years and I often feel characters I play are drawn from the many characters I met during those summers. My mum was a lovely woman and raised the five of us siblings—I'm the oldest—and she very sadly passed away in January of 2019."

And like many an actor, the path to the stage had detours. "We spent time each summer in Dublin," Keating recalled. "Dad is from the inner city. Keating's Pub on Store Street was owned by my grandfather. My father is a huge O'Casey fan and we grew up knowing so many of the famous lines from the trilogy. After I left college—I studied French and Politics at University of Limerick—I worked in Dublin for over four years as a public relations executive for a firm called Murray Consultants. I started to take weekend acting classes at Playwrights and Actors on North Frederick Street, and found that I just was mad about it and wanted to leave my career and try the theatre."

The acting bug had hit hard. "Taking these classes was so rejuvenating and exciting after a week's work," said Keating. "I also loved being around the other students and having the craic with them each weekend. I knew quickly that I wanted to try and do this."

Then luck struck. Keating landed a US visa through the annual lottery, and his path ahead was clear. "There I was, twenty-five, with four years professional work experience, a Green Card in my hand and single and I just went for it. I'd been in New York on work experience for six months when I was in college, I was nineteen, and had always yearned to go back. I thought, well, I can just go for a couple of years to New York and see if I can do some, even any work in the field and if it doesn't work out I can always come back and start again in Dublin."

NEW YORK, HERE I COME

Back in the day, Irish immigrants were often called greenhorns. And if there was one thing John Keating was, as an actor at least, it was green.

"When I came to New York," he remembered, "I knew exactly nothing about the business. In my first week, someone told me that the magazine *Backstage* was where jobs were listed, so I bought that and there were auditions for a tiny production of two Synge plays that very weekend. I went along and did a monologue and at the end, the director, David Brody, said he'd like to give me a 'call-back' but I didn't have a number on my resume. I said I didn't have a phone, and then I asked him what a call-back was (seriously!). He told me just to come back the following evening. I did and got the part in *Shadow of the Glen*. Months later he showed me where he had written on my resume, 'just off the boat—call-back.'"

"That job galvanized me," he recalled. "Suddenly, with an office job secured in a travel agency that summer and an apartment secured, I had acting work, almost unpaid, but acting work, a role. I started to learn about the industry in that show, but most importantly, I began to learn how to do a play, how to be in a play and behave in rehearsal and onstage. I never considered training after that."

And like many a New York actor, Keating had to find odd jobs to support himself. "In those first years in NYC with my green card (I've been here full time since 1994)," he recalled, "I would find myself getting a play, and then once the play finished would have to look for part time work. I did everything from proofreading in law offices to working in a travel agency to painting houses to working on Wall Street part time in a staffing firm (which my brother Michael now manages!). I suppose, as much as anything, it made me desperately want to find a way to work full time as an actor."

And Keating had a career plan. "A friend in a show in the late '90s advised me to try and get six months of work, and then never go back to other work once those jobs finished. It worked in 2002 when I did three plays back-to-back and I booked my first audiobook at that time and then on-camera work started to follow and I've made a full-time living since late 2002. I always know that work can come to an end for an actor at any time and I'm beyond grateful for the longevity. And the laughs! I just was lucky enough to start going from show to show, and then I began to do shows in large theaters outside New York City for a number of years, building a classical and contemporary resume. I've done at least fifty plays, as sometimes I direct too. I did twelve regional jobs (all in non-Irish roles and plays, a specific choice to not pigeonhole my resume) in many of the leading theaters in the US and stopped traveling the year before our kids were born in 2010. For the last decade I've worked extensively with both Irish Rep and Theatre For a New Audience (TFANA) in New York each year, while dipping into plays with other theaters here in the city and also into film and TV roles."

Firmly established in New York theater, Keating is also a family man, married to his wife Laura, who is also an actress, and together they have two children, Avonlea and Owen. "We live in Astoria close to Astoria Park. I suppose it's like living in New York City but not really, as it's so much quieter—it's lovely."

JUGGLING A CAREER

Keating went on to explain the challenges of working at both TFANA and the Irish Rep. "TFANA is the leading theatre in the US for Shakespeare," he said, "and has a long and deep relationship with England's Royal Shakespeare Company (RSC). I've been so lucky to be able to go regularly from something like *The Winter's Tale* there to a contemporary or classic play at Irish Rep, sometimes overlapping between the two. Both theaters are very nurturing of and hugely supportive of actors who work regularly with them, and both are also simply great fun! I love doing Shakespeare, his comedies are so hard that each time I do one I get to first preview and can't believe I'm doing another one as the humor is so old and difficult you have absolutely no idea if any of it resonates for today's audience until first preview—terrifying! But doing Shakespeare feeds your work on characters like Joxer in *Juno and the Paycock,* it just gives you more to draw from."

But Keating's staple remains the Irish Repertory Theatre on West 22nd Street. "As a friend of mine says more gracefully than I," Keating said with pride, "working at Irish Rep is just like being with family. Artistic Direct Charlotte Moore and Producing Director Ciarán O'Reilly have created a place like no other in NYC. I wonder if there is anywhere like it elsewhere? I have a feeling there's not. I've watched actors in conversation for years now—I did my first show there in 1995—talk about the shows they did there with such great fondness, both the work itself and for the environment. Irish Rep has built a large and loyal audience over time, it's work speaks for itself year to year and it represents to me the very best of the Irish and Irish-American Theatre experience. Stories by the greatest and the freshest, told superbly in a beautiful theatre. For many ex-pats, Irish Rep is extremely important also in providing a context for understanding the Irish-American experience. The *Wall Street Journal* only weeks ago referred to Irish Rep as 'Off Broadway's Leading Troupe.' It's taken them thirty years to build that reputation, and it's true."

And like any actor, Keating does have his favorites. "My favorite roles have been one's that push me the furthest," he admitted. "The Irish playwright and actress Laoisa Sexton wrote a play called *Pigeon in the Taj Mahal* in which I created the title character in a four character play. 'Pigeon' was a simple man who spoke at a rapid pace in a difficult dialect. Making him entirely understandable while retaining his core self was so challenging, the opening monologue alone in the play was almost thirty minutes of material which was layered but could seem like complete gibberish!"

He went on to list other favorites: "Brian Friel is a huge favorite of mine and playing Casimir in his *Aristocrats* at Irish Rep was a great experience. He, like Pigeon and Jim, in Conor McPherson's *The Weir,* which I've also played, are all characters which exist in one way or another on the periphery of society. I've always been drawn to and perhaps do okay by characters who are marginalized. Even Joxer in *Juno and the Paycock* has almost no back story or family mentioned whatsoever and how he even exists week to week is a mystery! My favorite Shakespearean role for TFANA is the wily servant Tranio in *Taming of the Shrew*. It is the largest role in that play but also has no history and exists entirely to serve the Kate/Petruchio story."

TV/FILM/AUDIOBOOKS—AND THE MANDATORY LAW & ORDER

Like every New York actor, Keating is very aware of the opportunities the city offers because so many films and television shows are shot there. He has already done his mandatory—for a New York actor—appearance on *Law & Order: SVU*.

"I've segued into half a dozen films and more than ten roles in episodic TV," he said. "I enjoy the process and the challenge and always try and set aside some part of every year to be available to audition for on-camera work. Smaller independent films—like Colin Broderick's *Emerald City*, which we shot in NYC in 2016, or Kerryman Seanie Sugrue's *Misty Button*, shot in NYC in 2018—are easily the best fun on camera as there is a great sense of camaraderie throughout the incredibly long days of shooting. I also loved shooting a large scene in Kelly Reichardt's new film *First Cow* this winter in Oregon, as she is someone whose work I have long admired. But I do prefer theater, no question."

Another source of income for actors is doing audiobooks and John Keating has thoroughly conquered the field. "I love recording audiobooks," he said. "I broke through with audiobooks as a narrator fifteen years ago and have now recorded close to two hundred books. I'm consistently very lucky with great material in an industry that's become so much more competitive since that time. My range is helpful in that I can go back and forward between my own accent and using an entirely British accent for books on end and particularly enjoy recording Harry Potter type books—there is little to compare, for me anyway, with playing some garrulous pirate in a seastorm in a recording studio on a dank Tuesday morning in February! Great fun, and the audio on its best days rivals the theater work for me."

The recording of audiobooks has become somewhat of a family affair. "My kids are the best judges of my work too, they will listen to snatches and tell me exactly what they think—enlightening and humbling, often in the same sentence! My wife Laura also records audiobooks and is a great touchstone for material for me. I won the Audie a few years ago (2013) for narrating *Gun Church* by Reed Farrel Coleman. I suppose it's the industry equivalent of the Oscars and it was lovely to be recognized in that way."

Speaking of awards, Keating just received the prestigious Actors' Equity Foundation's Callaway Award for his multiple roles in the Irish Rep's 2019 Sean O'Casey trilogy: *The Plough and the Stars, Shadow of the Gunman* and *Juno and the Paycock*. "The Callaway meant so much for two main reasons," Keating told me. "It's an award given by Actors Equity for the best classical character acting onstage in New York in a given year—one male and one female honoree—so it's from one's peers and that feels very special. And it was for work done at Irish Rep and working there and being honored for it is as special to me as it gets.

Although most know Keating from his work at the Irish Rep, people may also recognize him from *Boardwalk Empire*, in which he played Ernie Moran. "*Boardwalk Empire* was fun to do," he told me. "I was originally cast for one large scene, but they decided to develop the character—as one of Nucky's inner circle—so I was lucky to do multiple episodes. I remember Steve Buscemi, who played the central role of Nucky, being particularly sweet to work with and just so kind to everyone around him."

Somehow, Keating finds time to direct, too. "I occasionally direct plays. I don't pursue it as I don't have the time, but peers will ask me to direct something and I enjoy doing it so much. I also think it helps me as an actor later down the line, perhaps to get out of my own way and stop asking questions I don't need to!" Keating was being modest again. He won Best Director in the 2018 First Irish Festival Awards for Derek Murphy's *Dyin' For It*."

THE COMMUNITY THAT IS IRISH NEW YORK

Keating is deeply thankful for the acting community to which he belongs. "There is a large Irish and British acting community in New York," he said. "I imagine it's easily the largest in the US and my guess would be that the Irish community rivals London. There is a true sense of community in that people come to support each other's shows and readings all the time, and of course the Irish Rep is the epicenter of that community, with Origin Theatre and the Irish Arts Center also focal points. There is never a sense of being on one's own. I've often heard LA is like that and occasionally Irish actors do go there, but many more seem to come here."

And Irish New York is lucky that one who chose to come here was John Keating, late of Anacarty, County Tipperary.

CHAPTER FIVE
LARRY KIRWAN OF BLACK 47

NEW YORK IRISH RENAISSANCE MAN FROM WEXFORD: MUSICIAN, ROCK STAR, AUTHOR, PLAYWRIGHT

The first time New York heard of Larry Kirwan was when he teamed with Pierce Turner and was rocking Malachy McCourt's Bells of Hell saloon on West 13th Street in Greenwich Village in the early 1970s. To put it mildly, he was a long way from home in County Wexford.

Kirwan remembered his hometown fondly in his memoir, *Green Suede Shoes*: "Wexford was a town apart," he wrote. "It was incestuous, narrowminded, and up to its arse in everyone else's business. Before they self-destructed, it was run tighter than any Thomas Hardy novel by a theocratic Catholic clergy convinced of its own infallibility, and unafraid to self-righteously kick the bejaysus out of anyone with the least aspiration for freedom or self-expression."[9]

Wexford town was controlled by the church. It wasn't the church of Frank McCourt's time, but it wasn't all that liberal either as Kirwan grew up in the 1950s and '60s. Kirwan not so fondly remembers the Redemptorists priests and their terrifying retreats. They were, wrote Kirwan, "against Protestants, perverts, Freemasons, miniskirts, Socialists, Communists, horse thieves, wankers, spankers, and cross-dressers, and anyone else with even the remotest spark of individuality in them."

The Kirwan family consisted of his mother, Ita, and father, Jim, a seaman who was often gone for half of the year. At least in his dad he had an ally against the Redemptorists. Kirwan remembered that his father was "an unreconstructed atheist." During the nightly rosary the old man would mutter under his breath to young Larry, "Hail Mary full of grace, little Johnny won the race."

As for almost all Irish Catholics, devout or not, the religion had its effect, and it stuck to Kirwan. "Catholicism—this father of our fathers, this most mathematically precise and pragmatic of religions—made perfect sense to me," he wrote. "As a boy, I didn't question it. Indeed, I exulted in its confident certitude. Go to enough Masses, say enough rosaries, stay pious, pure, and far away from sex—whatever that was—and you were guaranteed a place in heaven nestled close to the blue veil of the Blessed Virgin, and within hailing distance of the handsome, Aryan, golden-haired Redeemer Himself."

At age ten Kirwan went to live with his grandfather, Thomas Hughes, and bachelor Uncle Paddy. Hughes would have a major impact on the young Larry. He had strong Republican sympathies and was purportedly recruited into the Irish Republican Brotherhood by 1916 martyr Seán MacDiarmada himself. "My grandfather, who raised me, was kind but a huge brooding presence for a small but strong man," said Kirwan.

> He had left school at 13 and apprenticed to his own father as a stonecutter. His father had witnessed the Great Hunger and described it to his family. Thomas Hughes, likewise, passed on to me the tales of people dying with grass stains on their lips. Hence, I believe, my grounding in Republicanism. On the other hand, my father's people were well off Fine Gael farmers—my granduncle John Kirwan had been killed while serving in the British Army in World War One. So, I was from a mixed family. With that background I've often written about the balance between principle and pragmatism, and the Irish Civil War was fought over those two principles. Should we accept a limited freedom and wait for better days or keep on fighting for what was probably unattainable at the time? Along with the three iconic Irish patriots Collins, Connolly and Sands, there are so many others in the Black 47 pantheon that I've tackled—Countess Markievicz, Bobby Kennedy, Paul Robeson. But I think the roots of my political songs come from the awful years of *An Gorta Mór*.

A visit from James Connolly, as witnessed by his grandfather, would influence Kirwan years later to write a song about the 1916 martyr. "Wexford was an industrial town with three main iron factories," said Kirwan in his memoir. "The bosses locked the workers out and told them not to come back if they were still union members. James Connolly came down from Dublin to lead the workers in their struggle. My grandfather often described the scenes of Connolly leading great torchlight processions through the town. The workers held out through a bitter winter but in springtime with their children starving they were forced to go back to work. When I was growing up people could still name the families who supported the workers and those who did not. History and politics were not something I learned about only in books. With the exception of the local friars, the church did not support the workers, so I'm sure that curried my attitude towards the establishment, both secular and spiritual. On the other hand I was a total believer in Catholicism until the age of 15 or so when I began to integrate Connolly, the Spanish Civil War, and any number of other radicals and conflicts into my worldview."

NEW YORK HERE I COME

By the time Kirwan reached manhood, the stagnant Irish political life and the heavy influence of the Church led him out of Wexford and into Dublin—where he said he lived "a Gingerman existence"—then onto New York.

His song "Land of De Valera" ("Got to get out of the land of De Valera") is his grand goodbye to Ireland. "Yeah," he told me, "when I jumped ship in 1972 it seemed like nothing would ever really change in Ireland. Despite the liberties of the 1960s there was a deep conservatism ingrained in the Irish psyche derived from a mass inferiority caused by British colonialism, allied with a belief and dependence on a very Irish form of Jansenist Catholicism. Artistically too, there was the feeling that we should leave that kind of thing to our betters. I had spent a summer in New York and the Poconos. I felt I could reinvent myself in New York. So, Pierce Turner and I left Ireland, formed Turner and Kirwan of Wexford and went to work at the Bells of Hell. 'Land of de Valera' was a parting shot. I resurrected the song in 1989 when Black 47 formed and it became a Reggae/Rap type anthem in those wild early years of the band."

Kirwan's image of America was formed early in his life—through the movies. "There we could link visions with Bogart, Cagney, and Audie Murphy, while measuring and memorizing the curves of goddesses the likes of Ava Gardner, Grace Kelly, and Rita Hayworth, not to forget our own dear Marilyn," he wrote in *Green Suede Shoes.* "Wexford was crazy for the 'pictures' and mad for Monroe's silky femininity. Some went every night and could recite whole films by heart; it was a rare person who didn't go at least twice a week. We spoke and acted like gangsters and cowboys: our accents a mélange of Brooklyn and Wyoming."

Why New York and not London? "I felt that British policy towards Northern Ireland was pigheaded in the extreme and would harvest nothing but blood and tears until Orange intransigence was finally faced up to," he wrote.

The U.S. government, in its wisdom and compassion, had offered the use of temporary social security numbers to impoverished Irish students. The idea is that we would work for the summer in Boston or New York and make enough money to fund the next year's education back home. All one needed was a student card to avail of this Holy Grail. The word spread like wildfire through the flatlands of Rathmines. Hundreds of drinkers, dossers, dreamers, and delinquents showed up at the American embassy with fake, and even occasionally, valid cards. So many were leaving that one wag in the Hideaway pub, waving a visa above his head, was heard to roar: "Last one out the door, turn out the lights!"

I didn't find it hard to leave Ireland at all.

I was always going and because my father was a deep-sea sailor, I was used to him going away for four or five months at a time. When Pierce and I got to NYC we caused a bit of a stir almost instantly. Then our holiday visas ran out. We went to an immigration lawyer who took our case but advised us not to go back until we had gained legal status, which we eventually did. That took three years and by the time I got back to Wexford I just didn't fit anymore. I had been living wild in the East Village—going home wasn't part of the equation anymore. Oddly enough I had outgrown my Gingerman days in Dublin too. And they were great. Apart from the sexual revolution hitting Dublin shortly before I arrived, at places like The Bailey on Duke Street you could be in the company of Luke Kelly, Phil Lynnott, Christy Moore, Donal Lunney. Not that I knew them, but you were just a 'how'ya' away. No one had any money, and yet we all managed to stay well-oiled on a fairly permanent basis. I'm not sure you could live the same life anymore; the economics are not the same. But in reality I exchanged Gingerman Dublin for a Rock and Roll Henry Miller type existence in New York.

If Trump and his anti-immigrant policies had been in effect in the 1970s, would he still have immigrated to New York? "It wouldn't have troubled me," he flat-out stated to me. "The U.S. has always had a hardcore 25–30 percent base of Know-Nothings. They were here when I arrived in Nixon's day, but they knew their place. Trump has just made ignorance cool. I was coming to the land of Walt Whitman, Henry Miller, James Baldwin, Bob Dylan, Otis Redding, Sly Stone, Stephen Foster, Bobby Kennedy, Paul Robeson, not some Fifth Avenue chancer who doesn't pay his bills. Besides, I had seen *Midnight Cowboy*. I went straight to Forty-Deuce."

LIVING LIFE AT THE BELLS OF HELL

"The Bells had its roots in the fabled Lion's Head on Sheridan Square," recalled Kirwan in *Green Suede Shoes*.

That is to say many of its core drinkers once frequented the latter establishment but now, for various reasons, chose to bend their elbows a little further uptown. Refugees from the Head included many alcoholics with aspirations to be novelists, hard-bitten journalists, rowdy lawyers, Communist seamen, contrary folksingers and the just plain horny.

The Bells added to this stew of very smart—if often masochistic—women, music critics, rockers, Vietnam vets, Bronx Irish, visiting anarchists, devotees of Aleister Crowley, gay ex–Christian Brothers and married priests, nurses from St. Vincent's, and a regularly rotating cast of adventurous young ladies from the Evangeline Residence some doors up the street. This jambalaya mixed with surprising ease and good grace under the watchful, taciturn eye of the manager and eventual owner, Peter Myers.

The fact that there was a huge cellar given over to the smoking of various herbs did not hurt matters. How the place never burned down, I have no idea, for Malachy was notoriously hostile to Con Edison and rarely paid their bills. In these blackout periods, patrons often wandered the back rooms like so many Florence Nightingales with candles and lamps, searching for toilets and other comforts while endeavoring not to trip over fornicating couples. This so infuriated Jimmy Gavin, a grumpy carpenter from Mayo, he cut a hole in the wall and jacked into the power of the apartment building next door. Malachy, ever the blasphemer, was heard to mutter, 'Let there be light,' as the electricity returned.

Word soon spread throughout the Village that Turner and Kirwan of Wexford were hot, which is surprising in that Kirwan never had a music lesson in his life. "Just picked up the guitar," he admitted to me, "a couple of people showed me where to put my fingers and I took it from there. I wish I had taken piano seriously. I figured out piano and guitar chords and learned how to place them, especially from writing songs—how to interject an obtuse chord that would necessitate a change in melody. I never took a lesson in playwriting either, learned everything the hard way, through listening to actors interpret your lines, and learning how to direct them. Same with novel writing, it's often seemed to me like a process of learning how to eliminate mistakes, with the occasional 'eureka' moment. But with all three it's a matter of telling a story. That's a primal talent, and one that we Irish—like most dispossessed people—have a talent for."

Of course, one of the regulars at the Bells was a schoolteacher from Stuyvesant High School, brother of the proprietor, named Frank McCourt, some thirty years away from a Pulitzer Prize for *Angela's Ashes*:

My first introduction to this remarkable gentleman happened on a warm afternoon. There was a bunch of us belly up to the bar, sharing nothing but the silence, some lager shandies, and the long lovely fleeting departure of a communal hangover aligned with the promise of yet another boozy night ahead.

The door opened, yet none could, at first, be bothered looking up from the contemplation of their drinks. A dozen or so teenaged boys filed in. They were led by a truculent-looking individual, clad in a disheveled suit and a shirt that had already seen a couple of days' wear. In a dismissive sneer, he ordered the boys to feast their eyes on us one and all. 'So you want to be writers?' Frank McCourt then inquired of his Stuyvesant High School English class. There was no answer. He shook his head in dismay and motioned to us. "Maybe you should take a look at the end result."

CRUMBLING NEW YORK WAS THE PLACE TO BE

The New York of the 1970s and '80s is today thought of as the city's nadir. The city almost went bankrupt in 1975 when President Ford would not go along with a federal bailout and the *New York Daily News* had the headline of the decade: FORD TO CITY: DROP DEAD. For all his fiscal restraint, it would cost Ford the election a year later when New York helped elect Jimmy Carter president.

While the city was broke, it was the place to be if you wanted to be a rock star. CBGB in the East Village was the place where the talented worked: Talking Heads, The Ramones, Debbie Harry, Dead Boys, The Clash, The Pistols, and Television. "New York is like that," wrote Kirwan. "It grips you like a mistress and won't let you think about home. The place is so all-enveloping and seductive, it is sometimes hard to remember that you had a life before you settled here. If time flows like a river through other communities, it rushes in flash flood through the concrete canyons of Manhattan."

Kirwan remembered the grimy New York of those days with affection. He told me:

I basically came to New York in order to grow. I had sensed I could do that on my first visit. I was interested in so many things and I wanted to experience life to the fullest. Right from the start I wanted—in some small way—to be a poet of the city, whether that meant being a musician, writer, playwright, or whatever. It was so incredibly inexpensive to live here in the '70s and there was no shame in having no money. Living in the East Village, hanging at The Bells, CBGB's, Max's Kansas City, I never met anyone who had much money. Women didn't expect it of you either.

Pierce and I could gig Friday and Saturday nights and make more than enough to live on. Anything else was gravy. Sure, it was decidedly unsafe, I once had a bayonet stuck in my throat during a mugging. But the nightlife was a blast—on a typical night I'd stay at The Bells until 3 a.m.—and you remember yourself the characters you might meet there, Lester Bangs, Pete Hamill, Malachy and Frank—not to mention Tom Waits, Warren Zevon, Joe Strummer—and then I'd go to the Kiwi on 9th Street and Avenue A, and stay until dawn or later. That was a Black/Puerto Rican afterhours where when you entered you put a five on the counter and were given two joints, a Heineken, and a buck change that you left as a tip. I have enough stories from those nights to write another five novels. Hemingway said, "To be young and in Paris!" Hey Ernie, it didn't hold a candle to New York in the '70s!

LARRY KIRWAN, BUSINESSMAN

One of the things about *Green Suede Shoes* is that it should be taught at the Harvard Business School as a primer on how *not* to get screwed by record companies if you are a recording artist. "Yeah, don't go into music or any other form of the arts unless you really have to," he surprisingly said.

> It's not a game for the weak of heart. I've seen so many people broken by "the music life." They've come away hating the thing they loved most. Despite all the high-jinx living, I had a business brain. So, I was curious about how things worked. I had a head for figures too, so could add, and learned early on that 2-and-2 rarely made 4 in the music business.
>
> Most "artists" also feel that art should be all they're responsible for—that someone else will take care of promotion, money, and the logistics of gigging. Wrong!!!! Think of someone who goes into hotel management or a cadet at sea. Each of those will have to learn how to scrub the pots and pans first, then work their way up through every department. Even though I was very much involved in the druggy drinking days of the '70s, I was observing and learning all the time, though I often didn't care to put what I knew into practice. But when Chris Byrne and I formed Black 47, I brought all of my past experience to bear on the business end of things. Chris was no slouch either—and even more importantly, he was a NYPD detective and had served his time on the streets. We were pretty unbeatable both onstage and in the business department. Talk about focus, and at the same time not giving a fuck what people thought of us. And yet we were loyal to everyone around us. That was the basis of Black 47. The music might have been original and at times transcendent, but there was an ethic and principle behind the band that people could—and still do—relate to.

CYNDI LAUPER HAS SOME ADVICE

Kirwan also learned "something very important" from Cyndi Lauper. "She made me question if this was the kind of life I wanted and, more important," wrote Kirwan in *Green Suede Shoes*, "if I had the drive to succeed at it."

"I loved Cyndi," Kirwan told me.

> Though we haven't been in contact since the '80s, I still think the world of her. She taught me that anyone can give 100 percent, it's what "do you got" at 115 or

120 percent that counts. I don't think she ever verbalized that, but it was her deeply ingrained MO. Pierce and I, as part of the Major Thinkers, toured with her from clubs up to stadiums—we had the same manager. Cyndi was going to make it or die in the attempt. I didn't really feel that way—still don't—so I had to question myself in the face of her sheer elemental force. It's an amazing thing being around someone like that and feeling the ripple of that life force. I think I also learned from her that you can't be afraid to fail—a very Irish trait. When I got back into music in 1989 with Black 47—after four years of learning how to be a playwright—I was very much aware that this was my last chance, and so I took everything I had learned from Cyndi and applied it. Neither Chris Byrne nor I were interested in showbiz glitz—we were after a certain political and musical commitment, not unlike that of The Clash or Bob Marley. We gave everything onstage and never less than at 120 percent. It was exhilarating and elemental, and it turned off a lot of Irish-born people—but we found a new audience, young and not so young Irish-Americans searching for their roots. As Paul Hill from the Guilford Four said, we "were a voice for the voiceless." How interesting that Cyndi Lauper helped unleash some of that.

KIRWAN TAKES A WRITING HIATUS

Larry Kirwan's musical metamorphosis went in three phases. First, there was Turner and Kirwan of Wexford. "We had only one interest—music," wrote Kirwan. "All else would provide for itself. We never gave a damn about tomorrow. That was a concept for the straight and the bored—two things we were most definitely not. On the plus side, we both could write, sing, play, arrange, produce, and go totally nuts onstage. I suppose we may have canceled each other out somewhat; but we were oblivious as to how the world perceived us. If there was magic in the moment, then the moment was what we were all about."

Turner and Kirwan of Wexford eventually became Major Thinkers. They toured for years and their last performance was on St. Patrick's Day, 1985—after the band was dropped by Epic Records. "This new reality or malaise went way beyond money, however," confessed Kirwan in his autobiography. "I had grown sick of the rock life and, not by coincidence, sick of myself, too. I had been on a nonstop roller-coaster ride for thirteen years and I couldn't even recall the original reason for stepping aboard. I had come to America for what? Some vague notion of 'making it?' But making what? I wasn't even sure what the concept meant anymore. I had no interest in a big house in Malibu. Nor was I desirous of owning fast cars or even faster women. But what the hell did I want? I had to confess that I didn't have a bull's notion. I did want to create. But what did that mean? Write songs? Form a band? None of it appealed to me anymore."

This led Kirwan to a four-year musical hiatus when he worked at the writer's craft, which he found challenging. "In no time at all," he wrote, "I realized why so many playwrights, and writers in general, become alcoholics. It's a bitch of a game with long hours, much loneliness, and little, if any, financial reward, not to mention that the perfect play has never been written. Still, I had plenty of time on my hands and nothing else on my plate. In other words, playwriting is not for the faint of heart! It takes time and it changes you—not always for the better."

Kirwan's first writing project was a play about the Beatles called *Liverpool Fantasy*. "I had been sketching out an idea for some time about what would have happened if the Beatles hadn't made it," he wrote. "I suppose I was still wrestling with the 'making it' syndrome."

To put it mildly, it caused a stir. "*Liverpool Fantasy*," Kirwan recalled, "almost shut down the house during the post-workshop discussion. What in the name of God was I thinking, and how dare I desecrate the memory of the warm and fuzzy Saint John? That seemed to be the majority opinion; while again, I had a sizeable body of supporters who thought I was only half-mad and deserved, at the bare minimum, the right of free speech. I decided that I'd put all my eggs in one basket and go for a production of *Liverpool Fantasy*. To say that I couldn't even get arrested with this play might be stretching a point, but it was certainly declined by the many theaters and producers to whom I submitted it."

As he had with the music business, Kirwan was soon to learn that the theater business was dog-eat-dog in its own unique way. "I received an amazing eye-opener into the convoluted theatrical world of New York City, its many delights and pitfalls. Coming from the cutthroat world of rock music with its much higher budgets and expectations, theater was at once archaic, far more principled, intellectual though often harebrained, and worlds away more bitchy."

With the help of actress-turned-director Monica Gross, Kirwan rewrote the play and got it performed off-off-Broadway at a little theater named El Bohio in Alphabet

City. *Liverpool Fantasy* was also performed at the Dublin Theatre Festival in the Eblana Theatre in the basement of Busaras. It was now directed (in a way) by Kirwan himself, and had a chaotic, albeit successful run.

Kirwan also had to find another way to earn a living during his playwriting period. "One of the ways I supported myself in the period between the Thinkers and Black 47," he wrote, "was by writing music for modern dance. In the East Village of the '80s there was great interaction between musicians, choreographers, and dancers on both a professional and social level. In fact, it was in this milieu that I met my own chore-ographer and, and later wife, June Anderson, and began composing pieces of music for her company."

His next playwriting project was called *Mister Parnell*, about the "Uncrowned King of Ireland," Charles Stewart Parnell and his fall from grace—helped tremendously along by the opposition of the Catholic Church—because of his affair with the married Catherine O'Shea. "I only had to look inside my own heart and mind," wrote Kirwan, "to witness firsthand the repression that dogmatic Catholicism fosters. As a boy, I had revolted against it because Catholicism failed to take account of our natural sexuality. I had also bucked against its Northern counterpart because it had allowed the good side of the message—the unhindered communion of the devotee with God—to become distorted into a discriminatory hatred of Catholics and Catholicism."

Mister Parnell was finally performed in the early '90s at Synchronicity Space in Soho. "I was surprised," said Kirwan, "that it never received another production as it's a hell of a story. My grandfather's family in Carlow had taken opposite sides in the split of 1891 over Parnell being named in the divorce of Catherine and William O'Shea. So, I had an inside look at the man through the eyes of my family. I might revisit it at some time but there's a claustrophobic Victorian darkness that tends to overshadow the tragedy."

BLACK 47

The idea for Black 47 came to Kirwan while on a wild tour of Eastern Europe with the poet Copernicus just as the Iron Curtain was coming down, but it was nurtured in its early days in the Bronx in 1989. "This was going to be an Irish band for sure," wrote Kirwan, "but a New York one—not Dublin, London, or Bally-de-back-of-fucking-be-yond." Black 47 would soon become known as "the house band of New York City"; it was also described by the yellow British press as "the musical wing of the IRA."

"Black 47 was always more than just a band," wrote Kirwan in *Green Suede Shoes*. "There was a political dimension, too. . . . From the start, we were perceived as Irish republican and we were. . . . But everyone knew Black 47 was subversive, had a left-of-center agenda, and meant business." With songs about Michael Collins, James Connolly, Countess Markievicz, and Bobby Sands, the Republican political slant was obvious. But the group also took sides on social issues, such as the AIDS crisis that hit New York especially hard in the 1980s and '90s.

Their song, "Danny Boy" about an immigrant gay Irish construction worker really hits home. "Irish America was past ready for a shaking up and, in our own crazy way, we were the boys to do it," wrote Kirwan. "As far as I was concerned, it was hypocrisy to be for civil rights in Belfast and Derry and be against gay rights in New York and Boston. We were in the business of kicking sacred cows as well as sacred ass."

"The East Village in the '70s and early '80s was a magical place," said Kirwan to me.

Every kind of outlaw hung out there. The Kiwi usually had transgender bartenders and the clientele was exotic and dangerous. I learned so much from those people. Back then gender fluidity was in your face. It didn't even have a name, but it possessed a fierce gentleness that could turn fiery when insulted. I once saw Carlita, a lovely trans person, take off one of her heels and drive it into a biker's forehead—and she was right. A whole generation of beautiful people got wiped out by AIDS not only because of sexuality but because it was considered an insult not to share needles with your friends. That's why I wrote 'Danny Boy' about a gay Irish construction worker, and every night I sang it with Black 47 I had to fight back the tears, because there was only one way that song could be sung—with love and defiance. Black 47 was huge at the time that song was released. Promoters of Irish festivals would request that we not perform it. I always replied, "Thanks so much for reminding me."

Another popular Black 47 song is "Funky Céili," a kind of jolly ode to a surprise pregnancy. "Because there was no legal birth control beyond abstinence," Kirwan told me, "every single person in Ireland of my youth was deathly afraid of pregnancy. So I wrote the song as a parable of sorts, warning young people that they should employ birth control or end up in the Bronx like the guy in the song. But the first night we performed it at the Irish Arts Center in 1990 everyone got up and danced and loved the song for what it was. To this day it's a thrill to see that it makes people so happy."

BLACK 47 ENDS AND THE WRITING BEGINS

Black 47 did their twenty-five years and disbanded in 2014. It was time for a new life for Kirwan. He has gone from doing 2,500 gigs with Black 47 to under twenty nowadays. "Many of those," he told me, "are two particular one-man shows for colleges and performing arts centers—A *History of Ireland through Music* and *The Story of Stephen Foster*. Occasionally I get a longing to do some rowdy rock and roll gigs and take those. But mostly I'm writing these days."

"I still do the big three—playwriting, novels, and songwriting," said Kirwan. "I really like the challenge of writing books, music, and lyrics to musicals. It's very difficult, but I find it fulfilling, although it does drive me crazy from time to time. I have two new musicals that take up a huge amount of time, *IRAQ* and *The Catacombs* about the life and times of Brendan Behan. I usually choose subjects that challenge me to learn or confront some new skill. For *IRAQ*, I had to come to terms with quarter-tone Arabic music and fuse it with the punk, hard rock and hip-hop sounds that the troops were experiencing during the early years of the war. And with the Behan piece I've fused Sean Nós with a Broadway sensibility. I also have a new novel, *Rockaway Blue*, that will be published by Cornell University Press. It's a post 9/11 novel and something that I've been working on for some time. For me New York is either pre-9/11 or post-9/11 and I wanted to show that through the eyes of a family who had to deal with great loss and make sense of it—if such a thing is possible."

REBEL IN THE SOUL AND THE CHARLOTTE MOORE INFLUENCE

In 2017, his play *Rebel in the Soul* was produced at the Irish Repertory Theatre in New York. It is the story of the Mother-and-Child Scheme that rocked Ireland in the early 1950s. Mother-and-Child was proposed by Dr. Noel Browne, the minister for Health in John A. Costello's coalition government and was supported by Seán MacBride, the minister for External Affairs. It was a health and insurance plan that sought to fight the high rate of child mortality in Ireland, much of it caused by the high incidence of tuberculosis. This seemingly good plan was opposed by Archbishop of Dublin John Charles McQuaid because it ran counter to "Catholic moral teaching."

Like most authors, Kirwan has a great affection for the people he is writing about: "They are all gloriously flawed—despite being three of the great men of their times. Because of the structure of the play we get a chance to observe them early on in private moments and can take their measure. They are soon caught up in a crisis, in many ways beyond their control, and we see them under pressure and often making wrong decisions."

Rebel in the Soul had been a work in progress for many years before it finally hit the stage. "It's not unusual for a play to take four or five years from conception to production," Kirwan told me in an interview. "There were some other factors in this case too. When we decided to disband Black 47 I went on the road for a long period and we made a final album, *Last Call*. Then my musical, *Hard Times*, became a success and is now being developed for a major production. These and other factors caused *Rebel in the Soul* to be put on hold for several years. But Charlotte Moore had always been attracted to the play, the era, and the characters; and I guess the timing was right for her. As ever it's great to work at the Irish Rep—like coming home to family. It's the perfect place to watch these fascinating Irish characters come to grips with an issue sixty-seven years ago that's roiling the US right now—healthcare and insurance. To add fat to the fire, the decisions they made under pressure back in 1951 led to the shaping of Ireland as we know it today."

Kirwan credits Charlotte Moore, the artistic director and co-founder of the Irish Rep, for helping him develop the play. "The first drafts of the play had only two characters, Browne and McQuaid. After an early public reading at the Rep, Charlotte suggested that I expand the work and include MacBride, since he was often mentioned in the text. Browne, MacBride and McQuaid are very dynamic characters who make mistakes under pressure—a good foundation for any play."

Writing *Rebel in the Soul* while out on the road in the final years of Black 47 had a therapeutic effect on Kirwan: "Writing keeps me sane while on the road," Kirwan told me. "There's an intensity, and a focus on the ego when you're touring and playing. But when I'm in a hotel room after the gig, and I begin to deal with three charismatic figures like Browne, MacBride, and McQuaid, I become a boy again back in Wexford, questioning my grandfather on politics and the times, and digesting his answers. The hours speed by as you turn historical figures into dramatic characters. Tighten the screws, heighten the pressure, deepen the intrigue, and you bring a special moment in time shimmering back to life. Before you know—it's morning, you're rip-roaring and ready to hit the road again."

DEALING WITH BRENDAN BEHAN

To say that Kirwan is prolific is a gross understatement. Besides his new novel, he has three playwriting projects underway. *Hard Times* is now called *Paradise Square* and looks as though it may reach Broadway in the next year. It had a very successful ten-week run at Berkeley Rep and has undergone many changes, although the basic story remains the same.

But his number one project is on Brendan Behan. "I'm presently recording the score for *The Catacombs*," he told me. "The book is written and I'm really happy with it. Behan has always been a difficult character to portray because of his alcoholism. But I was determined to capture him, his times, his music, and the politics of this controversial and influential man. We know so much more about him now—including the fact that he had undiagnosed diabetes for many years—my portrayal reflects that and other relevant information that's available now. Hopefully, people will get to see the piece in the next couple of years."

Behan has a special affection for Behan. "I always intended writing a musical about Brendan," Kirwan said, "basically because the man himself was so musically oriented. I don't think you can really capture him without song. I could also instantly hear in my head the type of music that would summon his essence. His alcoholism was the put-off. It touched too close to home for a working musician and is ultimately really depressing. I finally figured out how to excavate the real man from inside the alcoholic bubble and the ideas have flowed since.

"He's a very important figure in the Irish punk rock scene," Kirwan continued. "Shane MacGowan, although an original, adopted much of Brendan's trappings. The Tossers have a great song, 'Brendan O'Beachain'; Black 47 has 'The Ballad of Brendan Behan.' We musicians understand him and his lonely genius, because we've all been down part of his path, yet managed to get out alive. Brendan's the man!

"Brendan was one of us," opined Kirwan. "He said what he liked and did what he pleased. He was political, generous to a fault, and deadly afraid of slipping back into anonymity. Fame killed him. He drank too much and became a boor. But, oh, what a writer. Even re-reading *Borstal Boy*, you still get the feeling that you missed out on so much. His plays broke new ground and, with the right reimagining, can be relevant all over again. There's so much overlooked in Brendan's life and work. No matter, he'll always be 'our Brendan.'"

NO RETIREMENT IN SIGHT

When he's not writing plays or novels, Kirwan manages to host and produce a weekly SiriusXM radio show and pen a column for the *Irish Echo* newspaper. "I've always had insomnia problems," he told me, "and it's the one trait I share with our president. I enjoy both of these jobs so much. Doing an *Echo* column of seven hundred words every two weeks is a great writing workout. For about five years I did it every week but that became a bit too much. 'Celtic Crush' on SiriusXM is a three-hour music/talk show that I do without notes every week. The improv nature of the show keeps me sharp. It also led me to write *A History of Irish Music*—which is basically a memoir based on the various musicians I've met or admired in my life. So, as they say, one thing always seems to lead to another in my life.

"I've been fortunate to do just what I've wanted to in life and always enjoyed creating. To quote my dear friend, Malachy McCourt, 'I'll be working 'til I'm ninety—if I'm lucky!' "

PART THREE
IRISH LABOR PAINS

LABOR ORGANIZATIONS ON BOTH SIDES OF THE ATLANTIC WERE NURTURED IN IRISH NEW YORK: HOW A FIRE AND A COUPLE OF IRISHMEN NAMED MURPHY AND SMITH HELPED CHANGE AMERICA FOREVER

I t is extraordinary that the two greatest Irish labor leaders of all time—James Larkin and James Connolly—lived in New York during the first twenty years of the twentieth century. And their role as labor agitators and organizers in America would be followed and emulated by an acolyte of Connolly's, a tough ex-IRA man from County Kerry by the name of Michael J. Quill.

During these turbulent times a certain Irish Catholic Lower East Side politician named Alfred Emanuel Smith would come into prominence with a shove from a Tammany Hall chieftain named "Silent" Charlie Murphy. By 1928 Smith, this urban "Happy Warrior," would be the candidate for the Democratic Party for the office of president of the United States of America. He would lose dramatically, but the seed he planted would allow another Irish Catholic, John Fitzgerald Kennedy, to become president thirty-two years later. Between Ireland and New York, the way labor was looked at would be changed forever.

And it all started with a fire in Greenwich Village.

CHAPTER ONE

FIRE AT THE TRIANGLE SHIRTWAIST FACTORY

A COUPLE OF OLD SCHOOL IRISH NEW YORK POLS TO THE RESCUE

I t all started on a spring day, Saturday March 25, 1911. The Triangle Shirtwaist Factory was located at 23–29 Washington Place in New York's Greenwich Village, about a block east of Washington Square. It was payday and the workers, mostly Jewish and Italian women immigrants, were ready for their week to end. And their Saturday would end—in tragedy.

Triangle Shirtwaist was located on the eighth, ninth, and tenth floors of what was known then as the Asch Building, which is still there to this day, now part of NYU. The company made shirtwaists, which was what women's blouses were called early in the twentieth century. The factory was owned by a couple of Russian immigrants, Max Blanck and Isaac Harris, who had their own Horatio Alger stories but apparently had forgotten their humble roots. They liked to run things on the cheap. They were proponents of child labor, and when inspectors came by they would hide the children in a box. They also liked to save on such necessities as washrooms, closets, and toilets. They also had a history of arson at their factories. The thing they would not allow was a union. And they played dirty. Greed was their motto.

In 1909 a strike was called, and they shut their workers out. Their "replacement workers" were prostitutes from the Bowery who had no skills except that they could beat up women on picket duty outside the Asch Building. The Tammany Hall controlled police where no use either. "When the strikers fought back," David Von Drehle wrote in *Triangle: The Fire That Changed America*, "the Tammany police force intervened on the side of the owners. This was Tammany's custom. Strikers, after all, had no money, no 'sugar,' to pass around the station house. They added nothing to the stream of graft that powered the political machine." Blanck and Harris were truculent in their anti-union sentiments and urged other factory owners to follow their example during the heavy strikes that were to follow. To Blanck and Harris, it was war.

Blanck and Harris did the bare minimum to meet the inadequate fire regulations. "One inspector P. J. McKeon, who lectured in fire safety at Columbia University," wrote Terry Golway in his history of the FDNY *So Others Might Live*, "said that 'the place looked dangerous to me. There was a fire escape in the back and all that,' he said, 'and the regulations seemed to be complied with all right, but I could see that there would be a serious panic if the girls were not instructed how to handle themselves in case of a fire. I even found that the door to the main stairway was usually kept locked. I was told this was done because it was difficult to keep track of so many girls.'"[10]

It is believed that a carelessly discarded match or cigarette butt set off pieces of scrap cloth and started the fire on the eighth floor. Cotton cloth is very combustible and when you added the tissue paper used and the wooden tables, the fire had all the ingredients it needed. Most of the workers on the eighth floor escaped as the floor soon filled with smoke, but their compatriots on the ninth and tenth floors were not as lucky. Many escaped to the roof, where NYU law students from the adjacent building found ladders which they dropped down to save them. In the most ironic way, it was lucky the fire was on a Saturday, the Jewish sabbath, or the death toll would have been much higher.

IRISH NEW YORK TO THE RESCUE

And the first heroes on the scene were Irish. Passerby John Mooney saw the fire and pulled fire alarm box #289, which alerted the fire department's chief dispatcher, a man named Daniel Donahue. The first responders included a mounted cop on patrol, James Meehan, who saw the fire and rushed into the building. He ran up the stairs and directed the women out. On his way down, he forced open a locked door and freed many women escaping from the eighth floor. Within ninety seconds, the FDNY was on the scene. Engine Company 72 was the first to arrive with its contingent of Irish firefighters—Oliver Mahoney, Bernard McKenny, John McNulty, and Thomas Foley. They immediately fought their way into the Asch Building. Engine 72 was soon joined by Engine Company 18, rushing over from West 10th Street, only blocks away.

The fire quickly spread north above the eighth floor and soon New Yorkers would witness something that would not happen again for another ninety years until the

World Trade Center was attacked on 9/11—bodies becoming human missiles as women flung themselves out of windows from the top two floors. Firefighters and police kept victims of the fire in the building on the ground floor because they feared they would be killed by the falling bodies. Elevator operator Joseph Zito made repeated trips up and down to bring the deceased victims, packed over each other, down.

Everyone awaited the arrival of the Hook & Ladder companies. Their regular ladders would be thirty feet short of reaching even the eighth floor, but maybe their scaling ladders could save them. Scaling ladders, according to Golway, "looked like a homely cousin to the FDNY's larger and sturdier equipment. Firemen could extend their vertical reach by carrying this small ladder, which varied in height from 15 to 20 feet, to the top of their regular ladders. Consisting of a series of small rungs attached to a single central upright, its modest size and weight made it mobile, and that was the genius of it. The fireman positioned the scaling ladder so that it attached by a hook to a higher windowsill. It required a straight climb up and a straight descent—the scaling ladder wasn't fixed at an angle like regular ladders."

"Firefighters," wrote Golway, "including the veteran pioneer of the scaling ladder, John Binns, arrived within six or seven minutes of the fire's outbreak, but the fire spread with such speed and intensity that several victims already had jumped to their deaths as a growing crowd of horrified passersby looked on helplessly. Firefighters found their mangled bodies lying on the sidewalk. Above them, young women and a few men pleaded for help from windows and ledges."

The FDNY began to utilize life nets to try and catch the jumpers. David Von Drehle in *Triangle* relied on the work of William Gunn Shepherd, a young reporter for the United Press. Shepherd observed that "One girl tried to keep her body upright. Until the very instant she touched the sidewalk, she was trying to balance herself."

"Ladders were deployed quickly," wrote Golway, "but they reached only to the sixth floor. A young woman in a ninth-floor window, her skirt on fire, leaped for one of the ladders. She missed, and she fell to her death. Scaling ladders were brought out to reach to the upper floors, but by the time they were in place, the carnage was over. Those who dared had already leaped to their deaths. Those who couldn't were dead inside the building. Only about fifteen minutes passed between the death of the first jumper and the end of hope, when no more faces appeared in the windows."

Then there was the case of the gentleman jumper who, in an odd way, helped the women as they prepared to leap. "He held out a second girl in the same way," said

Shepherd, "then let her drop. Then he held out a third girl. They didn't resist." He kissed the next girl in line. Was it his sweetheart? "Then he held her out into space," continued Shepherd, "and dropped her. But, quick as a flash, he was on the window-sill himself. His coat flattered upward; the air filled his trouser legs; I could see that he wore tan shoes and hose. His hat remained on his head." When he landed, Shepherd inspected him. "I saw his face before they covered it. You could see he was a real man. He had done his best."

"A young firefighter with Engine Co. 18," wrote Golway, "recalled that the first thing he saw, as his engine pulled up to the scene 'was a man's body coming crashing down. . . . We turned into Greene Street and began to stretch in our hoses. The bodies were hitting all around us.'"

With the heat of the fire on them, a mass exodus began from the windows as Shepherd looked on in horror. "Girls were burning to death before our eyes," he wrote. "There were jams in the windows. No one was lucky enough to be able to jump, it seemed. But one by one the jams broke. Down came bodies in a shower, burning, smoking, lighted bodies, with the disheveled hair of the girls trailing upward. . . . There were thirty-three in that shower."

The fire was brought under control within an hour. Now the gruesome work began. The FDNY had to rig block-and-tackles to remove the bodies from the building. It would be midnight before every corpse was removed. The final count was 146 souls, 123 of them women.

"SILENT" CHARLIE MURPHY CHANGES THINGS

"The history of early twentieth-century New York," wrote Terry Golway in *Machine Made*, his colorful biography of Tammany Hall, "is defined not by a political campaign or an election but by a fire. . . . For Tammany, for the labor movement, for the burgeoning campaign for women's rights—even, some argue, for the nation itself—the Triangle fire has been considered a critical turning point, the tragic inspiration for the creation of a new social contract that foreshadowed the New Deal, which was put in place by a man who served in the New York State Senate at the time of the fire, Franklin D. Roosevelt."[11]

This burst of altruism by Tammany did not start with the Triangle fire. It started eighteen months earlier with a defeat at the polls in November 1909. Simply put, Tammany got clobbered.

The Grand Sachem—Tammany's leader—was a man named Charles Francis Murphy. He was born to Irish immigrant parents in 1858. It is believed that his father, a refugee from the Great Famine, hit New York in 1848.

Young Charlie dropped out of school at fourteen to go work in a wire factory. "He was a devout Catholic family man," wrote journalist Arthur Krock. "He would not take money from a whore or a criminal." With his first five hundred dollars he opened a saloon, Charlie's Place, at 19th Street and Avenue A in the neighborhood he was born in, the old Gas House District on the East Side. Although "honest," Murphy was a huge fan of patronage and thought nothing of steering a city contract to a friend or campaign contributor. It was the way of Tammany.

"He performed countless favors," wrote David Von Drehle in *Triangle*, "won thousands of friends, and eventually became district leader. Murphy liked to conduct the political business of the neighborhood while leaning against a lamppost on Twentieth Street. Anyone who needed a son out of jail, or a job, or relief from a hassling policeman knew that Mr. Murphy would hear pleas in the flickering glow of the gaslight."[12]

Tammany also had another problem—it was running out of Irish voters. "Murphy was being pressed by Big Tim Sullivan," wrote Von Drehle, "and others to do something significant to appeal to the new immigrants. And the largest percentage of those immigrants worked in garment shops or had loved ones that did. The Triangle fire struck directly at those people that Tammany needed most." Tammany could still count. There were five hundred shirtwaist factories, employing over forty thousand workers, almost all of them immigrants. Murphy was interested in these Eastern European Jews and Italians, especially the Jews because he thought they were more interested into assimilating into American society.

"In fact," added Golway, "Murphy and individual members of Tammany had been moving the organization toward the cause of reform—or, more to the point, to a new kind of reform shorn of its evangelical moralism—well before the Triangle fire."

"Silent Charlie listened silently to Smith and other young sachems like Wagner," observed Robert A. Caro in his titanic biography of Robert Moses, *The Power Broker.* "Murphy knew that Tammany must change. . . . Becoming identified with Progressivism, becoming known as the party of social progress, would be a way to shatter that image forever. Pushing to the forefront bright young men identified with such causes rather than with the ancient rituals of Tammany would be a way to spawn candidates who would shatter forever the unseen but heavy chains that weighed down the Irish Catholic in America."

"Most of the troubles of the world," Murphy himself once noted according to Von Drehle, "could be avoided if men opened their minds instead of their mouths."

"He was a listener and a watcher, and his taciturnity was legend," observed Von Drehle. "Murphy's silences always gave the impression that he knew more than he was saying; silence also saved him from making promises. This was important to Murphy, because any promises he made, he kept."

"He left no records and no formal speeches," wrote his biographer Nancy Joan Weiss, "and he granted no interviews of consequence. No letters survive and it is unlikely that they ever existed."

When he died in 1924, FDR would refer to Murphy, a nemesis to Roosevelt in his younger years, as a "genius." And the Triangle fire gave Murphy the perfect opportunity to prove his political acuity.

ENTER AL SMITH, IRISH MUTT

Murphy by the time of the Triangle fire was purging the old reactionaries of Tammany. He was embracing young pols like Al Smith, assemblyman from the Lower East Side, and state Senator Robert F. Wagner, a German immigrant, who represented a district in Manhattan. Soon Smith and Wagner came to be known as Murphy's "Tammany Twins." "Both grew up in poverty," wrote Von Drehle in *Triangle*, "scrapped for what education they had, and appreciated Tammany for the fairness with which it rewarded hard work and talent."

"Murphy not only advanced the political interests of his 'young men,'" wrote Weiss, "but he listened to their ideas and liked what he heard."

"Through Wagner and Smith," wrote Golway in *Machine Made*, "Charlie Murphy's control over Albany was enormous, for the new governor, John Alden Dix, was also a Tammany ally. The anti-Tammany Civic Leagued noted with anxiety that 'Murphy was in the saddle and Tammany controlled everything in sight.'"

So when flamed ripped through the Triangle Shirtwaist Factory two months after the ascension of Wagner and Smith, Tammany had in place the mechanism, the will, and the power to respond to the public's outrage—and the outrage of its young leaders. Wagner and Smith were named chairman and vice chairman, respectively, of the state Factory Investigating Commission (FIC) appointed in the fire's aftermath. No investigative body in the history of New York politics was given more sweeping powers than the FIC—it issued subpoenas, demanded access to private property (such as factories), hired staff without regard to patronage or politics, conducted public hearings, and sought alliances with advocacy groups, labor unions, and other interested organizations.

The point man was Al Smith. Smith was an Irish mutt—two of his grandparents were from Ireland, one from Germany, one from Italy. He liked to brag that he earned his "degree" from the Fulton Fish Market. Smith was a true man of the people. After the Triangle fire he even went to the city morgue to help his constituents identify the bodies of their loved ones.

The genius of Al Smith was that he knew intimately how Albany worked. When he first arrived in Albany it was like living on another planet. But while many of the legislators were part-timers, Smith never left Albany and started attending committee hearings that he was not assigned to. He read every bill and budget bill and when his time came, no one in Albany could pull the wool over Al Smith's eyes.

But as a Tammany man—and Charlie Murphy's man—the reformers were still suspicious of him. Slowly, as they saw him in action, their opinion of Smith turned to admiration. "First one and then another of the reformers," wrote Robert Caro, "began to tell their friends that they had really come to believe that maybe, just maybe, after decades of waiting, reform in New York had found at last, in the red-faced Tammany henchman, the instrument for which it had been waiting: the champion who would fight for their dreams in the political arena and turn them into laws. And some of the more romantic among them, examining Smith's long, slow rise through the ranks of Tammany, began to speculate that perhaps all the time he had been executing its dirty work he had been waiting for the chance to do good."

It seemed that Smith even surprised himself. According to Caro, Smith wondered how "an uneducated Mick from the Fourth Ward could rise so high."

With Smith on the Assembly side and Wagner on the Senate side, by 1913 twenty-five new labor laws had gone on the books. "Business leaders," observed David Von Drehle, "didn't quite know what had hit them."

Because of Murphy, Smith, and Wagner—and with the help of the likes of Frances Perkins, who would become FDR's secretary of the Labor in twenty years—lives were made better throughout New York State. The Democratic Party was refashioned by Silent Charlie Murphy and Al Smith, and the foundation was laid for the New Deal, which would rescue America from the greatest depression in its history.

"It is hard to imagine Al Smith's success in turning New York in the 1920s into a laboratory for the New Deal with the terrible fire to spur him on, and to inspire public opinion," wrote Terry Golway in *So Others Might Live*. "The fire came to symbolize the evil of passive government turning a blind eye to ruthless exploitation and criminal neglect in the workplace, which is why the Triangle Shirtwaist fire became far more than a local tragedy."

CHAPTER TWO

JAMES LARKIN

FROM STRUMPET CITY TO GREENWICH VILLAGE

J ames Plunkett captures the pre-revolutionary Dublin in his rich novel, *Strumpet City*. The use of the word "strumpet" makes it almost sound musical. But this Dublin City is not—it is the city of "whores," per Plunkett's not-so-subtle message, a city in deep poverty and unrest. Of course, it was also the city of labor leader extraordinaire James Larkin, who would be played by Peter O'Toole in the film version of Plunkett's novel.

Larkin owns a rich, albeit controversial, place in Irish history. He does not hold the reputation of fellow labor leader James Connolly—and it might be his own fault. He was a great orator but could also be a dilettante and a petty one at that. The one thing Jim Larkin was never accused of, however, was being boring.

A HARDSCRABBLE YOUTH

Larkin was born in 1874 in Liverpool to parents who immigrated from Ulster. He would later boast that his father had been a Fenian. By age seven, he was already working. He soon found that the world was not a God-like place for the poor. "I was taught the truth of eternal justice," he is quoted in *James Larkin* by Emmet O'Connor, "and I was taught the brotherhood of man was a true and living thing, and the fear of God was a thing that ought to cover all my days and also control my actions. And then I had occasion to go out into the world and found out there was no fatherhood of God, and there was no brotherhood of man, but every man in society was compelled to be like a wolf or a hyena, trying to tear down the other man that he might gain an advantage either by the other man's suffering, or by the other man's sorrow, or, which was more important, the sorrow of his wife, the sorrow of his woman, the sorrow of his daughter, the sorrow of his children.[13]

He was soon working the Liverpool docks, eventually becoming a foreman dock-porter. He then went to work for the National Union of Dock Labourers (NUDL) as a temporary organizer, then found a permanent post as a national organizer. By 1907 he was off to Belfast, where he began to make a name for himself as not only a labor organizer, but also as an orator. "A remarkable speaker and a man of seething energy," said one Vladimir Lenin. "Larkin has performed miracles among the unskilled workers."

"When Larkin spoke," wrote Bertram Wolfe, scholar, writer, and communist, "his blue eyes flashed and sparkled. He roared and thundered. . . . Sometimes an unruly forelock came down on his forehead as he moved his head in vigorous emphasis. Impulsive, fiery, passionate, swift at repartee, highly personal, provocative, and hot tempered in attack, strong and picturesque of speech, Larkin's language was rich in the turns of Irish poetic imagery sprinkled with neologisms of his own devising."[14]

Novelist David Garnett had a similar recollection of Larkin upon seeing him address a 1913 labor rally in the Albert Hall: "There, striding about the platform one beheld the whole of the sweated, starved, exploited working class suddenly incarnate in the shape of a gigantic Tarzan of all the slum jungles of the West."

By 1910 he was off to Dublin, soon to be replaced in Belfast by James Connolly, who had returned from New York.

THE LARKIN-O'CASEY FRIENDSHIP

Although Larkin had many detractors on both sides of the Atlantic, Sean O'Casey was not one of them. "The dynamic Larkin was probably the most important influence on the young O'Casey," wrote David Krause in *Sean O'Casey and his World*, "and the shaping of his proletarian view of life; Larkin the liberator, the 'Prometheus Hibernica' of O'Casey's autobiography, the fiery street orator and heroic union leader who came to Dublin to eliminate some of the worst slums in Europe and protect the people from the money-changers with his 'divine mission of discontent.'"

O'Casey joined the radical Irish Republican Brotherhood (IRB), but he was also a member of Larkin's ITGWU. "In later years," wrote Krause, "when he was asked why he lost his faith in the Church, he replied without hesitation, 'I never lost my faith, I found it. I found it when Jim Larkin came to Dublin and organized the unskilled workers. I found it in Jim's great socialist motto: 'An injury to one is the concern of all.' He was the saviour of Dublin. He put his faith in the people and their need to live a better and fuller life. And that's where I put my faith.'"[15]

"For Irish nationalists the Easter Rising of 1916 was the crucial event in Irish history," wrote Krause,

> but for the Irish working class, and for O'Casey, Larkin's general strike of 1913
> had launched the first blow for the liberation of the Irish people. As he did
> throughout his life, O'Casey put his socialism before his nationalism, and he
> turned out for the strike but not for the Rising. He chose to be a rebel worker
> rather than a rebel patriot."

O'Casey was upset when he learned that Padraic Pearse, of all people, was using the
"black trams" during the 1913 Lockout. For an IRB man to take this view of Pearse
and the Volunteers is, indeed, a radical insight by O'Casey, but there may be more to
it. His adoration of Larkin may have tainted his view of Connolly, who was looking for
an armed conflict with the British. "That Connolly joined the IRB caused distress to
some socialists," wrote Lorcan Collins in *16 Lives: James Connolly*, "including Seán
O'Casey, who said that 'Connolly had stepped from the narrow byway of Irish Socialism on to the broad and crowded highway of Irish Nationalism.' This nationalism
'became his daily rosary, while the higher creed of international humanity that had
so long bubbled from his eloquent lips was silent forever, and Irish Labour lost a
Leader.'"

O'Casey's antipathy toward Connolly finally resulted, with Larkin headed to
America, in his resignation from the ICA. "It would be wise when reading criticism
of Connolly by O'Casey," wrote Lorcan Collins, "to bear in mind the controversy
surrounding the secretary's resignation from the Irish Citizen Army. O'Casey was
annoyed that Markievicz was a member of the committee of Cumann na mBan as
they were clearly tied to the Irish Volunteers, an army which was 'in its methods and
aims, inimical to the first interests of Labour.' O'Casey called a meeting to discuss
this situation, but a vote of confidence in the countess was passed and O'Casey was
told to apologise to Markievicz. He refused to do so, on a point of principle, and
resigned his position and his membership of the ICA."

Larkin continued to influence the writing of O'Casey as witnessed by O'Casey's
character "Red Jim" in *The Star Turns Red*, published in 1940, an obvious reference
to Larkin. There is an interesting observation by Eileen O'Casey, Sean's wife, in her
memoir, *Sean*: "This summer Jim Larkin," wrote O'Casey, "the great Irish trade

unionist, travelled down to Devon for a single afternoon, arriving at midday and returning in the evening to London. Jim had always been Sean's hero; often he had told me of him and of how even his prison sentence had left him undaunted; they seldom come like Jim nowadays. Probably seventy at the time, he was a tall man, finely built, with a lovely head of hair and a compelling force. The children must have been at school; I remember that he and Sean, who was overcome by emotion at seeing him, sat in the kitchen to eat their meal and to talk over the past in a racing torrent of words."

Krause observes that in a 1956 letter to a despondent American socialist, O'Casey wrote: "Ireland misses Larkin just as the USA misses [Eugene V.] Debs, for such flames are rarely kindled; but they, in the work of others, will flame again, if not in America or Ireland, then somewhere else to lighten & warm the whole family of man."

Sean O'Casey was a Larkin man to the end.

THE DUBLIN LOCKOUT OF 1913

Several Irish patriots seem to have been put on this earth for a singular purpose. For Tom Clarke it was the Easter Uprising. For Michael Collins it was his genius at terrorism that resulted in the Anglo-Irish Treaty of 1921. For James Larkin, it was the Dublin Lockout of 1913.

Living in Ireland had spurred a strong nationalism in Larkin. For instance, Larkin's listing in the 1911 Irish Census. The Larkins are hard to find because they are listed under "O'Lorcáin," the Irish spelling of their name. This was somewhat surprising because Larkin didn't speak Irish, but it is not a move unprecedented among nationalist politicians in using the Irish of their names. However, his wife and sister, who was living with him at 27 Auburn Street on the north side of Dublin, said they are Irish speakers. It seemed his transformation from Liverpudlian to Dubliner was complete.

On one side stood Larkin, man of the people, and on the other William Martin Murphy, who Larkin described as a "blood-sucking vampire" and "a soulless, money-grubbing tyrant." Upon arrival in Dublin, Larkin had set up his own union, the Irish Transport and General Workers' Union (ITGWU), which included both skilled and unskilled workers. By 1913, Larkin numbered thirteen thousand members in the ITGWU. Employers in Dublin were beginning to become frightened.

William Martin Murphy was the Rupert Murdoch of his day. He was a media giant because he owned the *Irish Independent, Evening Herald,* and *Irish Catholic* newspapers. He also owned the Irish United Tramway Company, which was the major source of transportation around Dublin City. For good measure, he also owned Clery's, Dublin's most popular department store, and the B&I ferry company. He had it all and he wasn't about to share it. It was obvious that William Martin Murphy was not sleeping with another hundred people in a Dublin tenement like many of Larkin's members were.

In the summer of 1913 Murphy conspired with three hundred other Dublin employers to stop the ITGWU from organizing their workers. On August 31, 1913 workers rallied in Sackville (now O'Connell) Street and heard Larkin speak, arms upraised, just like his statue. He spoke from a balcony on the Imperial Hotel, also owned by Murphy, which must have delighted Larkin. It was at this point that the Dublin Metropolitan Police (DMP), batons at the ready, rushed the protestors. Two workers were killed, and three hundred others were injured. It would be the first "Bloody Sunday" in Irish history (to be followed by the one on November 21, 1920 when Collins's Squad shot fourteen British Secret Service agents and the British retaliated by opening fire on a football crowd in Croke Park, killing another fourteen; the final Bloody Sunday would be on January 30, 1972, when the British army murdered another fourteen innocent protestors in Derry.)

Tom Clarke, who refused to stock Murphy's papers at his two news agencies, was appalled by the carnage in Sackville Street: "Yet nothing I know of during my whole career can match the downright inhuman savagery that was witnessed recently in the [Dublin] streets . . . when the police were let loose to run amok and indiscriminately bludgeon every man, woman and child they came across," Clarke is quoted in *16 Lives: Thomas Clarke* by Helen Litton.

Larkin and Connolly were arrested for sedition and Murphy rejoiced, saying "I think I have broken the malign influence of Mr. Larkin and set him on the run." By September 22, twenty-five thousand workers were locked out. Tried for sedition and incitement to riot and robbery, Larkin got seven months' hard labor, but was released within weeks. On November 13, 1913, Connolly announced the formation of the Irish Citizen Army (ICA) to protect the workers in any future conflicts. By 1916, they would join ranks with the Irish Volunteers and fight in the Easter Rising. The lockout would last into early 1914 with the workers finally succumbing to the employers. It would be remembered by William Butler Yeats in "September 1913," maybe a preamble poem to events of 1916 and beyond:

> Romantic Ireland's dead and gone,
> It's with O'Leary in the grave.

"LONGFELLOW" GOES TO NEW YORK

By 1914, Larkin's wanderlust was picking at him again. "Larkin's interest in a world tour was common knowledge," wrote O'Connor in *James Larkin*, "and Connolly suggested he go to the U.S. to recuperate while fund-raising for the Labour Party, a proposal Larkin later twisted to allege that Connolly had beguiled him into travelling to America to be rid of his more popular superior." O'Connor added that "some, including admirers like Seán O'Casey, thought he wished to evade impending trouble over insurance money misspent during the 1913 struggle."[16]

Upon his arrival in New York, introduction from Connolly in hand, he "went directly to the Flynn household . . . and spent endless hours talking with 'my country-woman' Annie Flynn," wrote Helen C. Camp in *Iron in Her Soul: Elizabeth Gurley Flynn and the American Left*. Shocked after seeing young Elizabeth smoking, Larkin warned Mrs. Flynn about such "free ways," revealing the prude in him. On November 8, he spoke to fifteen thousand people in Madison Square Garden. The *New York Tribune* would soon refer to him as a "violent anarchist."

Like a lot of leftists, Larkin soon found his base in Greenwich Village—two times in Milligan Place, a little courtyard out of an O. Henry story near the corner of West 10th Street and Sixth Avenue, MacDougal Alley just off Washington Square Park and at 53 Jane Street, near the corner of Hudson Street, blocks from the river and the Cunard Line piers. With World War I raging, he soon found himself caught in the espionage world of John Devoy.

"Sometime around the time of Rossa's death," wrote Terry Golway in his biography of John Devoy, *Irish Rebel: John Devoy and America's Fight for Ireland's Freedom*,

> Irish labor leader James Larkin . . . asked Devoy to help arrange a meeting with German diplomats. Larkin, who was living on strong tea and little else, was prepared to take a German offer of cash in exchange for his support of the

German war effort. Larkin clearly wanted Devoy to be party to the deal so he could be a witness in case of trouble.

Sure enough, the Germans implored Larkin to help organize sabotage in American ports. One of Devoy's contacts at the consulate in New York, Wolf von Igel, took Larkin on a tour of Germany's secret sabotage center in Hoboken, New Jersey, just across the Hudson from Manhattan. Von Igel showed off an assortment of nasty devices designed to ruin the rudders of transatlantic ships. Larkin refused a formal offer to supervise sabotage operations on the American East Coast, but he agreed to continue to stir up labor trouble. How much Devoy knew of Larkin's involvement isn't certain. Devoy's letters from the period often refer to Larkin, usually under the code name Longfellow.[17]

"Some months earlier," wrote O'Connor in *James Larkin*, "Larkin had reactivated contacts with the Germans through Devoy. He now received an invitation from the German Minister in Washington, D.C., and subsequently arranged for Devoy to transfer monies from the Germans for anti-war agitation. The total sum received is unclear. Devoy recalled a request for the substantial figure of $10,000–12,000 being readily accepted, but not the period involved. Larkin always denied acceding to persistent German requests for him to engage in industrial sabotage, but this was less than the whole truth. He had first-hand knowledge of German sabotage operations, and supplied the Germans with intelligence and contacts."[18]

According to O'Connor, "The Germans briefed him on Roger Casement's 'Irish Brigade,' and he claimed that, in 1915, he had collaborated with them in a futile attempt to join Casement in Spain."

It is still a wonder today how Larkin, and especially Devoy, avoided arrest for espionage in 1917–1918.

THE EASTER RISING FROM NEW YORK

Back in Dublin, James Connolly was rattling sabers, much to the chagrin of Tom Clarke. Clarke was worried that Connolly and his Irish Citizen Army would go off on their own and preempt his own planned insurrection at Easter. Clarke "kidnapped" Connolly and, over several days, with the help of Seán MacDiarmada and Joseph Mary Plunkett, brought him into their Easter conspiracy.

It appears that Larkin, three thousand miles away in New York, was getting the same vibes from Connolly. "Connolly's insurrectionary intentions worried Larkin," wrote O'Connor, "and his brother Peter and Francis Sheehy Skeffington carried home messages for Connolly to 'pull out of it.' In late 1915 or early 1916, Larkin cabled him 'not to move.' The Rising came as a bombshell. Larkin knew he had been upstaged on a grand scale and, for several days, he remained incommunicado."

That the Rising was a technical failure doesn't seem to have fazed Larkin. The execution of Connolly and the subsequent adoration of him as a martyr got under Larkin's skin. "The Rising and Connolly's new stature," wrote O'Connor, "never ceased to rankle him, and in private he frequently traduced his old underling."

This jealousy over a dead man stuck a raw nerve in Larkin's craw. When he returned to Dublin in 1923, according to O'Connor, "Larkin asserted, and this he reiterated over the coming weeks, that he had gone to the U.S. in 1914 to procure munitions at the behest of James Connolly, Tom Clarke and Pádraig Pearse. In the climate of the time, this is not just bumptious, but irreverent. Mrs. Kathleen Clarke wrote to the press asking for evidence, and she was supported in the ensuing controversy by Lillie Connolly, John Devoy and O'Brien, who developed a fixation about Larkin's claim. Larkin was to make no response."

It is interesting that in 1914 Clarke and Connolly, although friends, did not have a close working relationship and Pearse, although picked by Clarke to be the voice of the insurgents, was not on the level of, say, a Seán MacDiarmada. "Connolly's status really nettled him," wrote O'Connor, "'He agreed that it was the sacrifices of James Connolly that built up the Union, but who sowed the seed?'"

LIFE AT SING SING

While Michael Collins was waging his brutal guerrilla war against the British Secret Service in the streets of Dublin, Larkin had his own problems in New York. He was arrested in MacDougal Alley for "criminal anarchy" and released on fifteen-thousand-dollars' bail, of which five thousand was supplied by—who else?—Devoy. Larkin defended himself—did someone say, "a fool for a client"?—in court and was convicted, getting five-to-ten in Sing Sing. To keep him away from giving interviews to newspapers he was moved to the Clinton Correction Facility in Dannemora, New York—nicknamed "Little Siberia" for its brutal climate near the Canadian border—before being returned to Sing Sing. He denounced the Collins Treaty on December

10, 1921. His celebrity persisted in prison with visitors such as Charlie Chaplin and the Countess Markievicz.

He was briefly released by an appeals court in 1922, but quickly rearrested on another charge of criminal anarchy and served with a deportation warrant.

With the likes of Patrick Joseph Cardinal Hayes, the Sinn Féin–leaning arch-bishop of New York, in his corner his case came to the attention of Irish Catholic Al Smith, who was elected governor of New York in November 1922.

"Smith," wrote O'Connor, "concluded that this was a 'political case where a man has been punished for the statement of his beliefs.' At 5:00 p.m. on 17 January [1923], convict number 50945 left Sing Sing with a free pardon."

"The Happy Warrior [Governor Smith]," wrote Camp in *Iron in Her Soul*, "said that New York was secure enough to tolerate 'an erroneous, and even an illegal, polit-ical doctrine,' as long as no overt act had been committed."

But Larkin's New York decade was over. He was charged with being an "alien anar-chist," and deported in April 1923 back to Britain.

"Larkin had eventually made an impact in the U.S. as an anti-war agitator, a founder of American communism and a famous political prisoner," O'Connor wrote. "Nevertheless there was an air of unfulfilled promise about his stateside sojourn. To his comrades on the far left, he seemed a strange, lonely, implacable rebel wasting his energies on the fringe when he might have been leading his people at home. His time spent in prison had created a tragic image of him as a gaunt idealist for whom 'life is crushing.' It also won him international renown as a revolutionary political agitator, and that was the path he intended to pursue."

DUBLIN AND THE ANTICLIMACTIC YEARS

Larkin returned to Dublin and found the city of his 1913 fame changed. Also, the present leadership of the ITGWU was not crazy about his return and intervention in the union. A disastrous dockers' strike sealed his fate, and on March 14, 1924, he was ejected from the union that he had formed. He continued union organizing, but clearly he was past his prime.

There was a softening of the fiery Larkin over the final twenty years of his life. He was three times elected to the Dáil and was often solicited by Eamon de Valera's gov-ernment for his opinion on the social issues of the day.

Larkin died in Dublin on January 30, 1947, with Archbishop of Dublin John Charles McQuaid at his bedside. McQuaid called Larkin his "most treasured conversion." And in the true fashion of an honest labor leader, he left an estate of only twenty pounds.

"He revolutionized trade unionism in two respects," wrote Emmet O'Connor in *James Larkin*. "Firstly, in developing the ITGWU, he delivered a terminal blow to the crippling policy of dependence on British labour and laid the foundations for the modern Irish labour movement. Secondly, in industrial relations, he introduced a method of struggle which made possible the unionization of unskilled workers, without whom labour could not have become a force of any significance. He then made the method heroic and enduring by embedding it in a set of moral values. The spectacular success and popularity he enjoyed exacerbated his personality problems, with disastrous results."

But when his time came in the Dublin Lockout of 1913, James Larkin was there for the ITGWU and his country, and no one can ever take that away from him.

CHAPTER THREE

JAMES CONNOLLY

THE COMMANDANT-GENERAL WAS ONCE A NEW YORKER

Of all the sixteen martyrs of 1916, Commandant-General James Connolly of the Irish Citizen Army is probably best remembered. Why? Because he was the only one who was wounded and was shot while sitting in a chair because he couldn't stand for execution. The British couldn't wait.

Connolly, like his fellow labor leader James Larkin, was to spend time in New York and be influenced by it, but unlike Larkin, he managed to get back to Ireland in time for the 1916 Rising. In fact, it was Larkin's decision to go to America that propelled Connolly to the forefront of both the Irish labor and nationalist movement. His life was unbelievably hard from his birth to his execution, but his fierce spirit in the face of dire economic, personal, and professional obstacles, marked him as a special man.

Perhaps no one put it better than Michael Collins, who was with Connolly in the GPO in 1916, when he observed: "Of Pearse and Connolly I admire the latter the most. Connolly was a realist, Pearse the direct opposite. There was an air of earthy directness about Connolly. It impressed me. I would have followed him through hell had such action been necessary. But I honestly doubt very much if I would have followed Pearse—not without some thought anyway."

BORN INTO POVERTY

James Connolly was born in Edinburgh on June 5, 1868 to parents born in Ireland. It is interesting to note that on both the 1901 and 1911 Irish Censuses—perhaps trying to prove his Irish bonafides—he falsely claims to have been born in County Monaghan. He was also born into abject poverty. His father, in perhaps a metaphor for the family's terrible finances, could find work only as a manure carter for the Edinburgh Corporation. By age eleven, young Connolly was out of school and into the printing trade, which, ironically, would come in very handy in helping him produce journalism in the years to come. But the stigma of working from an early age left an imprint and years later Connolly wrote "Work is not pleasure for children."

The family's poverty eventually forced Connolly to join the British army. He was soon shipped to Cork which was his introduction to Ireland. During his time in the army he was also stationed in the Curragh in County Kildare and Dublin. His army experiences did not impress him. He described the British army as a "veritable moral cesspool corrupting all within its bounds."

The British army caused one good thing to happen to Connolly—he met his wife Lillie while stationed in Dublin. Lillie was Church of Ireland, which meant nothing to the secular Catholic Connolly. When they decided to marry, Connolly, fearing his unit was being shipped off to India and nearing the end of his seven-year hitch, decided to go AWOL. He was done with army life—until later in life.

TARGETING A "VULTURE ARISTOCRACY"

Married life soon bought babies and more brutal poverty. He opened a cobbler shop which failed because he was a terrible shoemaker. By this time Connolly was agitating for a socialist agenda and rights for the workers. But Connolly's poverty continued unabated until he received an offer from the Dublin Socialist Club in 1896 to become a club organizer at the princely sum of one pound a week. Connolly went right to work, immediately changing the Dublin Socialist Club into the Irish Socialist Republican Party. He also began contributing articles to newspapers, which raised his profile.

It was about this time that he came into contact with Maud Gonne. Together they worked to make June 22, 1897, an unforgettable day for Queen Victoria's Diamond Jubilee Day. Gonne hung a name on Victoria that sticks to this day—"The Famine Queen." And Connolly reminded the Irish people just how magnificent her reign was: "this glorious reign Ireland has seen 1,225,000 of her children die of famine; starved to death whilst the produce of her soil and of their labour was eaten up by a vulture aristocracy—enforcing their rents by the bayonets of a hired assassin army in the pay of the 'best of the English Queens."[19]

Together Gonne and Connolly decided to put on a little theater to mock the Famine Queen. A black coffin with the words "British Empire" was driven all over town. They were on their way to bury the British. They were halted by the Dublin

Metropolitan Police (DMP) at O'Connell Bridge. An altercation followed with the DMP, and Connolly tossed the coffin into the Liffey shouting, "To Hell with the British Empire!" which got him arrested.

The DMPs advanced up O'Connell Street to Parnell Square, where Gonne had produced a magic lantern show, using a new-fangled invention called a "projector." They attacked mostly women and children who were fascinated by the advanced technology of the day. One old woman died. This demonstration of DMP cruelty was a precursor to the Bloody Sunday of 1913 where the DMPs again brutalized Dublin citizens. One wonders if the two incidents, sixteen years apart, had an effect on Connolly not hesitating in 1913 to form the Irish Citizen Army to prevent future DMP brutality.

NEW YORK IS NOT KIND TO JAMES CONNOLLY

As the names in this book document, New York has been very generous and welcoming to Irish dissidents. Not so with James Connolly. He was brought to the attention of the American Socialist Labor Party by his pamphlet, *Erin's Hope: The End and the Means*, and an invitation for a speaking tour of America was forthcoming. So in August 1902 Connolly left his family at their home in the Liberties neighborhood of Dublin and sailed for New York for three-and-a-half-months of touring.

The *New York Times* welcomed him with "Agitator Connolly Here" when he spoke at Cooper Union on September 15, 1902. The Socialist Labor Party was a little more welcoming than the Old Gray Lady. Their proclamation at Cooper Union declared: "Whereas James Connolly in his mission to destroy the influence of the Irish Home Rulers and the bourgeoisie in Ireland, and their allies who trade on the Irish vote in this country to the economic detriment of the Irish working men in this country."

Connolly, in turn, commented, "No person can be economically free who is not politically free and no person can be politically free who is not economically free."

After Cooper Union, Connolly hit the road on a brutal schedule that left little time except for travel and speeches. Connolly hardly missed a hamlet while in America: every major city plus places like Salt Lake City, St. Paul, New Bedford, Syracuse, Buffalo, Louisville. If there was a socialist there, Connolly would speak to them. The tour finally ended in late December, and Connolly returned to Ireland.

Back in Ireland things were in turmoil. There was acrimony in the Irish Socialist Republican Party, and Connolly had trouble keeping his newspaper, *Workers'*

Republic, in print. He left to lecture in Scotland, leaving his family in Dublin, always one step ahead of the poverty that had pursued him from the day of his birth. Finally, in July 1903 he decided to return to America to start a better life for his family. But he left Ireland with a bitterness in his mouth: "Men have been driven out of Ireland by the British Government, and by the landlords, but am I the first driven forth by the 'Socialists'?"

A TERRIBLE OMEN

Connolly hoped to settle in New York, but when no job was forthcoming he traveled north to Troy, New York, where he had friends and family and took a job with the Metropolitan Life Insurance Company, agitating for socialist causes in his free time.

By August 1904, the rest of the family was ready to join him. Just before the family was scheduled to leave for New York, Connolly's daughter, Mona, was burned to death in an awful kitchen accident. It was a terrible omen for what would be the start of the Connollys' seven-year sojourn in America. By the winter an economic depression hit, and Connolly lost his job when people couldn't afford to pay their premiums. In search of work, he spent more time away from the family at Jack Mulray's place in Greenwich Village.

By 1905, things picked up when he somehow talked his way into a job as district manager for the Pacific Mutual Life Insurance Company of California. He freely admitted "I was playing the American capitalists at their own bunco game, and succeeded so far," he is quoted by Lorcan Collins in *16 Lives: James Connolly.* His insurance job was to be short lived. By the fall he had moved to Newark, New Jersey, while working at the Singer Sewing Machine Company.

A BRONX TALE IN "THIS CURSED COUNTRY"

During his time in America, Connolly joined the Industrial Workers of the World, affectionately known as the "Wobblies." Organized by the likes of "Big Bill" Haywood, Eugene V. Debs, and Mary Harris "Mother" Jones, it was an organization that put an American imprint on Connolly's socialist philosophy. By 1907, the Wobblies offered Connolly a job as head organizer of the District Council of New York City, and the family moved to 684 East 155th Street in the South Bronx, close to where his friend Elizabeth Gurley Flynn lived.

By 1908, Connolly was back in the journalism business with his new newspaper, *The Harp*. The content was so good that John Devoy reprinted several articles in his paper, the *Gaelic American*. But the slugging was hard, as Elizabeth Gurley Flynn testified. "It was a pathetic sight to see him standing poorly clad, at the door of Cooper Union or some other East Side hall, selling his little paper. None of the prosperous, professional Irish, who shouted their admiration for him after his death, lent him a helping hand at that time."[20] He longed for Ireland and called America "this cursed country."

But everything was not doom and gloom. In 1909, Connolly managed to get a book, *Socialism Made Easy*, published, which put some much-needed money in the family's pocket. And once again, to the angst of his family, Connolly hit the road to promote the book, this time staying out for a grueling eleven months. He looked to Ireland for salvation and wrote union organizer William O'Brien in Dublin. According to Lorcan Collins in *16 Lives: James Connolly*, he told O'Brien, "I may confess to you that I regard my emigration to America as the great mistake of my life, and, as Jack Mulray can tell you, I have never ceased to regret it."

His plan to get back to Ireland now focused on *The Harp*. By the beginning of 1910 the printing of *The Harp* was transferred to Dublin. According to *16 Lives: James Connolly* by Lorcan Collins, "Larkin was taken by the first Dublin issue of *The Harp* and decided to offer his managerial services, much to Connolly's delight."

Unlike in *Casablanca*, it would not be the beginning of a beautiful friendship; it would be a death notice for *The Harp* but would signal revolution for Ireland. So on Tuesday, July 14, 1910 Connolly was given a goodbye dinner at Cavanaugh's Restaurant on West 23rd Street near Eighth Avenue. James Connolly's unhappy seven-year sojourn in America was finished. Next stop, Belfast.

LARKIN VS. CONNOLLY

There are two prominent statues in Dublin—James Larkin in O'Connell Street, and James Connolly outside the Customs House, just across the street from his home base of Liberty Hall on the Liffey. The two statues tell the story of the two men precisely. Larkin, arms upraised in anger during the 1913 workers' strike, and Connolly standing quietly, dignity shouting out of every bone in his body. The two most famous labor leaders in Irish history had, strangely, a very uneasy relationship. And it probably had more to do with Larkin's prickly personality than their beliefs. Larkin was the oil to Connolly's water.

"Larkin always lashed back *ad hominem* when under attack," wrote Emmet O'Connor in his biography of Larkin. "Indeed, attacked or not, he preferred to go for the man rather than the ball."[21]

When Connolly returned to Ireland, Larkin was persuaded, according to O'Connor, "to appoint James Connolly as northern organizer. Up to this point, jealousy had caused Larkin to decline . . . requests to give Connolly a job. Connolly had mixed feelings about working for Larkin and thought him 'an overgrown schoolboy.'"

Connolly soon found that working for Larkin, even separated by the one-hundred miles between Belfast and Dublin, was not easy. "I don't think I can stand Larkin as boss much longer," Connolly said. "He is singularly unbearable. He is forever snarling at me and drawing comparisons between what he accomplished in Belfast in 1907, and what I have done. . . . He is consumed with jealousy and hatred of anyone who will not cringe to him and beslaver him all over." He confided to William O'Brien that "[Larkin] does not seem to want a democratic Labour movement; he seems to want a Larkinite movement only."[22]

And although the personalities of Connolly and Larkin were combustible, their politics were converging. "If Larkin was the more emotively nationalist of the two," O'Connor wrote, "Connolly was the more separatist." They shared a contempt for both the Irish Parliamentary Party, the fantasists of Home Rule, and the Ancient Order of Hibernians who refused to help the Irish Transport and General Workers' Union (ITGWU) in its hour of need.

THE LOCKOUT INSPIRES THE CREATION OF THE IRISH CITIZEN ARMY

William Martin Murphy thought he would destroy the ITGWU, but instead he set in motion the events that would end up establishing the Irish Free State.

Connolly traveled to Dublin from Belfast when the lockout was called and was arrested. "Connolly was taken from Liberty Hall by the DMP," wrote Lorcan Collins, "and charged with incitement to cause a breach of the peace on the previous night. Connolly refused to be bound over and informed the court that he did not recognize the English government in Ireland. This treasonous talk resulted in a sentence of three months." Connolly was conveyed to Mountjoy Prison, where he immediately went on a hunger strike, becoming one of the first Irish patriots to use this method of resistance. The strike worked and Connolly was soon released on the orders of the Lord Lieutenant of Ireland to convalesce at Countess Markievicz's house.

On November 13, 1913, Connolly announced the formation of the Irish Citizen Army with incendiary rhetoric: "I am going to talk sedition. The next time we are out for a march, I want to be accompanied by four battalions of our own men. . . . When you draw your strike pay this week I want every man who is willing to enlist as a soldier to give his name and address, and you will be informed when and where you have to attend for training. I have been promised the assistance of competent chief officers, who will lead us anywhere. I say nothing about arms at present. When we want them, we know where we will find them."

Later in the *Workers' Republic* he told the reasons behind the formation of the ICA: "Three men had been killed, and one young Irish girl murdered by a scab [during the lockout], and nothing was done to bring the assassins to justice. So since justice did not exist for us, since the law instead of protecting the rights of the workers was an open enemy, and since the armed forces of the Crown were reservedly at the disposal of the enemies of labour, it was resolved to create our own army to secure our rights, to protect our members, and to be a guarantee of our own free progress."[23]

Larkin was soon off to America and Connolly was running the ITGWU and the ICA. The fun was about to begin.

THE GREAT WAR BRINGS OPPORTUNITY

On August 4, 1914, war was declared between Britain and Germany. Connolly and other nationalists saw opportunity. "Should a German army land in Ireland tomorrow," Connolly wrote, "we should be perfectly justified in joining it if by doing so we could rid this country once and for all from its connection with the Brigand Empire that drags us unwilling into this war."

He was not the only Irishman thinking like this. Tom Clarke was on a parallel path to revolution. "Connolly was a far more impetuous man than Clarke," wrote Helen Litton in *16 Lives: Thomas Clarke*, "and felt that the IRB was dragging its feet."

Litton also tells a wonderful story about the funeral of Jeremiah O'Donovan Rossa's funeral when Clarke solicited Connolly to join in preparations. "'When are you fellows going to stop blethering about *dead* Fenians?" Connolly demanded of Clarke. "Why don't you get a few *live* ones for a change?"

"Send him to me," Tom Clarke said. "I'll fix that."[24] And he did.

"As a mark of Clarke's respect for Labour," wrote Lorcan Collins in *16 Lives: James Connolly*, "Connolly was included as a member of the Guards and Procession sub-committee. This ensured the ICA and Volunteers would guard Rossa's remains and jointly form the guard of honour at his funeral."

Connolly soon joined the Irish Republican Brotherhood, which did not please Sean O'Casey. "That Connolly joined the IRB caused distress to some socialists," wrote Lorcan Collins, "including Seán O'Casey, who said that 'Connolly had stepped from the narrow byway of Irish Socialism on to the broad and crowded highway of Irish Nationalism.' This nationalism 'became his daily rosary, while the higher creed of international humanity that had so long bubbled from his eloquent lips was silent forever, and Irish Labour lost a Leader.'"

EASTER 1916

"The odds are a thousand to one against us," Connolly told his Irish Citizen Army. "If we win, we'll be great heroes; but if we lose, we will be the greatest scoundrels the country ever produced. In the event of victory, hold on to your rifles, as those with whom we are fighting may stop before our goal is reached. We are out for economic as well as political liberty. Hold on to your rifles!"[25]

Connolly also emphasized to the ICA the value of guerrilla warfare and not fighting the British on their own terms, which would mean certain defeat. This may have been the greatest impression he made on Michael Collins, who would define guerrilla warfare—the British would call it "terrorism"—against the Crown to finally force them out of twenty-six counties.

The Rising was supposed to start on Easter Sunday, but Eoin MacNeil, the titular head of the Irish Volunteers, countermanded the order, which caused massive confusion. It was decided instead to go on Easter Monday. Connolly, Clarke, and Pearse assembled at Liberty Hall then marched down Lower Abbey Street to O'Connell Street, turned right, and marched to the General Post Office (GPO). Connolly gave the command, "Left turn. The GPO, charge!"

The rebels entered the GPO and started smashing out the windows. Pearse came out front to read the Proclamation. When he finished, Connolly grasped his hand and said, "Thanks be to God, Pearse, that we have lived to see this day!" The Rising was on.

Connolly was the military commander of the Dublin Division and part of his duties forced him to leave the GPO and examine and advise his men in the field. It was on one of these sorties that he was wounded, first in the arm, then in his ankle, which was shattered into a compound fracture. He was wounded around Liffey Street, near the Ha'penny Bridge. The local legend said he was taken into what is now the Lotts Café Bar at 9 Liffey Street before being removed back to the GPO. Gangrene soon set in and he was in excruciating pain. When asked how he was doing, Connolly, according to Lorcan Collins, replied, "Bad—the soldier who wounded me did a good day's work for the British government." Connolly was evacuated from the burning GPO on Friday and taken with the rest of the rebels to Moore Street, finally settling at #16.

TRIAL AND EXECUTION

When Pearse issued surrender orders to the men on Saturday, Connolly agreed with them and told the men and women of the ICA, mostly associated with the St. Stephen's Green command, to also lay down their arms. While the rest of the rebels were marched off to Richmond Barracks, Connolly was taken to the Red Cross Hospital in Dublin Castle.

His kangaroo court trial commenced on May 9, 1916. He was charged with two offenses:

1. Did an act to wit did take part in an armed rebellion and in the waging of war against His Majesty the King, such act being of such a nature as to be calculated to be prejudicial to the Defence of the Realm and being done with the intention and for the purpose of assisting the enemy
2. Did attempt to cause disaffection among the civilian population of His Majesty.

He pleaded "Not Guilty" to both charges.

Not trusting the prevaricating British, Connolly made a statement, according to Lorcan Collins, which was smuggled out with the help of his daughter Nora. In it he declared: "We went out to break the connection between this country and the British Empire and to establish an Irish Republic. . . .

We succeeded in proving that Irishmen are ready to die endeavouring to win for Ireland their national rights which the British Government has been asking them to die to win for Belgium. As long as that remains the case, the cause of Irish freedom is safe. Believing that the British Government has no right in Ireland, never had any right in Ireland, and never can have any right in Ireland, the presence in any one generation of even a respectable minority of Irishmen ready to die to affirm that truth makes that Government for ever a usurpation and a crime against human progress. I personally thank God that I have lived to see the day when thousands of Irishmen and boys, and hundreds of Irish women and girls, were equally ready to affirm that truth and seal it with their lives if necessary.

Despite his eloquence, Connolly stood no chance and was found guilty of the first charge and innocent of the second. The sentence was death.

At midnight on May 11, Connolly's wife Lillie and daughter Nora were called to Dublin Castle. According to Lorcan Collins, in a heartbreaking scene Connolly said, "I suppose you know what this means?" He told them he was to be shot at dawn. His wife started crying, and Connolly said, "Don't cry, Lillie. You'll unman me."

Early in the morning of May 12, Father Aloysius arrived to hear Connolly's confession and give him Holy Communion. According to Collins, Father Aloysius asked him to forgive the men in the firing squad. Connolly replied "I do, Father. I respect every man who does his duty."

He then had his last meal in bed. Still dressed in his pajamas, he was put in an ambulance and driven straight into the breaker's yard at Kilmainham Gaol.

It is here that the legend of James Connolly is solidified. Since he couldn't stand he was placed in a chair. The twelve-man firing squad took aim and fired. Connolly was hit in the head twice and the chest and the force of the bullets blew the chair in half.

His execution was highlighted in an iconic song called "The Patriot Game" by Dominick Behan, Brendan's brother, which immortalized Connolly.

James Connolly was the last rebel to be executed in Kilmainham in 1916, and, with his blood sacrifice, he pumped new life into rebel Ireland that would deliver in less than six years the Irish nation he happily gave his life for.

CHAPTER FOUR
MIKE QUILL

FROM THE IRA TO THE IRT: FREEDOM FIGHTER, UNION ORGANIZER, CIVIL RIGHTS ICON, QUINTESSENTIAL NEW YORKER

I vividly remember sitting in a car, waiting for a traffic light to change, on Perry Street in New York's Greenwich Village in the early days of 1966. The radio was on and the voice of Michael J. Quill came on. "The judge," roared Quill in a thick brogue, "can drop dead in his black robes!" My County Louth–born father howled in delight. I think, now, it was my introduction to Irish revolutionary politics.

In those cold January days, Quill—whose Transit Workers Union (TWU) had struck the subways and buses and brought the world's greatest city to its knees—was vilified in the eyes of New Yorkers. How dare he, that Commie, "Red Mike"! But he didn't care. Nothing could frighten Quill. He had fought the Black and Tans back home in his native County Kerry. He had gone against the Treaty and fought the Free State army during the Irish Civil War. And he had come to New York and fought the thugs the transit bosses used to terrorize subway workers to keep them in their place.

To understand Quill, you have to understand the Irish and what makes the Irish so Irish. Quill was a unique combination of revolutionary Michael Collins—a brilliant organizer who was not afraid to innovate on the go and use guerrilla tactics when he had to—and Barry Fitzgerald, the Oscar-winning Irish actor who was never afraid to steal a scene no matter how big the star he was playing against. Quill even looked like Fitzgerald, and you could imagine Quill leading John Wayne by the hand in *The Quiet Man*. It was a rare combination of wit, guile, and charisma that made him one of the greatest American labor leaders of the twentieth century.

FROM THE IRA TO THE IRT

Michael Quill was born in Gortloughera, Kilgarvan, County Kerry, on September 18, 1905. His father was a farmer with a keen sense of justice. "My father," Quill is quoted in his wife Shirley's biography of her husband, *Mike Quill—Himself*, "knew where every fight against an eviction had taken place in all the parishes around." This sense of justice resulted during the War of Independence in Quill, as a teenager, becoming a member of the 3rd Battalion, Kerry No. 2 Brigade Headquarters of the IRA.

Shirley Quill documented her husband's IRA time in her biography: Mary Healy Shea, daughter of Tim Healy, the intelligence officer for Quill's brigade, remembered his exploits: "Michael was only fifteen at the time. He was on a scouting mission and stumbled on a patrol of Black and Tans asleep in a ditch at the foot of the mountain. He was alone. Instead of running away, he stole all their ammunition without rousing them and gleefully returned to Gortloughera with his loot."

We know much about Quill because of the work of his second wife, Shirley, and her outstanding biography, *Mike Quill—Himself: A Memoir*, which was published in 1985. "Michael," wrote Shirley, "graduated to a rifle and organized thirty lads in the village into an IRA Scout group, which conducted drills several times a week.

"Almost every important leader connected with the movement passed through Gortloughera at some time: Liam Deacy, Tom Barry, Sean Moylan, Seamus Robinson, Dan Breen, Liam Lynch, Eamon de Valera, Erskine Childers, Humphrey Murphy. Michael met them all. Before he left Ireland, many were dead, ambushed, executed. He had had the rare opportunity as a teenager to be in touch with the minds and hearts of some of Ireland's most inspired patriots."[26]

Quill went against the Treaty and fought Michael Collins's National Army. Of all the western counties, Kerry suffered the most. Led by General Paddy O'Daly, the former leader of Collins's Squad, atrocities were committed by the Free Staters at Ballyseedy and elsewhere, resulting in the deaths of twenty-three anti-Treaty soldiers who were murdered by dynamite. This unbelievable brutality and injustice was to mark Quill for life.

Being on the wrong side of the Treaty, there were few jobs available and Quill set out for America. Quill arrived in New York on the day before St. Patrick's Day in 1926. He stayed at his Aunt Kate's railroad flat on East 104th Street in Harlem. He had $3.42 in his pocket.

To say Quill became an American jack-of-all-trades would be an understatement. Quill's occupations in the years after his arrival in New York included salesman, elevator operator, able seaman, railroad trainmen, booze smuggler during Prohibition, ditchdigger, coal passer, and peddler of roach powder and religious pictures. It was during his peddler days he saw the terrible conditions that people in the Pennsylvania coal country lived in and wrote his father, according to Shirley Quill, "that the cows and pigs in Kerry were better housed and fed than were the miners' children in America."

AN ACOLYTE OF JAMES CONNOLLY

After his ramblings Quill returned to New York and secured a job working for the Interboro Rapid Transit Company (IRT), where he became ticket agent Michael J. Quill, Pass Number 3355, making thirty-three cents an hour.

The IRT was becoming a haven for the diaspora of Irishmen who were on the wrong side in the Irish Civil War. Why were there so many Irish working the subways? "Because they spoke English," Quill said, according to his wife's biography. "They could read, write, make change and communicate, in some fashion, with the riding public. The immigrant wave of the twenties brought strong young men from the farmlands; they could withstand the rigors of working twelve to fourteen hours each day, seven days a week. They were a hardy breed."

But the Irish were not the only ones working underground for the IRT and Quill knew all of them. "Negro workers could get jobs only as porters," remembered Quill. "They were subjected to treatment that makes Little Rock and Birmingham seem liberal and respectable by comparison. . . . I saw Catholic ticket agents fired by Catholic bosses for going to mass early in the morning while the porter 'covered' the booth for half an hour. Protestant bosses fired Protestant workers for similar crimes—going to church. The Jewish workers had no trouble with the subway bosses—Jews were not employed in the transit lines."

Working the twelve-hour overnight lobster, or graveyard, shift, Quill began his education. He brought with him a hundred-watt light bulb to replace the generic fifteen-watt IRT-issued bulb. Then he began to read.

His greatest inspiration was James Connolly, the leader of the Transport Workers Union in Dublin who was executed by the British for his part in the 1916 Rising. "Connolly's two basic theories," wrote Shirley Quill in her biography of her husband, "were to guide Mike Quill's thinking for the next three decades: that economic power precedes and conditions political power, and that the only effective and satisfactory expression of the workers' demands is to be found politically in a separate and independent labor party, and economically in the industrial union. . . . James Connolly had provided the blueprint: raise an army to fight the exploiters as once the Irish had fought the British tyrants. The instrument of liberation was theirs to create. The torch had been lit. Mike Quill had stumbled across the threshold of a new cause."

Years later when Quill was the president of the TWU he only had two pictures on the wall in his office—Abraham Lincoln and James Connolly.

ORGANIZING THE TWU

The terrible working conditions in the IRT had to end and Quill knew that the only way that would happen would be to organize the workers into a union.

At first, Quill went to Irish Catholic organizations in New York for support. "We went to the Friendly Sons of St. Patrick," Quill said according to his wife, "but they would have nothing to do with the idea of organizing Irishmen into a legitimate union. We went to the Ancient Order of Hibernians, and they threw us out of their meeting hall. They wanted no part of Irish rebels or Irish rabble. That was the reception we got from those conservative descendants of Ireland's revolutionists of a hundred years ago."

Quill soon found himself embracing the old Irish adage that "the enemy of my enemy is my friend" and found himself courting the Communist Party. "Sure," said Quill, "I worked with the Communists. In 1933 I would have made a pact with the Devil himself if he could have given us the money, the mimeograph machines and the manpower to launch the Transport Workers Union. The Communist Party needed me, and I needed them. I knew what the transit workers needed. The men craved dignity, longed to be treated like human beings. The time had come to get off our knees and fight back."

As Quill often noted, "You will get only what you are strong enough to take. You will have to fight for your rights—they will never be given to you. And you cannot win if you fight alone."

The union was organized using the methods of the Irish Republican Brotherhood (IRB), the secret society pledged to the violent overthrow of British rule in Ireland. "For now," wrote Shirley Quill, "the organizers evolved a plan to form secret groups of five; that way no man would know the names of more than four other workers in the organization. Should there be a spy amongst them, only four men would be in jeopardy. Their inspiration: the Fenian movement in America." Messages were sent in half-Gaelic and half-English to confuse company spies, known as "beakies."

The charismatic Quill became the star of the union movement and was fired by the IRT in 1935. Quill, according to Shirley, "performed as if to the microphone born." He proved irascible on many fronts, even toward his new communist friends. Quill had a dim view of the Communists and knew he wanted no part of them when they thought he should attend "Workers School" for indoctrination. Mike Quill would be indoctrinated by nobody.

"He had a dream," said Shirley. "Connolly's dream—that the working people could be liberated from lives of despair, disease and degradation, that they could be the instruments of their own liberation through the power of industrial unionism."

NEW DEAL, NEW TIMES

But, as Bob Dylan would write thirty years later, the times they are a-changin'. Franklin Delano Roosevelt was now president and Senator Robert F. Wagner of New York had succeeded in getting his Wagner Act through congress and signed by the president. The Wagner Act (aka, the National Labor Relations Act) guaranteed workers in any industry engaged in interstate commerce "the right to self-organization, to form, join or assist labor organizations, to bargain collectively through representation of their own choosing, and engage in concerted activities for the purpose of collective bargaining or other mutual aid or protection." Mike Quill and the TWU were in business.

Quill succeeded in getting his nascent union into the Transport Workers Union, Lodge 1547, International Association of Machinists, American Federation of Labor. He then started unionizing the other transportation companies of New York: The Third Avenue Railroad system (the "El"), the Brooklyn-Manhattan Transit (BMT) and Independent (IND) subway systems, Fifth Avenue Coach Company, and the New York City Omnibus Corporation.

In January 1937, the BMT dismissed two boiler room engineers from their power plant in Brooklyn because of their union activity. Mike Quill had his battle and he was going to win it. He immediately called a sit-down strike. "This is no seizure," Quill told the public in a strike bulletin, "This is an orderly *stay-in* for legitimate union demands—reinstatement of two competent workers discharged for union activity, and recognition of the union in the spirit of the Wagner Labor Relations Act. . . . The labor policy of the BMT—low wages, long hours, union discrimination—has been so vicious and ruthless that the men have taken this action as the last remedy."

Fourteen and a half hours after the "stay-in" began, the BMT surrendered to Quill and the TWU.

Soon the TWU separated from the Machinists Union and the AFL and joined John L. Lewis's militant Congress of Industrial Organizations (CIO). With Lewis handling the negotiations, the TWU won a $2,500,000 contract package. The TWU was here to stay—and so was Michael J. Quill.

MIKE QUILL: IRISH SEX SYMBOL

Mike Quill was a man way ahead of his generation. The same can be said for his sex habits. Today, Donald Trump's sexual escapades makes Quill look like a monk. But in the 1930s and '40s in Irish Catholic New York they would have been considered sinful and, if known, would probably have ended his career.

Quill was never much of a Catholic, and that can be traced back to the Irish Civil War. Shirley in her book recalled that "Mike and [his brother] John were cut to the heart when their parish priest refused to request temporary amnesty for them to attend their mother's funeral [when they were on the run] . . . [Mike] remained hostile and angry."

His experiences in New York with "respectable" Irish Catholics also left a foul taste in his mouth. "When we first started to organize the union," he is quoted in *Mike Quill—Himself*, "we asked for help from the Knights of Columbus and the Ancient Order of Hibernians. We were booed and booted out. The Irish organizations did nothing *for* us and the Church campaigned actively *against* us."

He was also incensed when a Catholic nun went against the wife of a union member: "She was given a lecture about the Godless, Communist subway union; it was a sin for the child's father to belong—the woman must help save her husband's soul by insisting that he quit TWU immediately."

"Mike could not separate," Shirley said, "what he called church politics from basic spiritual concepts. He was bitter over the church's open hostility to the nationalistic cause during the Irish Civil War, outraged by the Vatican's accommodation with Mussolini and the devotion of the church in Spain to the fascist Franco."

Mike Quill's religious beliefs were succinctly summed up in these words according to his wife's biography: "I believe in the Corporal Works of Mercy, the Ten Com-
mandants, the American Declaration of Independence and James Connolly's outline
of a socialist society. . . . Most of my life I've been called a lunatic because I *believe*
that I *am* my brother's keeper. I organize poor and exploited workers. I fight for the
civil rights of minorities, and I believe in peace. It appears to have become old-fashioned to make social commitments—to want a world free of war, poverty and disease.
This is my religion."

So, Quill had little time for the New York Catholic power structure when it came
to politics—and even less when it came to marriage and sex. His first marriage to
Mollie Theresa O'Neill was one of the strangest courtships in the annals of Irish
romance. It was so odd that it could be filed under the old joke about an Irish marriage proposal: "Would you like to be buried with my people?"

Quill and Mollie had met at a dance for Irish exiles in New York. They had
courted, but with the onset of the Great Depression Mollie became unemployed and
decided to return to Ireland. They continued their "courtship" with three thousand
miles of ocean between them for years. Finally, after Quill was elected to the New
York City Council, he returned to Ireland, married Mollie, and the two returned to
New York. The union soon produced a son, John, but it was a cold arrangement
between two people who barely knew each other.

"His fiancée had been patient and undemanding," wrote Shirley in *Mike Quill—
Himself*, "writing dutifully every week about the nonevents of her little village; for four
years Mike (or his secretary) had sent envelopes bulging with newspaper clippings.
No intimacies exchanged, none expected. He was en route to the most important
event of his adult life, his marriage, and he felt nothing. . . . Two well-intentioned
people had married, only to discover they were strangers. It was a marriage of conve-
nience."

During Quill's reelection bid in 1943 for the City Council a nice Jewish girl from
Brooklyn named Shirley Ukin was bought in to help Quill's campaign in the Bronx.
Shirley, a fire-breathing ex-communist, soon became a star on the flatbed sound
truck that worked the various neighborhoods of the Bronx. Quill took notice and as
Bogey said in *Casablanca*, it was the beginning of a beautiful friendship.

"After the first painful year [of marriage to Mollie]," Shirley wrote, "Mike found a
weekend ally in a bottle of whiskey. Later he found the companionship of women far

more satisfying than a quart of scotch. It wasn't the first time I had listened to the story of the unhappy husband looking for extramarital romance, but this man I believed, and I could not refuse to see him. It no longer mattered that people were gossiping about us. What was important was to be with Mike. . . . Sometime during that campaign we became lovers."

Shirley couldn't contain herself. "His healthy appetite for sex was interwoven with a sizable chunk of guilt for being 'unfaithful' to his long-absent fiancée. 'It was part of the baggage I brought from the other side,' he explained uneasily."

"Mike was the most exciting man who had ever stumbled across my path. We had an enormous physical attraction for each other. I was in love with everything about him: his keen intuition, his sensitivity, his restless searching mind, his sharp wit—the passion, the fun, the blazing energy that charged everything he did. When I was with him, I was alive and knew it."

But, of course, Mollie was still in the picture—and Quill had no intention of divorcing her. Shirley was patient—to an extent. During their twenty-year affair, Shirley married twice, but quickly returned to Quill's side. "He had jettisoned many of his orthodox religious beliefs," wrote Shirley, "but he was obviously not prepared to become the first divorced Quill in the family." They finally married after Mollie's death in 1959—but strangely not until 1961. Perhaps one Shirley quote explains this strange, yet loving, relationship: "You've had me and your Irish respectability."

QUILL TAKES ON THE HUAC

Quill was always great theater. He had an opinion about everything and was not shy about sharing it with the public.

He was hauled before a House Un-American Activities Committee (HUAC) run by the appropriately named congressman Martin Dies. Quill was not going to play their "gotcha" game and went right after the ranking Republican, Congressman J. Parnell Thomas of New Jersey. Quill revealed that Thomas had changed his name from Feeney to his mother's maiden name. To put it mildly, Thomas's Irish constituents were not amused. Quill could always smell a rat, and he had Thomas in his crosshairs from the beginning. And he was right. Thomas was caught in a kickback scandal and pleaded the Fifth Amendment, something he used to castigate witnesses before his HUAC committee for, and ended up doing time in Federal prison.

FOR AMERICA AND AGAINST BIGOTRY

"I never forget how it feels to be an immigrant in the damn big city without a shilling in your pants pocket," said Quill, according to his wife's biography. "You'll never know what it means to be able to talk to someone from home, someone who understands and cares. You'd have to be an immigrant to know what I'm talking about. I hope I never lose that interest."

At a time in America where the term "immigrant" is spat out by half the population, it's important to remember the brilliant egalitarianism of Michael Quill. He did not see people as Irish, or African American, or Italian, or Hispanic, or Asian, or Jewish—he saw people. One of the plays he saw with Shirley was *West Side Story* and you can just image the kick he would have gotten out of Rita Moreno singing "America," a song that closely resembled his own immigrant experience.

Quill hated bigotry, and he was early in the fight against Nazism and the bigotry of the likes of Father Charles Coughlin. "Anti-Semitism," said Quill according to his wife' biography, "is not the problem of the Jewish people alone. It is an American problem, a number one American problem. We all know how Hitler came into power—while he was persecuting one section of the people, other sections of the people were asleep. The merchants of hate picked their spot and picked their cause. We too must pick our cause—freedom of all peoples in a democratic America." And he had a way of making his membership, still overwhelmingly Irish Catholic, understand why standing up to the anti-Semites was important: "As a Catholic, I know that if Jews are abused, Catholics will be abused; if synagogues are violated, churches will be violated. That's what happened in Germany, and wherever I am and whatever position I occupy, I am going to do my best to prevent it from happening here."

But not all union members shared his idealism. Especially outside of New York, Quill had to lay down the law as to why he was a friend of Jews, blacks, and other minorities. Pan American Airways employees in Miami wanted workers' rights, but did not want to share these rights with their fellow employees of color. "This union isn't asking you to love Negroes or to marry them," Quill bluntly told them. "The bosses hired you and the same bosses hired the blacks. You are on one payroll, you come to work and leave through the same gate; you punch the same time clock. Unless there is one union to protect all of you, the employer will train these men and use them to displace you—at half your wages. Unless Negroes are unionized under the same union contract that protects whites, they will be an open-ended source of cheap labor and there will be no future for you in this industry."

And in the deep South, things could get sticky. When organizing bus drivers in Houston, one of the drivers pulled a gun out of his lunch bucket and placed it in front of him. This stunt did not faze the old IRA man. "Without missing a syllable," wrote Shirley, "he deliberately picked up the gun and examined it. Still talking, he emptied the bullets into his pocket and returned the gun to its owner. There was a burst of applause from the workers, who had not heard a word he said as they followed his performance."

Quill was a great admirer of the Dr. Martin Luther King, Jr. and stated so publicly at the TWU's eleventh convention in 1961: "[W]e are reaching the turning point in America. I don't think any leader since Abraham Lincoln has done as much to unite the American people, black and white, as Dr. King has done in the past fifteen years. . . . His tactics are very similar to the tactics that we use in the trade union movement— the sit-down strike, the outright strike, the boycott. . . . Dr. King adopted the methods of the great Mahatma Gandhi, who after a hundred years, freed the Indian people from imperialism by his special and unusual tactics. . . . We are anxious about this struggle. We are anxious that it be finished in our time."

When challenged by TWU members in Tennessee for supporting Dr. King and the Freedom Riders, Quill lashed out: "The trials and tribulations of all America are 'things of the union'! Wherever there are ignorant, racist Ku Kluxers . . . trying to destroy our country, it is the business of the TWU. Wherever Americans do not have the right to vote, it comes under the heading of 'things of the union.' . . . When America is sick and endangered by the cancer of segregation, it is cause for concern by all organized labor—and by each and every member of TWU."

"Do you know what I'm most proud of?" Quill told a reporter at a press conference near the end of his life. "That in TWU we have eliminated racial discrimination in hiring and in promotions and within the union's ranks. Blacks, Hispanics, Orientals, American Indians and women are holding appointive and elective office. A few years ago we finally eliminated the word *colored* from the Pennsylvania Railroad's employee passes. We've come a long way from the pan and the broom, as Lou Manning, one of our Negro International board members, describes the employment of black workers thirty years ago."

THE GREAT TRANSIT STRIKE OF 1966

Like his hero, James Connolly, Quill decided it was time to stand and deliver, especially after his young opponent, Mayor John Vliet Lindsay, decided that he had to get
tough with the TWU. Lindsay was the perfect foil for Quill—the aristocratic WASP
sent by central casting. Jimmy Breslin caught it brilliantly in his column in the *New
York Herald-Tribune*, "[Lindsay] was talking down to old Mike Quill, and when Mike
Quill looked up at John Lindsay he saw the Church of England. Within an hour, we
had one hell of a transit strike."

Quill and Mayor Robert Wagner, the son of the man the Wagner Act is named
after, got along well. They huffed and puffed, but always came to an agreement. May-
or-elect Lindsay did not want to negotiate with Quill until he was royally sworn in as
mayor on January 1, 1966. He found to his horror his opponent—a man who had
taken on the terrorist Black and Tans—was not fighting with the Marquis of Queens-
bury rules.

"He stands alone in the moral wreckage of the union movement," wrote Pete
Hamill of Quill, "the last man in the country who once worked with his hands and still
speaks to us in the voice of the thirties. . . . He may be an anachronism . . . but the old
guy still has some iron in him. This could be his last hurrah and he knows it. . . . Quill
is the last union leader we have who will go to his grave cursing employers."[27]

Quill, as cited by Shirley in her biography, came out swinging at Lindsay, citing
Lindsay's "abysmal lack of knowledge of the fundamentals of labor relations." And he
didn't stop there. He torn into Lindsay as "a pipsqueak, a juvenile" and found his
intellect lacking: "we explored his mind yesterday and found nothing there." And, of
course, in that thick Kerry brogue he expertly mispronounced the mayor's name as
"Linsley," delighting men like my father all over America.

Quill, after four heart attacks, knew it was his last hurrah. But he would go out the
way his hero, James Connolly, had gone out—with defiance and bravado. Then Lindsay made a dramatic mistake, jailing the old rebel. Quill would not go quietly: "The
judge can drop dead in his black robes!"

"No one would have ever called him Saint Mike," wrote Hamill, "but he went off
to jail like a Christian going forth to meet the lions."

He was treated harshly by New York, its people, its politicians, and its newspapers.
He had another heart attack and was sent to the shabbiest of city hospitals. The only

person to call and ask Mrs. Quill if he could be of service was Senator Robert F. Kennedy of New York. The rest hoped he would die.

And you know what? Quill won.

While in hospital a deal was hammered out giving a 15 percent wage increase along with improvements in the health, welfare, and pension systems. In all, it was worth over sixty million dollars.

The strike over, he was released from police custody. He came marching out with his wife Shirley, a big smile on his face and flashing his shamrock cufflinks. Three days later he would be dead.

In this age of gutless, useless, amoral politicians, eunuch labor leaders, and Americans consumed by apathy and a thorough lack of decency, we'll never see the likes of Michael J. Quill again. And that's America's loss because men like Quill built America and his passing marked the end of the fighting American worker.

In the Epilogue to *Mike Quill—Himself*, Quill's wife Shirley quotes Dr. Martin Luther King, Jr. on the contributions of her husband: "Mike Quill was a fighter for decent things all his life—Irish independence, labor organization, and racial equality. He spent his life ripping the chains of bondage off his fellow-man. When the totality of a man's life is consumed with enriching the lives of others, this is a man the ages will remember—this is a man who has passed on but who has not died."

Even the august, yet stale *New York Times*, which had been lambasting Quill for years, seemed to know they had lost a favorite antagonist. In an editorial they declared: "His contemporaries long ago recognized that the acting profession was the loser when Michael J. Quill chose unionism as his career. He was a man who loved to have the last word and to make his entrances and exits with a dramatic flourish. He enjoyed life too much ever to have welcomed death, but he would doubtless have taken a wry satisfaction from the fact that he made his final exit from the stage of life just as his most memorable scene ended. From conference table to jail to hospital to final press conference, he held the attention of all New York in these last weeks. We would be less honest if we retracted now our many criticisms of Mike Quill when he was living; but there is no doubt that his departure leaves this city not quite so interesting or so colorful."[28]

Quill remained a wonderful enigma to the end. He requested a Catholic burial to make his death more "bearable" for his family. "For the first time ever," said Shirley in her book, talking about her husband in his coffin, "I saw him with rosary beads in his hands." The funeral mass was held at St. Patrick's Cathedral, and his coffin was draped with the Tri-colour of the Irish Republic he had so bravely fought for. But he had one last "respectable" thing to do—he was buried next to his first wife, Mollie, at Gate of Heaven Cemetery in Westchester County, New York.

All in all, not bad for a lad from Gortloughera, County Kerry, who found success and triumph in the dank subways of the City of New York.

PART FOUR
LITERARY IRISH NEW YORK

If there is one thing that infuriates the British it is that they forced their language on the Irish and the Irish turned around and used the same language in ways they never imagined. James Joyce reinvented it; Samuel Beckett fractured it; Yeats exposed their imperialism with it; while Shaw and Heaney raised it to a new level. In the twentieth century alone, the tiny island of Ireland produced four Nobel Laureates in Literature—Yeats, Shaw, Beckett, and Heaney. The biggest surprise is that Joyce, the most famous of all, did not crack the list.

And as the Irish moved to New York they took along their literary genius.

New York became a refugee for many an Irish writer including eccentric *New Yorker* writer Maeve Brennan, the rambunctious Brendan Behan, Joyce's friend/foe in the flesh Oliver St. John Gogarty, censor-fracturing Barney Rosset, the kidnapped New Yorker Frank McCourt, Marianne Moore, the Irish poet who loved baseball, and the three outer-borough tabloid columnists who ruled New York for decades—Jimmy Breslin, Pete Hamill, and Joe Flaherty.

They loved their city, New York, and they wrote about it. And because of that New York continued to lead the world in thought and character. This is their story.

CHAPTER ONE

WAS HOLLY GOLIGHTLY FROM *BREAKFAST AT TIFFANY'S* INSPIRED BY MAEVE BRENNAN?

DID THE EXTRAORDINARY DUBLIN WRITER, DAUGHTER OF REVOLUTION, PLAY MUSE TO TRUMAN CAPOTE?

Every time I see *Breakfast at Tiffany's* on TV I think of Dublin-born writer Maeve Brennan.

Why?

Because she may have been the inspiration for Audrey Hepburn's sexy and totally eccentric—and morally challenged—Holly Golightly.

Brennan made her mark as "The Long-Winded Lady" at the *New Yorker* magazine, but she was born in 1917 at the beginning of the War of Independence in Dublin to Robert Brennan, one of the most important Republicans of his day. In fact, she was born while her father was serving time in prison for his rebel activities.

DAUGHTER OF A REVOLUTIONARY WHO HAD A "DISLIKE OF COLLINS"

Maeve was very much her father's daughter—highly intelligent, highly rebellious, and highly literate. If you read her father's witness statements about the War of Independence at the Irish Government's Bureau of Military History you are struck that her father was an exceptional—and wordy—writer, too. Brennan must have nearly six hundred-manuscript pages at the Bureau concerning his adventures during the rebellion. Many of them are riveting.

Mostly, he did PR and journalism for the movement, but he had daily involvement with every important person, from Eamon de Valera, to Arthur Griffith, to Michael Collins. He did not like Collins, but had a great, grudging respect for him.

He first met Collins in Dublin. Collins, always the man with the money, paid Brennan and his friends from Wexford their expenses. Brennan asked his companion who the man with "the tremendous . . . shoulders" was and was told it was Collins. "I don't like him," Brennan said.

He may not have liked him, but there is nothing but admiration in his description of him. "This initial dislike of Collins," Brennan freely admitted in his witness statement, "I never quite got over. I tried to do so later, because I had a lively appreciation of the great work he was doing and of the risks he ran. His energy was terrific and his self-confidence unbounded. Though he was dynamic, he was never flurried. He built up from nothing at all an almost perfect intelligence department. His secret agents were to be found later in almost every British institution up to the highest level.

"Against odds," Brennan continued, "which would have disheartened most men, he carried on the heavy work of the Finance and Communications departments. His memory for detail was faultless and his office system, harried though it was by having to remain underground and subject to constant raids, was well-nigh perfect. Any one of his departments—Intelligence, Finance, Army, Communications—would have taxed the ability and time of a very able administrator, but Collins managed them all without apparent effort. Not merely that, but because he was inpatient of delays, he encroached on the domain of nearly every other government department and thus spurred his colleague to greater effort.

"I knew all this," Brennan admitted, "and yet I could not bring myself to like him. Perhaps it was because he was ruthless with friend and foe; because he could brook no criticism or opposition; because he was vain and loved power. Some of his admirers give Collins all the credit for such success as we had. I think this is a pity. It is true that without him Sinn Féin could not have achieved the success it did in the time it did, but this is not less true of Eamon de Valera or Arthur Griffith."

MAEVE WITNESSES THE BRUTALITY OF THE BRITISH

Brennan mentions his daughter only once in all his writings for the Bureau. Being a prominent propagandist for Sinn Féin, his offices and homes were subject to raids by the British. He recounts one such raid and the effect it had on his family:

"When I got over the wall," Brennan wrote, "I saw [his wife] Una standing at the window, pale and silent. I had never seen her so near a break. She had been crying. They had kept her downstairs all night away from the children and they had grilled her and our eldest child, Emer, aged nine, for hours, on my activities and whereabouts. Una had very narrowly missed having a bayonet run through her at the foot of the basement stairs in the dark. The rooms looked as if a herd of wild cattle had been through them. The two younger children, Maeve, aged three, and Deirdre, one and a half, were hysterical, which was not to be wondered at. It was of this raid that Erskine Childers wrote: 'This is not civilised war.'"

MR. BRENNAN GOES TO WASHINGTON . . . AND TAKES MAEVE WITH HIM

Brennan, devoted to de Valera since their prison days after the Rising, went against the Treaty, and, of course, Collins. But by 1932 de Valera was back in power and Brennan, after a stint as general manager of de Valera's *Irish Press*, found himself in Washington, first as secretary of the Irish Legation, then Chargé d'Affaires, and finally as the top man, Irish minister to the United States, which basically was the Irish Free State's ambassador to Washington. (Still officially holding dominion status in the British Commonwealth of Nations, Éire technically could not have an ambassador of its own.)

Maeve arrived in 1934 and, apparently, became Americanized fairly quickly. She took to fashion and because of her extraordinary looks, fashion took to her. She studied library science at the Catholic University of America, but even then you can see her attitude changing toward Ireland after de Valera's 1937 Constitution put restrictions on the women of Ireland and what jobs they could hold. According to Angela Bourke's biography of Brennan, *Maeve Brennan:* Homesick *at* The New Yorker, she corresponded with the fiercely Republican writer Dorothy Macardle, who warned her what de Valera's Ireland had become to many feminists like Macardle: "I am glad to know you are making steadily for library work. But how I hope you won't encounter heartbreak and frustration when you come back here. The country is going through a phrase when scarcely anybody is interested in anything but money and factories. People who care about thinking and reading are getting desperate. If you find you can't do your best work here I think you'll just have to go where you can do it."[29]

Bourke describes Maeve as "popular, witty and wickedly clever." Even her attitude toward revolutionary Ireland—the Ireland her parents had put their lives on the line to achieve—was changing. Apparently, she was also sexually active—something that a girl her age back in Dublin would probably not even consider. She fell in love with a Jewish man, who rejected her because of her Catholicism. Apparently, the great love of her life was Walter Kerr, a renowned theater critic. Kerr dumped Maeve for a woman ten years his junior. That woman, Jean Kerr, would gain some fame in 1957 by publishing *Please Don't Eat the Daisies*. Maeve's heart was broken, and she was learning quickly that life in America was not a Doris Day movie.

By the early 1940s, she found herself in New York City working for *Harper's Bazaar* magazine. Eventually, she made her way to the *New Yorker* where she rubbed elbows with editor William Shawn and such writers as Brendan Gill (perhaps another lover), and a southern fellow named Truman Capote.

Her two sisters married and stayed on in America, but her family returned to Dublin in the late 1940s. Maeve remained in New York, where she morphed into the Maeve Brennan we celebrate today. Her pieces on everyday New York, written under the byline of "The Long-Winded Lady" told of a New York and its peculiarities: its glamour, its quirkiness, and, yes, its loneliness. The thing about the pieces that sticks out, even over fifty years later, is how alone Maeve seemed to be. Already divorced, she was a gypsy, moving from apartment to apartment and hotel to hotel, the only anchor being her love for Greenwich Village. In many stories, she related her tales as she sat alone in restaurants and observed the world around her. Her stories are magical, and as someone who grew up in Greenwich Village during that period, they always strike me as being right-on in capturing that bohemian period of the 1950s and '60s.

HOLLY GOLIGHTLY BRENNAN?

Since her death in 1993, which was preceded by years of mental illness, Brennan has been positively reevaluated, and her reputation has grown. The late Eileen Battersby, literary correspondent at the *Irish Times*, argued that her short stories are such master-pieces that "no one could dispute that Brennan's Dublin stories are best compared with James Joyce's *Dubliners*."

On the hundredth anniversary of her birth, a bit of a cult seemed to have grown up around Brennan. Her comeback began in 1997 when Houghton Mifflin published *Springs of Affection: Stories of Dublin*. This was followed by Counterpoint in 2001 publishing her nonfiction pieces: *The Long-Winded Lady: Notes from The New Yorker* and *The Visitor*, her novella which was only discovered in 1997 at the University of Notre Dame and was unpublished during Brennan's life. All these publications were followed by Angela Bourke's biography in 2004. Actor Eamon Morrissey, who lived in the same Dublin house that Maeve grew up in, premiered his one-man play, *Maeve's House* at the Abbey Theatre in September 2013. At one point the Irish Arts Center in New York City even had a walking tour celebrating her haunts in Greenwich Village.

One of the tantalizing unknowns surrounding Maeve is that she may have been the avatar for Truman Capote's Holly Golightly in *Breakfast at Tiffany's*. Maeve and Capote worked together at the *New Yorker* in the early 1950s and were friends. I interviewed Angela Bourke when her biography of Brennan first came out and she had some interesting things to say about that mystery. "Truman Capote's Holly Golightly may owe quite a lot to her," Bourke told me.

"I think it is a speculation," continued Bourke.

It doesn't do justice to the totality of who she was, because Holly Golightly comes across as a bit of an airhead and Maeve was emphatically not that—she was an intellectual and a worker. But certainly "Miss Holiday Golightly, Traveling," as you see on the doorbell in the first chapter of *Breakfast at Tiffany's*: Maeve called herself a "Traveler in Residence." Maeve always had a cat. Maeve wore big glasses. She would have worn the little black dress and the hair piled high. And that kind of elusive quality. It wouldn't surprise me in the least if she had been the model for Holly Golightly. I refer to *Breakfast at Tiffany's* in the book, but I didn't want to lay any weight on that because I don't want to reduce her. Holly Golightly's a wonderful character, but she's not Maeve and Maeve's not like Holly Golightly, but I think some of the ways she influenced people and the way people saw her, there was that incredibly attractive, very elusive, maddening kind of quality about her. She'd be absolutely charming—then she'd be gone.

MAEVE VS. HOLLY

But there may have been more to Maeve being Holly than Bourke was willing to admit. In *Breakfast at Tiffany's* Joe Bell, the bartender who did not make the cut to the movie, says of Holly, "I know she had her ways. . . . I see pieces of her all the time, a flat little bottom, any skinny girl that walks fast and straight." You see Audrey Hepburn—and Maeve Brennan—in that remark.

Her moving about New York seems to be echoed when Holly says, "I'll never get used to anything. Anybody that does, they might as well be dead."

On her mailbox it declares: "Miss Holly Golightly, Traveling." One wonders if Capote is echoing Brennan's Irish past as he invokes the gypsy in her, particularly the use of the word "travel," invoking thoughts of Irish travelers, pejoratively known in those days as tinkers.

Maeve's New York wanderlust and restlessness is also echoed in Holly: "After all, how do I know where I'll be living tomorrow? So I told them to put *Traveling*. Anyway, it was a waste of money, ordering those cards. Except I felt I owed it to them to buy some little *something*. They're from Tiffany's."

Her sexuality in the book is a great mystery. "If there's one thing I loathe, it's men who bite," she says. One wonders if she's just a free spirit or something more. "Of course I like dykes for themselves," she enigmatically exclaims. "Of course people couldn't help but think I must be a bit of a dyke myself. And of course I am. Everyone is: a bit. So what? That never discouraged a man yet, in fact it seems to goad them on."

In the book, Holly, it turns out, is really Lulamae Barnes, who married Doc Golightly when "she was going on fourteen." Is this the dramatic makeover Maeve underwent when she went from Dubliner to New Yorker like Holly?

And like Maeve, Holly has a way with words: "Never love a wild thing, Mr. Bell . . . you can't give your heart to a wild thing: the more you do, the stronger they get."

"Whiskey and apples go together." How Irish is that?

And who can argue with the wonderful thought: "I want to still be me when I wake up one fine morning and have breakfast at Tiffany's." Or: "Leave it to me: I'm always top banana in the shock department."

Even better is her remark about her adopted city: "I love New York, even though it isn't mine."

So, the next time you see *Breakfast in Tiffany's* and hear the haunting score of *Moon River*, I hope you think of a great Dublin writer with a great Irish pedigree and history and remember the woman, Maeve Brennan, who is now considered one of the best Irish writers of the twentieth century.

CHAPTER TWO

HOW BARNEY ROSSET BROUGHT SAMUEL BECKETT TO AMERICA

HALF IRISH, HALF JEWISH, ALL REBEL, ROSSET FOUGHT CENSORSHIP ALL HIS LIFE

R ebellion runs in my family's blood," wrote Barney Rosset in his posthumous autobiography, *Rosset: My Life in Publishing and How I Fought Censorship.* "We have never shown a willingness to accept unthinkingly what authorities told us was right or wrong, in good taste or bad. The repression of imposed conformity has always been something we fought against, no matter what the odds."[30]

Rosset changed publishing in many ways. As the publisher of the Grove Press he was essential, along with Richard Seaver, in bringing the works of Samuel Beckett to a wide American audience. He was also instrumental in fighting the United States government and having the censorship ban on D. H. Lawrence's *Lady Chatterley's Lover* and Henry Miller's *Tropic of Cancer* lifted.

Rosset is the product of what used to be called a "mixed marriage." His father was a non-religious Jew and his mother, an Irish Catholic. Liberal politics, not religion, played the most important part when he was growing up as his mother was a big Al Smith supporter. As for religion, he said he "declared myself an atheist at an early age."

There is absolute pride as he discussed his rebel Irish family in his autobiography: "On July 10, 1884, in Carrick-on-Shannon, County Leitrim, Ireland, my great-grandfather, Michael Tansey, was sentenced to death for the murder of one William Mahon." Mahon was a "British landlord's man" and gamekeeper and his job was to keep poachers off the land. Rosset's great-grandfather was convicted on trumped-up charges. However, he was spared the death penalty, and Fenianism became part of the family's DNA. His grandfather eventually made his way to Michigan, where Rosset's mother Mary was born in 1891.

It is obvious that the Irish side of his family had the greatest impact on him as he was growing up: "My maternal grandparents, Roger Tansey and Maggie Flannery, retained their undying hatred for the English. No explanation of this was ever given to me. But I do vaguely remember hearing something about the Black and Tans from time to time. Although my grandparents spoke in Gaelic when they did not wish me to understand, I got the message quickly and never forgot it. British colonialism had brutalized Ireland and its native people. Indeed, Roger had left Ireland with a price on his head. Nevertheless, he was a very gentle man, tall, handsome, and the patriarch of the immediate neighborhood, which was largely made up of working-class people. Roger worked for the city, building and maintaining sewer lines."

HOOKING UP WITH BECKETT—WITH THE HELP OF RICHARD SEAVER

Rosset may have been the American who published Beckett, but Richard Seaver is really the American who discovered Beckett. Seaver, who went on work with Rosset and Beckett at Grove and eventually started his own company, Arcade, first came across Beckett when he lived in Paris after World War II. Seaver wrote an essay on the then unknown Beckett and Rosset came across it.

On the centennial anniversary of Beckett's birth in 1906, I interviewed both Seaver and Rosset about catching up with the reclusive Beckett. "Barney wrote me a letter," Seaver told me, "saying, 'I read your piece and I'm coming to Paris in the spring [of 1953] and can we meet?' I said absolutely. We had lunch together and we talked a lot about Beckett. Barney wanted to meet Beckett and I said, 'I'm not allowed, because Beckett was very secretive. I can't give out his address. But here's the name of his publisher and I will call the publisher and say you're going to come by and see him.'"

"We met him at the Pont Royal Hotel in Paris," Rosset told me. "He came in very jaunty, wearing a raincoat. Said he didn't have much time. That would have been around seven and we stayed with him until four in the morning. It was very calm and very wonderful." For a thousand-dollar advance, Beckett became a Grove author.

In 1959, Seaver joined Rosset at Grove. "I got a wonderful letter from Beckett saying, 'I'm so glad you're there, that's where you should be, now we're together again.' So for the next ten or twelve years I was at Grove I edited his work. It was an enormous pleasure. He's the most impeccable writer I have ever worked on."

WALTER WINCHELL THINKS *WAITING FOR GODOT* IS A COMMUNIST PLAY

"The problem of who was going to translate *Godot* into English was a thorny one," Rosset wrote in his autobiography. "Perhaps when Beckett wrote in French, no one looked over his shoulder, and he could achieve a more dispassionate purity. Perhaps he was also angry at the British for failing him as publishers. His novel *Murphy* and a short story collection, *More Pricks Than Kicks*, had achieved little notice in England. Perhaps Beckett felt he was too lyrical in English. He was always striving to strip away as many of his writer's tools as possible before finally ceasing to write altogether—taking away tools as you would take away a shovel from a person who wants to dig." Eventually, after much prodding, Beckett agreed to do his own translation.

Beckett was also worried about being censored, but Rosset told him not to worry about it. "And in 1956," Rosset wrote in his autobiography, "Bert Lahr himself would perform the role of Estragon in the first American production of *Waiting for Godot*, which opened in a new theater, Coconut Grove, in Coral Gables. When it opened, Walter Winchell proclaimed it a Communist play. The joke of the week was: 'Where is the hardest place in Miami to get a taxi?' Answer: 'Standing in front of the Coconut Grove after the first act of *Waiting for Godot*.' Now the theater proudly celebrates the fact that the first American production of *Godot* was put on there."

BECKETT COMES TO NEW YORK AND MEETS THE METS AND BUSTER KEATON

Beckett only came to the United States once, in 1964. He came to make a film with silent film star Buster Keaton which, Beckett being Beckett, was called, naturally, *Film*.

Rosset told about the Beckett-Keaton collaboration in his autobiography: "Sometime after *Film* was finished and being shown, Kevin Brownlow, a Keaton/Chaplin scholar, interviewed Beckett about working with Keaton. Beckett said, 'Buster Keaton was inaccessible. He had a poker mind as well as a poker face. I doubt if he ever read the text—I don't think he approved of it or liked it. But he agreed to do it and he was very competent. He was not our first choice. . . . It was Schneider's idea to use Keaton, who was available. . . . He had great endurance, he was very tough, and, yes, reliable. And when you saw that face at the end—oh. At last.'"

During his time in New York Beckett was brought to a Mets baseball game by Seaver, who, by the way, was a second cousin of New York Mets Hall-of-Fame pitcher Tom Seaver. The 1964 Mets were awful and hopeless, so naturally Beckett took to them. These Mets played baseball as if they were in a Beckett play:

Ever tried.

Ever failed.

No matter.

Try again.

Fail again.

Fail better.

The Mets won the first game of the doubleheader and Beckett insisted on staying for the second, which surprised Seaver. The Mets, astonishingly, also won the second game. Seaver, in his wonderful memoir, *The Tender Hour of Twilight*, recalled: "As we stood to depart, Beckett said with a sly grin, 'Perhaps I should come to see the Mets more often. I seem to bring them good luck.'"[31]

Except for the Mets, it seems that Beckett did not take to New York, as Rosset tells the tale. " 'This is somehow not the right country for me,' Sam told us at the bar. 'The people are too strange.' Then he said, 'God bless,' got on the plane, and was gone, never to return to the United States again."

ROSSET PUBLISHES CASEMENT'S *BLACK DIARIES*

Beckett was not the only controversial Irish author Rosset would publish. He also took a great interest in Sir Roger Casement's notorious *Black Diaries* and decided to publish them.

"The British," wrote Rosset, "said he was homosexual and the Irish said he wasn't. But he was. He had written diaries while he was in the Congo, mostly about the treatment of people there, but he also wrote about his love affairs. The British brought out the diaries and the Irish said they were forgeries. What ultimately happened is the British came to the United States and got the Catholic Church to stop Irish Catholics from supporting Casement because they were raising all kinds of money for his defense. Maurice [Girodias] obtained the original diaries and published part of them and made him seem very sympathetic. I published the book here and received marvelous comments from Paul O'Dwyer, who said Casement was not homosexual. He understood immediately Casement's importance. If you don't get somebody mad, no one is ever going to hear about it. This was all due to Maurice, who wanted the world to know that Casement was a political renegade who was fighting for the rights of people in the Amazon and the Congo, who also happened to be gay."

FRIENDS TO THE LAST

Rosset sold Grove Press to heiress Ann Getty with the promise he would continue to run the company. It was not to be, and he was soon fired. Beckett, a man who Richard Seaver called "the most faithful of writers," took this as a personal affront. And like a lot of Irishmen, he had a long memory. Rosset told the story in his autobiography:

A later, thornier encounter at Le Petit Café involved Beckett and Peter Getty, son of the famously wealthy Ann Getty, who, with Lord George Weidenfeld, had bought Grove, in a sad story to come, from me in 1985. (After Getty and Weidenfeld promised to keep me as CEO, they would wind up ousting me without ceremony the following year.) Smart and young, Peter Getty, who often borrowed subway fare from Grove employees to get uptown to his Fifth Avenue apartment, had learned I was meeting Beckett in Paris soon after my ouster, and asked to be introduced. I agreed, and Getty flew over, checked into a suite at the Ritz, and taxied out to Beckett's unlikely hangout, Le Petit Café, with a book he wanted autographed.

This was the only time Sam was not friendly to someone I introduced him to. It was a short, tense meeting. After autographing the book, he glared at Peter and asked, "How could you do this to Barney, and what do you plan to do about it?" Peter was very embarrassed, and mumbled something about consulting with his mother. Later, I heard that Beckett had told another supplicant from Grove, "You will get no more blood out of this stone," and he never allowed them to publish anything new of his again. To me and a group of others assembled in his honor at La Coupole he said, "There is only one thing an author can do for his publisher and that is write something for him." And he did exactly that. It was the little book called *Stirrings Still*. It was to be his last prose work, and he dedicated it to me.

Their relationship was so close that Rosset named one of his sons "Beckett."

Samuel Beckett died in Paris in 1989 at the age of eighty-three. Barney Rosset died in New York in 2012 at the age of eighty-nine. Together their respective genius, once it came together, made publishing history.

CHAPTER THREE

OLIVER ST. JOHN GOGARTY

BUCK MULLIGAN COMES TO NEW YORK

What's the best opening line of all time in a novel?

"Call me Ishmael," from *Moby Dick* by Herman Melville?

"It was the best of times, it was the worst of times," from A *Tale of Two Cities* by Charles Dickens?

"It is a truth universally acknowledged, that a single man in possession of a good fortune, must be in want of a wife," from *Pride and Prejudice* by Jane Austen?

Or was it "Stately, plump Buck Mulligan came from the stairhead," from James Joyce's *Ulysses?*

Most Irishmen would go for the latter, the first line in what is arguably one of the best novels ever written, a day in the wonderful life of one of the most wonderful cities in the world on June 16, 1904.

Buck Mulligan was based on the character of Oliver St. John Gogarty. And Gogarty, to put it mildly, was a character. Born in 1878 on Rutland (now Parnell) Square in Dublin, he went on to become a writer, a noted physician, wit, friend—then enemy—of Joyce, a patriot of the highest order in his duty to Ireland, and, ultimately, a robust New Yorker for the final two decades of his life.

DEDALUS AND BUCK

The relationship between Gogarty and Joyce was, to say the least, prickly. Friends and roommates at the Martello Tower in Sandycove where *Ulysses* opens, they became estranged. Joyce soon escaped to Paris, but it seems that Gogarty could not escape the specter of Joyce.

In his excellent biography, *Oliver St. John Gogarty: The Man of Many Talents*, J. B. Lyons cites several instances where Gogarty, while living in New York forty years after their relationship ended, was haunted by Joyce's reputation and success.

According to Lyons, he once commented on Joyce: "That's what we've come to! The fellow once spent an evening with me in Holles Street Hospital and now some character in Canada is probably getting a Ph.D. for analyzing his profound knowledge of midwifery."

He wrote a piece called "They Think They Know Joyce" for the *Saturday Review of Literature* in which he called Joyce "the most predamned soul I have ever encountered"; *Ulysses*: "one of the most enormous leg-pulls in history"; and *Finnegans Wake*: "It is infantile Mairsy Doats!"[32]

"He poked fun at the James Joyce Society," wrote Lyons, "and literary societies in general ending his letter with a swipe at Joyce. 'There is an amount of squalor inseparable from his work which the impertinence of a loose association with Homer will not hide.'"

When I was in college, one of my professors was Edward C. McAleer, former chairman of the English Department at Hunter College. He knew Gogarty and was a fellow faculty member with him down in Virginia around 1950. McAleer told a story in class about how he and Gogarty were walking along and McAleer innocently asked him, "Why did you call Joyce *Kinch, the knifeblade* in *Ulysses*?" Gogarty exploded at him: "None of your fucking business!"

Gogarty would be reminded of Joyce again, in 1937, when Joyce's Paris secretary, Samuel Beckett, would contribute to his Dublin demise.

BORN INTO PRIVILEGE

Gogarty led a privileged, full, and colorful life. He was born at an important time in Irish history, just as the Gaelic League and a new nationalism was about to hit Ireland. He had his enemies—Joyce and Eamon de Valera being two of them—but he also had many important friendships too, such as Arthur Griffith, the founder of Sinn Féin, Irish revolutionary Michael Collins, and a deep, lasting relationship with the Archpoet, William Butler Yeats, who called Gogarty "one of the great lyric poets of our age."

He was a complicated man. He shunned the conventional Catholic education of the time—unlike Joyce he would attend the Protestant Trinity College and not the

Catholic National University—and he would partake in the rambunctious Dublin of his youth, being a regular in Nighttown.

Nighttown—AKA "The Kips," or "Monto" because Montgomery Street ran through it—was Dublin's Red Light District, made famous by Joyce in *Ulysses*. It ran from the Customs House north to Mountjoy Square and extended out to Amiens Street (now Connolly) Station in the east. It is estimated that by 1900 over 1,600 prostitutes worked the carnal trade, servicing everyone from Joyce himself to the prince of Wales and every British soldier and sailor who passed through Dublin.

One of its most colorful characters was the Madam Extraordinaire, Becky Cooper. Joyce disguised Becky as "Bella Cohen" in the Circe's chapter of *Ulysses*. Gogarty was also a client and remembered Becky fondly:

> *Italy's maids are fair to see*
> *And France's maids are willing,*
> *But less expensive, 'tis to me,*
> *Becky's for a shilling.*

PHYSICIAN AND PATRIOT

But it was not all fun and games with Gogarty. After studying in Vienna, he became one of the most noted physicians in Europe and one of the most sought-after ear, nose, and throat doctors, operating out of the Meath Hospital. He held court at his townhouse at 15 Ely Place, just beyond St. Stephen's Green. His salon was one of the intellectual meeting places in Dublin.

With the Easter Rebellion in 1916 he became friends with both Arthur Griffith and Michael Collins. He was Griffith's personal physician when the president of the Dáil died of a stroke while under his care on August 12, 1922. Ten days later Collins was gunned down in County Cork, and, as he had done with Griffith, he had the gruesome job of autopsying and embalming the Big Fellow. Further adding to Gogarty's agony, he found his own latchkey to Ely Place, which he had given to Collins for safety, in the general's clothing.

He became a strong supporter of the new Free State government, run by his friend, President William T. Cosgrave, and supported the government as an Irish senator.

This support brought him to the attention of the anti-Treaty forces during the Civil War of 1922–1923.

In November 1922, he was kidnapped by the irregulars and was about to be murdered when he made a daring escape by leaping into the Liffey River and swimming clear of his captors. The Civil War was to cost Gogarty dearly. His country house in Renvyle, Connemara, was burnt to the ground and he was forced to evacuate his family to London for the remainder of the conflict. Upon his return, he was accompanied by President Cosgrave and W. B. Yeats when he donated swans to the Liffey in thanksgiving for surviving his kidnapping. He was an archfoe of new President Eamon de Valera ("Every time he contradicts himself, he's right!") and remained a senator until de Valera abolished the Senate in 1936.

GOGARTY VS. BECKETT

> *Two Jews grew up in Sackville Street*
> *And not in Piccadilly,*
> *One was gaitered on the feet,*
> *The other one was Willie.*

In 1935 Gogarty published *As I Was Going Down Sackville Street*, a reminiscence of the Dublin he knew so intimately. He was sued for libel by Harry Sinclair, a Dublin Jewish art dealer, charging that Gogarty had attacked his deceased twin brother, William, and also his grandfather who had been convicted, as Gogarty wrote, for "entic[ing] little girls into his office." Gogarty claimed the characters were composites and had nothing to do with the Sinclairs. Adding to the strange situation, according to Bair, it seems that William Sinclair and Gogarty were apparently friends and often played billiards together.

The trial started on November 23, 1937, and Dubliners were licking their chops in anticipation. "The case created a sensation in Dublin," wrote Ulick O'Connor in *The Times I've Seen: Oliver St. John Gogarty, A Biography*. "There is an illusion common among Dubliners that they are potential writers or barristers. The opportunity of seeing both professions simultaneously was not to be missed. There were queues for seats in the gallery of the court."[33]

"At the beginning of the trial," wrote Deirdre Bair in *Samuel Beckett: A Biography*, "all Dublin was on Sinclair's side, hoping that he could indeed 'get Gogarty,' who had many enemies. Sinclair's testimony, however, in which he actually produced records of his grandfather's alleged indiscretions and readily agreed to their veracity, created a quandary for Dublin's citizens. How could they support Gogarty, whose vicious pen had castigated them all at one time or another, who mocked Dublin and all in it while still claiming to be more Irish than anyone? But even more difficult, how could they rally to the side of a man who would produce in a public court evidence of his grandfather's guilt in a disgusting and disgraceful crime? It was a relief when Beckett was ushered to the stand to give testimony, as he was more easily classified by the spectators as someone at whom they could laugh."[34]

Enter Samuel Beckett, then an unknown struggling novelist, who had just returned to Dublin after being Joyce's amanuensis (literary assistant) in Paris. Anyone who knows Beckett's history knows that he was an honorable and courageous man, which he proved during World War II when he was a member of the French Resistance. However, during this trial it appears that Beckett fudged the truth when it came to his relationship to the Sinclairs.

It must be remembered that Harry Sinclair was his uncle by marriage because Harry's twin brother William ("Willie" of the Gogarty poem) was married to Beckett's aunt Cissie, his father's sister. Bair describes William as "the penniless Jew of great charm, good looks, and no profession." Cissie and "Boss" William, as he was known, led a bohemian existence that Beckett admired.

Beckett was also interested in Cissie's daughter Peggy, described by Bair as "a cool, green-eyed beauty who always wore green and was openly artistic and unorthodox in her behavior. Beckett was entranced; she was such a fascinating, quicksilver creature that he wanted to know more about her and the branch of the family that no one in Cooldrinagh [the Beckett home] seemed willing to speak about."

According to Bair, "Shortly before he went to Paris, Beckett gave the following affidavit:

> I purchased a copy of the book, *As I Was Going Down Sackville Street* from
> Green's Library, 16 Clare Street, Dublin. My attention had been called to it by
> the many advertisements I had read and the notoriety of its author. On reading
> the paragraphs . . . I instantly inferred that the lines . . . referred to Mr. Henry

Morris Sinclair and the late Mr. William Abraham Sinclair and that the words 'old usurer' and 'grandsons' referred to the late Mr. Morris Harris and his said two grandsons. I also considered that the words constituted a very grave charge against the said Henry Morris Sinclair and his late brother.

As recounted by J. B. Lyons in his Gogarty biography, under cross-examination by Gogarty's attorney, J. M. Fitzgerald, Beckett felt the heat:

Fitzgerald: You have made an affidavit in which you led the court to believe that you were an impartial, independent person, but you forgot to tell the Court that it was your uncle-in-law who suggested that you should buy the book?

Beckett: I said in my affidavit that my attention was attracted by the book because of the notoriety of the author and the advertisement it had received.

"Beckett added that he had been asked to buy the book by Sinclair," wrote O'Connor, "before he identified him in it. He made no reply when it was suggested that he had made an Affidavit at a previous hearing in the High Court, implying that he was an impartial witness, but had not referred to his relationship with the Plaintiff."

Beckett's work, *Horoscope*, also came under the microscope. Fitzgerald in his summation referred to Beckett as the "bawd and blasphemer from Paris"

All the fireworks were for naught, as Gogarty lost the suit and was fined nine hundred pounds in damages plus costs. An angry Gogarty exclaimed, "The Jew sold his stinking past, dug up a skeleton! Ah well."

"That a fellow-writer like Beckett should have given evidence against him hurt him deeply," wrote Ulick O'Connor in his biography. "He never forgot it. In 1956, he wrote to the biographer [O'Connor] referring to a talk given on the Third Programme of the BBC: 'I am sorry you praised Beckett's play (*Waiting for Godot*). It's nothing but a long wail."

The verdict was the beginning of the end for Gogarty in Ireland. "Gogarty lost more by the libel action than the £2000 he had to past costs and damages," wrote O'Connor. "The sale of the book was affected, and his expectancy of a sizable sum from that source was not fulfilled."

Soon thereafter Gogarty self-exiled himself—ironically, à la Joyce—to New York City for the rest of his life.

GOGARTY AND NEW YORK CITY, A LOVE AFFAIR

With the beginning of World War II, Gogarty offered his services as a physician to the RAF. He was turned down because of his age—he was in his early sixties. He then left his wife Neenie and headed out to America for a previously scheduled speaking tour. His tour done and stuck in America because of the war, he again offered his services to the Canadian Armed Forces and was again turned down because of his age. He decided to settle in New York City. It was mutual love at first sight.

He initially planned to work as a physician. "He intended to practice as a doctor in New York," wrote Ulick O'Connor, "but a State examination was compulsory before he could do so. He felt too old to sit for an examination at his age. He continued his profitable journalism and lecturing, in the intervals writing novels and poetry."

According to Lyons, the Chrysler Building became Gogarty's metaphor for his love of his adopted city: "He could not tire of watching the Chrysler building," Lyons wrote, "he liked to linger in 43rd Street just off Fifth Avenue feasting his eyes on it; he studied it from Tudor City and looked at it down Lexington Avenue. Unforgettable, bathed in sunlight, unimaginable at nightfall. 'When the lights come out in New York they are like so many fire-flies shining in a honey-comb. Light after light a delight to the beholder.'"

"That is what I meant when I said that 'skyscraper' was a misnomer in New York," Lyons quotes Gogarty, "for the sky is so lofty that it stands far above its towers. How well they balance each other, these soaring pavilions of the sky. The loveliest building on earth is the Chrysler building. Who dreamt of that mighty tower lightening off into that tenuous pinnacle as tapered as the snout of a sword-fish? And the way its roof is designed: shell upon shell, dark as lead during the day but see it with the sun from East River upon it and it can hardly be endured that brilliance supernal making invisible the exquisite spire that is lost in light."

He soon found lodging at 45 East 61st Street and out of staid Ireland, he began to blossom again. Asked if he intended to return to Ireland he replied, "Why should I? In Dublin I'd spend most of my time sitting in pubs talking to people for nothing. Here I make a comfortable living saying the same thing for money."

He became a regular at the Russian Tea Room, Donohue's Steakhouse on Lexington Avenue, Costello's bar on East 44th Street, and Sardi's in the theater district. By 1943 he was a social butterfly, taking in all the culture that Manhattan had to offer. He went to see Sonja Henie's ice-skating show at Madison Square Garden and saw Katharine Hepburn—"tall, gaunt, big eyes and big mouthed"—on Broadway in *Without Love.*

Gogarty found that he could make a good living with his writing. "I have finished a book and am starting another," Gogarty wrote. "Also giving 'lectures.' There's a livelihood in it and no banks to worry about."

"He found he could make a pleasant living there writing articles and lecturing," wrote O'Connor. "His fame soon spread, and he was in demand once again, as he had been in London in the Twenties, at fashionable gatherings and house parties, as a conversationalist and storyteller."

The frenzy of New York City seemed to reinvigorate him: "A week goes like a weekend," he wrote to a friend, per Ulick O'Connor, "and there is a dint in the moon the day after she is full. My three years here have gone like one. Maybe it was the relief from petty dislikes and frustrations that made me for the first time in my life experience freedom."

THE LAST YEARS

Although he was a New Yorker now, the war over, he managed to spend several months a year during the summer in Ireland. He visited his wife, whose health was failing, and his children. But he always returned to New York. "Their mode of living is a profusion," he told those who asked him why he liked America. "And they want you to share it with them."

He was still vigorous as he advanced into his middle seventies. In December 1954 he received a five-thousand-dollar fellowship from the Academy of American Poets. "The younger Irish writers," observed Lyons, "who knew him in New York do not seem to recall him as an old man, though they invariably refer to him as a lonely man."

Gogarty planned to retire back to Ireland in 1958, but he suffered a heart attack while walking on a New York street. After a few days stay in hospital, he passed away on September 22, 1957. His remains were flown to Ireland and he was buried at his country home in Renvyle in the Connemara countryside. The mourners included former President Cosgrave and his son Liam, a future Taoiseach, Sean MacBride, and his biographer, Ulick O'Connor.

"His later disillusion with Ireland does not lessen the dedication he showed to it as a young man," said poet and novelist Brendan Kennelly, according to J. B. Lyons. "One thing is certain: if Gogarty left Ireland, Ireland never left Gogarty."

So the next time you're in New York and walking down Lexington Avenue, look up at the silver spire of the Chrysler Building and think of New York's own Dr. Oliver St. John Gogarty.

CHAPTER FOUR
BRENDAN BEHAN, NEW YORKER

"TO AMERICA, MY NEW-FOUND LAND. THE MAN THAT HATES YOU HATES THE HUMAN RACE."

B rendan Behan was an addict. He was addicted to two things—booze and New York City. Together, in less than four years, they would combine to kill him at the ridiculously young age of forty-one. To put it mildly, Behan and drink did not mesh. And he seemed to know it. "One drink is too many for me," he once said, "and a thousand not enough."

New York has always acted as a magnet for the Irish. Behan was no different. Most people think of Behan as the quintessential Dubliner—and he was. But New York could give Behan what Dublin couldn't—fame and fortune. He loved the attention as much as he loved the taste of booze.

Ulick O'Connor in his revealing biography of Behan, *Brendan*, said, "While he was sober in New York, Brendan was happier than he had been anywhere else, except Dublin. He found certain literary circles there congenial and less inhibited than in London. The artist seemed to have fewer layers of encrusted social background to break through in order to find himself."

Seldom has an Irish writer—Oliver St. John Gogarty may be the exception—rhapsodized so loquaciously about his love for the City of New York as Behan. In *Brendan Behan's New York*, he waxes poetic about his adopted city:[35]

"I have never felt so much at home anywhere as I do in New York."

"I am not afraid to admit that New York is the greatest city on the face of God's earth. You only have to look at it, from the air, from the river, from Father Duffy's statue. New York is easily recognizable as the greatest city in the world, view it any way and every way—back, belly and sides."

"Broadway is not lonely at any hour of the day or night because it is a complete blaze of colour and you can get anything you want there twenty-four hours a day."

"London is a wide flat pile of redbrick suburbs with the West End stuck in the middle like a currant. New York is a huge rich raisin and is the biggest city I can imagine. I'd say it is the friendliest city I know."

"Lenin said that Communism is Socialism with electricity. New York is Paris with the English language."

"I go there for spiritual regeneration. When I arrive here from Canada I am so grateful that I am in the United States that even Howard Johnson's architecture in Buffalo cheers me up."

"The only space I am interested in for the rest of my life is that between Father Duffy and George M. Cohan in Times Square."

"New York is the only place on this Continent where you have an excuse for Behan."

UNDERSTANDING BEHAN

Behan was born into the slums of Northside Dublin on Russell Street—although it should be pointed out that the tenement he grew up in was owned by his granny. To understand Behan the writer, I think one must understand his virulent Republican background.

His mother Kathleen's brother, Peadar Kearney, wrote the Irish national anthem, "Amhrán na bhFiann," ("The Soldiers' Song") and his father was in the IRA, most prominently helping to burn down the Custom House in Dublin in 1921. While his father was imprisoned, his mother went to see Michael Collins in search of money. She always called Collins her "Laughing boy." Behan remembered that and at the age of thirteen penned the sweet and gentle poem, "The Laughing Boy," about Collins's death:

> 'Twas on an August morning, all in the dawning hours,
> I went to take the warming air, all in the Mouth of Flowers,
> And there I saw a maiden, and mournful was her cry,
> "Ah what will mend my broken heart, I've lost my Laughing Boy."

At the age of sixteen, as a member of the IRA, he went to England with plans for blowing up a Royal Navy destroyer. He was apprehended and sent to a borstal for boys, memories of which years later he turned into the compelling autobiographical *Borstal Boy*. In 1941 he was locked up again, this time by the Irish, for gunplay in Glasnevin Cemetery. He was released five years later in an amnesty and began his life for real. He worked as a housepainter and started writing.

But his writing was always to be infected by his desire to drink. His three greatest works were written before liquor grabbed him by the knees. *Borstal Boy* is a superb book, full of insights, howls, and absolutely beautiful writing. His two plays, *The Quare Fellow*, about a man—the "quare" fellow himself—about to be hanged, and *The Hostage*, about a British soldier held by the IRA as a prisoner, are also superior works. *The Quare Fellow* was made into a movie in 1962, starring the American actor Patrick McGoohan. *The Quare Fellow* also contains one of the most beautiful songs—written by Behan himself, "The Old Triangle," about the lonely life of an inmate in Mountjoy Gaol.

BRENDAN BEHAN DISCOVERS NEW YORK—AND VICE VERSA

Behan landed in New York for the Broadway premiere of *The Hostage* in September 1960. "Brendan staged his arrival superbly," wrote Ulick O'Connor in his Behan biography. "He got off the ship with a bottle of milk in his hand. 'I'm on the wagon,' he told reporters. 'It's not easy to smile when you're drinking this stuff. I may need a stomach pump.'"

The play was a hit and it, and its author, seemed to energize the Big Apple at the end of the Sominex Eisenhower era: "New York was dead in those days," O'Connor quoted Norman Mailer in his biography. "It was the end of the Eisenhower regime, a puritan period. Brendan's *Hostage* broke the ice. It was a Catholic Hellzapoppin. It made the beatnik movement—Keruoac, Ginsberg, myself and others—respectable up-town. Before Brendan, we were in exile down in the Village. *The Hostage* was adored because of its outrageousness and its obscenity, and because of Brendan's captivating humour and personality. He was an ice-breaker, and the times needed an ice-breaker."

He would return to the city for periods of time over the next three years. He took to the city—and the city took to Behan. He was a celebrity, appearing on TV with the likes of Jack Paar, David Susskind, and Jackie Gleason. This was the celebrity-gilded life he had been seeking.

Behan made a bucket list of things he wanted to see in New York for the *New Yorker* magazine, which Rae Jeff's repeated in her biography of Behan: "I would like to see the Rockefellers' paintings by Diego Rivers. I would also like to see in New York the Rockefeller who said that he would like to see me in Ireland. I would like to see and pay my respects to Big Daddy Burl Ives, Lee Tracy, Studs Lonigan, Billy Graham, Tom Lehrer, the Empire State Building, the Saint Patrick's Day Parade on Fifth Avenue, Costello's saloon on Third Avenue, Robert Frost, Marilyn Monroe, back and front, the most unforgettable character you know, the Mafia, the Mizrachi, the Daughters of the American Revolution, the Ivy League, Niagara Falls, Nick the Greek, the Governor's pitch in Albany, William Faulkner, the Yankee Stadium, a love nest, a hot dog stand, a jam session, the Golden Gloves, and the candidates for the presidential election."[36]

Behan's first New York go-around in 1960 went relatively well. The only incident was when he took to the stage drunk at the Cort Theatre, but he thought that sort of thing helped sell tickets. He went home to Dublin at Christmastime and returned to New York in February 1961. There was an incident in Canada where he was jailed for public drunkenness, and he was banned from New York's St. Patrick's Day parade by Judge John J. Comerford, ironically an ex-IRA man himself, for being a "disorderly person." But Behan, a master of the media, turned the episode with a positive spin. "There are three things I don't like about New York," O'Connor quotes him in his biography, "the water, the buses and the professional Irishman. A professional Irishman was one who was terribly anxious to pass as a middle-class Englishman." Take that, Judge Comerford!

He was invited to the Jersey City St. Patrick's Day Parade by Mayor Witkowski and given the key to the city. Behan responded with the classic line: "At the end of the Holland Tunnel lies freedom. I chose it."

TRYING TO WRITE IN NEW YORK

Without a doubt, the best descriptions of Behan in New York are supplied by his editor at Hutchinson publishers in London, Rae Jeffs, in her superb book *Brendan Behan: Man and Showman*. It is a no-holds-barred biography that will have you marveling at Jeffs' Job-like (and job-like) patience.

"It was inevitable that Brendan should fall in love with New York," wrote Rae Jeffs, "for it was nearer to his dream of Never-Never-Land than he would ever find elsewhere: a city which never appears to go to sleep, and a fancy fair of brilliant lights where at any time of the day or night he could walk without fear of being lonely. His restless and inquisitive personality found a thousand avenues to explore, and always a friendly face to accompany him, to sit and enjoy a cup of coffee or a glass of orange juice whenever he felt the need." She went on to add that "the Americans love a celebrity and he was very high up on their list."

Jeffs had been working with Behan since Hutchinson had published *Borstal Boy* in 1957. She was sent to New York to get three books—*Brendan Behan's Island, Confessions of an Irish Rebel,* and *Brendan Behan's New York*—out of him. She soon realized that his "appalling thirst," as she called it, had destroyed any discipline he may have once had as a writer.

When Jeffs arrived in New York, she had a celebrity tour guide—Brendan Behan. "For the next few days Brendan introduced us to the city which he had come to regard as his second home," wrote Jeffs, "pointing out the famous landmarks with an air of lairdship."

Jeffs was in New York for five weeks working on *Confessions of an Irish Rebel,* Behan's autobiographical follow-up to *Borstal Boy.* They got fifty thousand words down on tape despite all the distractions: "Brendan had managed to produce a solid structure upon which to build his book."

"He certainly never read the two books which were produced by means of the tape-recorder," wrote Jeffs, "*Brendan Behan's Island* and *Brendan Behan's New York,* nor would he even edit the raw material. And he died before the tapes of *Confessions of an Irish Rebel* had been fully transcribed. He was ashamed that he had lost the will-power and the concentration to work and was forced to resort to book-making in this manner." It is not surprising that Jeffs titled her chapter on Behan in New York: "America: Triumph and Disaster."

By 1963 Jeffs found herself working at the Chelsea Hotel with a Behan totally out of control. His wife, Beatrice, was also in New York and pregnant with their first child. The work on *Brendan Behan's New York* was going poorly.

The alcohol, diabetes, and liver ailments had begun to take their toll and his health began to deteriorate with alcoholic seizures. He was removed to a hospital and at one point thought he was in Grangegorman, the Dublin lunatic asylum.

By the fall of 1963 he was back in Dublin. "On the few occasions that he spoke," wrote Jeffs, "he made it clear that his chief regret at leaving the city of his heart was a persistent doubt that he would ever see it again. Indeed, the extent of his affection for New York was such that for the first time he made no attempt to drown his sadness, but preferred to savour and remember soberly his last remaining hours in the place."

The fall of '63 was very traumatic for Behan. Jeffs tried to get as much of *Brendan Behan's New York* on tape as she could and became not only its editor, but its writer. "Using *Borstal Boy* as my guide," she wrote, "I would pace the floor in an endeavour to force myself to become a second-rate understudy."

On Friday, November 22, 1963, *Brendan Behan's New York* was finished, and they went out to celebrate at the Bailey restaurant in Duke Street. They were soon to learn that John F. Kennedy had been assassinated that day in Dallas. Two days later, November 24, Behan's only child, Blanaid Orla Mairead, was born. In thanks for all the work she had done with Brendan, Rae Jeffs was made the child's godmother.

Brendan's time was limited, he knew it, and continued to drink in any pub—and there weren't many—that would allow him on the premises. Less than four months after his daughter's birth, he was dead.

THE VERY ODD *BRENDAN BEHAN'S NEW YORK*

Brendan Behan's New York is only 159 pages long. A clear one-third of the book is drawings by Paul Hogarth, so the book has barely a hundred pages of text. The book is rambling in context, but, strangely enough, it gives some very good insights into the thinking of the secret Behan. There is no doubt that it was spoken into a tape recorder and not written.

The book is bulked with shameless name-dropping: Ethel Merman, Paddy Chayefsky, Supreme Court Justice William O. Douglas, Governor Averell Harriman, Norman Mailer, James Baldwin, Jack Dempsey, Gene Tunney, Jack Paar, Arlene Francis, Alexander Woollcott, Franchot Tone, Arthur Miller, Elizabeth Gurley Flynn, Tallulah Bankhead, Allen Ginsberg, Thornton Wilder, James Thurber, Jack Kerouac, Samuel Beckett, Lauren Bacall, Jason Robards, Jr., and Jackie Gleason.

He doesn't miss many Irish saloons either: McSorley's, Costello's, P.J. Clarke's, the White Horse, and Chumley's. Another bar down in the Village he mentions is Stefan's on Christopher Street. Behan said in the book, "I understand the barman one time was not very complimentary about me as a man, although he liked my plays. No harm to him. He is entitled to his opinions, the same as everybody else." I happen to know that the barman was the late Nick Pinto, a close friend of mine for over thirty years. Pinto told me his Behan story and it was not pretty. It should be noted that Nick was one of those men who loved almost everyone—except, apparently, Behan. Nick worked in the bar business as either a restauranteur or barman for over fifty years and he was not going to put up with Behan's act. Behan, Nick told me, would be okay at first, but the more he drank the more chaos he caused. Finally, one day he stuck his head in the bar and Pinto let him have it, "Get the fuck out of here you fucking Irish pain-in-the-ass!" The "86" worked and Pinto never saw Behan again.

THE GAY BEHAN

The big revelation of Ulick O'Connor's biography was that Behan was bisexual. "There was a YMCA gymnasium across the road and . . . Behan went there regularly for work-outs," wrote O'Connor. "Brendan would punch the bag inexpertly but vigorously, do some press-ups and swim interminably up and down the pool. Afterwards he would sweat it out in the steam bath, his eyes lighting up, a member recalls, as he saw young men pass by naked on their way to the shower."

In *Brendan Behan's New York*, Behan reveals part of his YMCA life: "I am extremely fond of swimming and opposite the Hotel Chelsea is the Young Men's Christian Association where I used to swim quite a deal. And they have a rule that you cannot wear bathing trunks and before you dive into the pool, you have to take an ankle bath and you have to take a soap shower."

"At this time he was never sure that some enterprising journalist would not spring the story of his affair in New York," continued O'Connor. "This explanation would be used in Ireland to explain his frequent visits to America. His past homosexual encounters might be raked to the surface. Brendan was still hot news, and any hint of scandal would be amplified a hundred times."

"In New York in his last year," said O'Connor, "he would sometimes ask an acquaintance to arrange a rendezvous with negro youths who took his fancy, but would always fail to turn up himself for the appointment."

In *Brendan Behan's New York*, he has a whole paragraph on homosexuality, prompted by a visit to Fire Island. It is a little disturbing that he sees the age of consent at only fourteen. "Later that evening," he wrote, "somebody asked me if I was a homosexual, because apparently Cherry Grove, a part of the Island near to where we were staying, was a sort of haven for these fellows. Now I think that people have much more to trouble them than how adults behave. I am of course of the opinion, like every reasonable man, that any kind of sex with any sort of interference with kids, of say under fourteen, should be prohibited by law. There is no point in talking about homosexuality as if it were a disease. I've seen people with homosexuality and I've seen people with tuberculosis and there is no similarity at all. My attitude to homosexuality is rather like that of the woman who, at the time of the trial of Oscar Wilde, said she didn't mind what they did, so long as they didn't do it in the street and frighten the horses. I think everyone agrees that with young people it is a bad thing for society, but amongst consenting adults, it is entirely their own affair."

THE END

Behan died at the Meath Hospital in Dublin on March 20, 1964. The *New York Times* in their obituary reported the cause of death as "diabetes, jaundice and kidney and liver complaints—aggravated by his renowned bouts with drink."[37]

And after his battles with the Church he would, of course, die a Catholic death. "I suppose I am inclined to believe in all that the Catholic Church teaches," he once told the *New York Herald Tribune*. "I am accused of being blasphemous, but blasphemy is the comic verse of belief. I am a religious man only when I am sick or up in an aeroplane. On the aeroplane coming over, a nun sat next to me. There were moments when I felt like snatching the Rosary Beads out of her hand and doing a little prayer myself."

"When I die I want to die in bed surrounded by fourteen holy nuns with candles," he once said. "I am a Catholic. A damn bad one according to some. But I have never ridiculed my faith. Even when the drink takes to me I find that when darkness falls I think of my prayers."

"To those who regarded him with disdain," the *New York Times* noted, "a view held among some Irish intellectuals—he was a stage Irishman, a strange mixture of the naive and the sophisticated. His plays were looked upon as a shapeless collection of bright quips that could be given polish only by a talented director. To his admirers, who are many, he was a writer of immense talent, capable of transferring people live and warm from their natural habitat to the stage or printed page."

Whatever you think of Brendan Behan, he was one unique talent and personality. He is buried in Glasnevin Cemetery in Dublin. I have seen his grave. It is close to the south gate which is right outside John Kavanagh's Gravediggers Pub. Somehow, I feel that Brendan rests easier because of this friendly juxtaposition.

CHAPTER FIVE

MARIANNE MOORE

"I AM TROUBLED, I'M DISSATISFIED, I'M IRISH"

I think the most devastating poem ever written about being Irish was not by Yeats, Heaney, Stephens, Kavanagh, Gogarty, or any other Irish-born poet.

It was written by an American Presbyterian named Marianne Moore and any Irish person who reads it will feel the immediate punch.

It is called "Spencer's Island" and it recalls the brutality by the British on the Irish.

Back in 1596 English poet Edmund Spenser wrote "A View of the Present State of Ireland." In it he stated that "Ireland is a diseased portion of the State, it must first be cured and reformed, before it could be in a position to appreciate the good sound laws and blessings of the nation." His solution? Destroy the natives' language, customs, and culture. A man two-and-a-half centuries ahead of his time, he thought famine might do the trick.

"One of the reasons the Irish have such a way with English is that they had no choice," Irish American author Rosemary Mahoney told me. "There was a time when the Irish were forbidden to speak their own language, forbidden to practice their religion, so the only thing left to them was to adopt the language of their oppressor. As you know, they more than succeeded in that." So, as the English came to Ireland and took the Gaelic language away from the Irish. The Irish, in revenge, took the English language and turned it upside down, commandeering it as a form of rebellion against the English, proving that the pen was, indeed, mightier than the sword.

Over three hundred years later Spenser's threats were not forgotten, especially by Marianne Moore as she wrote in "Spenser's Island" with the devastating final line:

I am troubled, I'm dissatisfied, I'm Irish.

DRAWN TO NEW YORK LIKE A MAGNET

Marianne Moore was born in 1887 in Kirkwood, Missouri. Her Irish roots go back to County Monaghan. "The great-great-grandmother, Susan Henderson, was a Scot by birth," wrote Linda Leavell in *Holding on Upside Down: The Life and Work of Marianne Moore*. "She married an Irishman, John Riddle, against *her* parents' wishes. In 1815 they left the Riddle family home in County Monaghan and brought their large family to New York." Like United Irishmen revolutionaries Theobald Wolfe Tone, Robert Emmet, and Lord Edward Fitzgerald, she was of solid Presbyterian stock. "It was primarily through her Craig relatives," wrote Leavell, "that Marianne learned about her Scotch-Irish heritage."[38]

Moore's father suffered from mental illness and she never met him. She was brought up by her mother, Mary, and they would be inseparable until Mary's death. They moved around regularly—St. Louis, Pittsburgh, and Carlisle, Pennsylvania. She graduated from Bryn Mawr College in 1909 and by 1916 she had made her way, mother in tow, to Chatham, New Jersey. By 1918, she was drawn to Greenwich Village like so many other Irish, including James Connolly, James Larkin, Dorothy Day, and Eugene O'Neill.

She finally settled at #14 St. Luke's Place, an 1852 townhouse on one of the Village's most beautiful streets. She was comfortably nestled between New York's ninety-seventh mayor, Jimmy Walker, at #6 and writer Theodore Dreiser at #16. Her commute to work consisted of walking across the street to the Hudson Park branch of the New York Public Library.

"After the first year at St. Luke's Place," wrote Leavell, "Marianne accepted a half-day position at the public library branch across the street. The thirty dollars a month she earned the first two years and the fifty dollars she earned thereafter made little difference to the Moore's standard of living. [Her mother] Mary sent it all to her banker in Pittsburgh for Marianne to use to go to Italy someday. But the job did provide respite from Mary's hovering presence. Marianne usually wrote in the mornings and worked afternoons at the library. And while she had no access to her money and little sense of its value, she took pride in accumulating it.

"Marianne kept the job almost six years. She liked working half days and liked the work itself. On a typical day, she might help a man research the composition of concrete for a business he was starting, recommended a list of romantic novels to a lonely woman, and help a literary society plan its program for the season. The library patrons

came from all social classes and sometimes spoke little English. Marianne was generally good with people as well as books. She received high praise from her superiors
and advanced quickly."

She also stayed in the Village while she was the editor of the literary magazine
Dial, located at 152 West 13th Street. She edited it from 1925 until it folded in 1929.

THE EASTER RISING INSPIRES MOORE

Moore was very proud of her Scotch-Irish Presbyterian background. But something
about the 1916 Easter Rising seemed to startle the Irishness in her. "After the Easter
Rising of 1916," wrote Leavell, "Marianne called herself Irish rather than Scotch-Irish
yet proudly identified with her ancestors. 'I am Irish by descent,' she told Ezra Pound,
'possibly Scotch also, but purely Celtic.' Like many Americans, she supported the
Irish nationalists who led the Easter Rising and opposed the Scotch Irish who sided
with the Crown. Her poem 'Sojourn in the Whale,' written in 1916 praises Ireland's
ability to survive 'every kind of shortage' and to 'rise automatically,' like 'water in
motion,' 'when obstacles happened to bar the path.' Resistance to tyranny, in its various forms, is her poetry's most pervasive theme."

In "Sojourn in the Whale," Moore seemed to invoke a vision of Cathleen Ní Hou-
lihan as other Irish writers like Yeats, Joyce, and O'Casey did:

> [S]he will become wise and will be forced to give in.
> Compelled by experience, she will turn back;

"Spenser's Ireland" would be included in a collection published at the beginning of
World War II. She was clearly "troubled" by Ireland's neutrality during their "Emergency."

"'We are out of humor with Ireland just now,' Marianne told Mary Shoemaker as
she was assembling poems for *What Are Years* [1941]," wrote Leavell. "She had one
more poem to write, 'Spenser's Ireland.' While she could appreciate the frankness of
the French, the poem indicates that she identified with Irish credulity. The world
could do with less 'obduracy' and more Irish 'enchantment,' the poems says. 'You're
not free until you've been made captive by/supreme belief.' This is the most obviously
autobiographical poem in Moore's oeuvre: she mentions her great-great-grandmother
and proudly claims her Irish heritage.

"Whereas Moore chastised Ireland for its neutrality in 'Spenser's Ireland,'" wrote Leavell, "in 'A Carriage from Sweden' she praises another neutral country for being 'responsive and/responsible' and for providing sanctuary to Denmark's eight thousand Jews."

NO INTEREST IN SEX

Unlike many who descended on Greenwich Village, including Dorothy Day, Moore was not consumed by sex and apparently had no interest in either sex. Her own mother said she had "no man-instincts whatever."

"Marianne showed no more sexual interest in women than she did in men," wrote Leavell. "Her lesbian friend Bryher called her 'a case of arrested emotional development,' who 'haunt[ed] places full of potential victims' (victims, that is, of her inadvertent seductiveness). Marianne repeated the diagnosis late in life to explain why she had never been 'matrimonially ambitious.'"

Despite her reluctance to engage sexually, men found her attractive. "Moore is most familiar to us with her gray hair and three-cornered hat," wrote Susan Edmiston and Linda D. Cirino in Literary New York, "but William Carlos Williams described how she looked as a young woman: 'Marianne had two cords, cables rather, of red hair coiled around her rather small cranium . . . and was straight up and down like the two-by-four of a building under construction.' Alfred Kreymborg said that she was 'an astonishing person with Titian hair, a brilliant complexion and a mellifluous flow of polysyllables which held every man in awe.'"

She may have had some kind of eating disorder. At one point she was down to an alarming seventy-five pounds. "Too little body fat," concluded her biographer Leavell, "causes both amenorrhea and the loss of libido."

Her slight weight may have also been some kind of statement to the world. "She did like the streamlined, androgynous body of the New Woman," wrote Leavell. "Throughout the 1920s she wore a mannish suit that hung loosely on her shoulders and revealed nothing of her shape."

MARIANNE TAKES TWO AND HITS TO RIGHT

While sex did not excite her, the sound of ball hitting bat truly aroused her. Alfred Kreymborg, poet, novelist, playwright, literary editor, and anthologist, found out first-hand when he took her to a baseball game at the Polo Grounds in April 1917.

"Never having found her at a loss on any topic whatsoever," Kreymborg said, "I wanted to give myself the pleasure at least once of hearing her stumped about something." Finally, the game began. "Strike!" yelled the umpire.

"Excellent," was her response.

"Do you happen to know the gentleman who threw the strike?" he asked.

"I've never seen him before," said Moore, "but I take it it must be Mr. Mathewson."

"Why?" gasped Kreymborg.

"I've read his instructive book on the art of pitching," she responded, "And it's a pleasure to know how unerringly his execution supports his theories."

Kreymborg was shocked that Moore even knew who Christy Mathewson was, although he was not pitching that day, having retired in 1916. He joined the army in 1918 and was accidentally poisoned by gas in Europe. Moore may have had an affinity for him because Mathewson was also a writer. She had read his book, *Pitching in a Pinch*, and he also wrote a play, *The Girl and the Pennant*. His lungs compromised by the gas, he developed tuberculosis and died in 1925 at the age of forty-five.

After her early days in the Village, Moore moved to Brooklyn where she became a fan of the Brooklyn Dodgers. In 1956 she wrote an ode to the Dodgers' Syn-PHONY Band, a rag-tag musical outfit that played it more for laughs than anything else. The poem was rejected by the *Hudson Review*, the *New Yorker*, and *Sports Illustrated*. "Moore sent it at last to the *New York Herald-Tribune*," wrote Leavell in *Holding on Upside Down*. "To her surprise . . . the newspaper printed it on the front page to mark the opening day of the 1956 World Series, when the Dodgers again faced their Goliath, the New York Yankees." It didn't, however, help the Dodgers. They lost the series in seven games.

After the Dodgers deserted to Los Angeles following the 1957 season, Moore became a Yankee fan. "Baseball and Writing" is an epic poem to the great Yankee teams of the early 1960s. Everyone is remembered from Elston Howard, to Roger Maris, to Mickey Mantle, to Hector Lopez. And she didn't miss many either, including Moose Skowron, Johnny Blanchard, Bobby Richardson, Tony Kubek, and Clete Boyer. Michael Burke, president of the Yankees, invited her to throw out the first ball of the 1968 season.

THE OCTOGENARIAN CELEBRITY

Marianne Moore hit the jackpot in 1951. Her *Collected Poems* hit the literary trifecta, winning the National Book Award, the Pulitzer Prize, and the Bollingen Prize. T. S.

Eliot, in his introduction to the collection, said, "My conviction has remained unchanged for the last 14 years that Miss Moore's poems form part of the small body of durable poetry written in our time."

During the 1960s her celebrity continued to grow. She wrote the liner notes for Cassius Clay's record album, *I Am the Greatest*. "This was before he defeated Sonny Liston to become heavyweight champion and before he became Muhammad Ali," wrote Leavell. "The queen of understatement and self-abnegation praised the poetry of Clay's braggadocio decades before rap musicians and Henry Louis Gates, Jr., taught white listeners about the oral black folk tradition of 'playing the dozens.' She invoked Shakespeare and Sidney to describe Clay's rhymed taunts. Clay is 'a master of hyperbole' and 'a master of concision.' When asked, 'Have you ever been in love?' he said, 'Not with anyone else.' Noting also his 'fondness for antithesis,' she called him 'a smiling pugilist.'"

Moore was also a champion of the black athlete, going back to when Jackie Robinson broke the color barrier on her beloved Dodgers in 1947. "Marianne liked athletes who persevered against their rivals and admired especially those who prevailed against personal and racial obstacles," wrote Leavell. "She had been a Jackie Robinson fan from the time he joined the Dodgers in 1947 but became a Dodgers fan, she later claimed, while watching Roy Campanella, who joined the team the following year. She liked the swagger of his gestures and idiom as well as his skill as a catcher. An automobile accident paralyzed Campanella from the neck down in 1958, and his autobiography, *It's Good to Be Alive*, came out the next year. 'This book is more persuasive— inherently—as emphasizing the injustice, indeed hatefulness, of race prejudice, than any book I know,' she wrote the publisher. 'What an incentive to accept grief and disability, not just stoically but with joy.'"

Her politics were liberal, and she became friends with James Baldwin (who she called "a fine youth"), Langston Hughes, and Harry Belafonte. She appeared on *The Tonight Show* while Johnny Carson was on vacation and Belafonte was guest hosting. She had, however, a different take on John F. Kennedy and Lyndon B. Johnson than most Americans. When Belafonte asked what she thought of the assassinated president, she said she "did not like that young man" and did not have time to give him "the thousand reasons."

Her take on LBJ was even more provocative: "She lauded Lyndon B. Johnson's stance on Vietnam," wrote Leavell, "as strongly as she did his stance on civil rights.

Unlike her friend Robert Lowell, who publicly refused an invitation to Johnson's inauguration as a way of protesting the war, Marianne called herself 'one of Mr. Johnson's most fervent admirers—both of his objectives and of his words in defining them.' Only her frail health prevented her from accepting her own invitation to the inauguration" in 1965.

THE PERFECT EPITAPH

In late 1965, she moved from Brooklyn back to the Village, taking an apartment on the seventh floor of 35 West Ninth Street, only a few blocks from Washington Square Park. The move did not prohibit her celebrity. "She earned $5,000 for appearing in Braniff Airways historic 'When you got it, flaunt it' advertising campaign," wrote Leavell, "that paired unlikely celebrities such as Andy Warhol and Sonny Listen in adjacent airline seats. Warhol explains the significance of soup cans to Liston, and pulp fiction author Mickey Spillane explains the power of words to Marianne. 'Tough Mickey Spillane and gentle Marianne Moore always fly Braniff,' said the voice over."

A Moore protégé, poet Elizabeth Bishop, also experienced a trifecta triumph, winning the Pulitzer Prize, the National Book Award, and the National Book Critics Circle Award. Her whimsical poem "Invitation to Miss Marianne Moore" captures the spirit of the poet:

> From Brooklyn, over the Brooklyn Bridge, on this fine morning,
> please come flying . . . Please come flying . . .

Moore died on February 5, 1972 at the age of eighty-four. Outside her Ninth Street apartment building there is a simple, but terrific plaque. In twenty-one simple words and numbers they summed up the superb life of Marianne Moore:

> 35 West 9th Street/Last Home of
> MARIANNE MOORE
> (1887–1972)
> Pulitzer Prize-Winning Poet, Baseball Enthusiast
> And Lifelong New Yorker

It was the perfect epitaph for a special Irish New York poet.

BRESLIN-HAMILL-FLAHERTY

THE TRINITY OF NEW YORK TABLOID COLUMNISTS DOMINATED IRISH NEW YORK IN A TIME WHEN NEWSPAPERS RULED

I n my youth—B.I., Before the Internet—the New York thing to do was go down to the newsstand, in my case in Sheridan Square in Greenwich Village, and wait for the *Daily News* truck to show up around 8 p.m. It was a ritual when neighbors could stand around and chat and it was a great excuse to get out of the house.

The *New York Post* was the afternoon paper and you could pick it up after work as you hit the subway. The *News* was early evening and the august *New York Times* would slam around 11 p.m. when most working-class Irish were already tucked in to be ready for the next day's work.

We knew most of the news—the Commies were after us, the Mets had lost, the Yankees had won, so what else was new?

What we lived for were the columnists. Those guys who made us laugh or inflamed us. In New York in the '60s and way into the twenty-first century, two of those guys were Jimmy Breslin and Pete Hamill. For a short fifteen years they were joined by Joe Flaherty. They were all Irish to the core, all from the outer boroughs. Breslin from Queens and Hamill and Flaherty from Brooklyn. To put it mildly, they knew how to cut through the bullshit.

Pete Hamill is still with us and still writing books. He more than any other writer in this city was the conscience of New York. He never lets his city off the hook. His thoughtful, beautifully crafted columns remind us of the good in us and what the alternatives can be. He can be quixotic in his hopes, but if one can't hope what's the point of being alive?

Joe Flaherty was the opposite of Hamill. He used his pen as a blunderbuss and his shout was meant to shock you into action. He was also the funniest man I ever met, but with a humor so broad and at times ribald that you'd be grabbing your sides in convulsions. Cancer took Joe from us much too soon, but his books and columns give a poignant look into the chaos that New York City was from the 1960s to the '80s.

But I think it's fair to say that it was hard for Hamill and Flaherty to compete on equal ground with Breslin. For Breslin was more than a talented writer. He was a gadfly, a politician, a performer. He proudly carried a New York swagger as he defended his city against all comers. And it was never just New York to Breslin, it was always "The City of New York."

CHAPTER SIX

JIMMY BRESLIN

HE LOVED TO "COMFORT THE AFFLICTED AND AFFLICT THE COMFORTABLE" IN REAL IRISH NEW YORK

I grew up with Jimmy Breslin.

In 1963 I was having my first romance. It was with a terrible baseball team called the New York Mets. Breslin had just written a book called *Can't Anyone Here Play This Game?* about the 1962 Mets who were, unbelievably, worse than the '63 version I was currently romancing.

My heroes were a young hustling second baseman named Ron Hunt, an old Dodger icon named Duke Snider, and a tough young black sinkerball pitcher named Alvin Jackson, who Mets broadcaster Bob Murphy always called "Little Al Jackson." I also had a place in my heart for a young black catcher with the unlikely name of Choo Choo Coleman, who couldn't hit and could barely catch. I asked my brother why they called him Choo Choo and he told me that his real name was Clarence. "What would you rather be called?" he asked me. "Clarence or Choo Choo?" I suddenly, at the age of twelve, realized Choo Choo's dilemma, although I didn't know what a "dilemma" was. But I felt for Choo Choo and his dilemma.

Breslin wrote about New York, but he also wrote about the great working-class City of New York, a city that had half its heart cut out of it when both the Brooklyn Dodgers and New York Giants left the Big Apple to become California dreamers. The one thing that always stuck in my head was the last three paragraphs of the book.

"The Mets lose an awful lot?

"Listen, mister. Think a little bit.

"When was the last time you won a lot out of life?"[39]

It was a *Real* Irish New York lesson I never forgot. It was a warning for a young kid how tough life could be. Years later, when interviewing Breslin, I asked him if Casey Stengel actually used the line, "Can't Anyone Here Play This Game?" and he admitted to me that he made it up. A pretty good make-up for a writer.

THE "GRAVEDIGGER'S THEORY"—A POWERFUL LAMENT FOR JFK

The next time I remember Jimmy Breslin was later in that fateful year of 1963. It was the weekend President John F. Kennedy was shot. To say that the country—especially Irish New York—was in shock is an understatement. That weekend, as America prepared for the president's state funeral, Breslin did something unique and nothing short of genius. Breslin went to Arlington National Cemetery in search of a gravedigger.

On Sunday, November 24, Breslin found himself at the White House looking for a story to write. He stood in the White House press office with the rest of the media and decided that his story would not come in the form of a press release.

In 1996 I interviewed Breslin for *Publishers Weekly*, the trade magazine of the publishing industry, and Breslin told me how he came to write what he called his "gravedigger's theory."

"I went to the White House in the morning," he told me. "I walked into the lobby and that was packed, and I said this is not for me. So, I saw Art Buchwald and we talked for a second and I said, 'I can't do any good here. I'm going to go over and get the guy who dug Kennedy's grave.' 'Yeah, that's a good idea,' he told me, instantly. And I left there right away. I just turned and walked right out of the place and over to Arlington cemetery, and they got me the guy."

Breslin's guy was African American Clifton Pollard, forty-two years of age, who, Breslin noted, was "an equipment operator, grade 10, which means he gets $3.01 an hour." Pollard was called into work on short notice and his boss said to him, " 'Sorry to pull you out like this on a Sunday.' 'Oh, don't say that,' Pollard said. 'Why, it's an honor for me to be here.'"

Pollard climbed into his reverse hoe and "at the bottom of the hill in front of the Tomb of the Unknown Soldier, Pollard started the digging."

"One of the last to serve John Fitzgerald Kennedy," wrote Breslin, "who was the thirty-fifth President of this country, was a working man who earns $3.01 an hour and said it was an honor to dig the grave."

When I reminded Breslin, who never finished college, that his outside-the-box gravedigger's story is taught in every journalism school in the country, he came alive. "Yes! They should, too," he exclaimed. "It's the gravedigger's theory."

VIETNAM AND BEYOND

The next time as a kid I remembered Breslin was during the Vietnam war. It was about 1965 or '66 and he wrote a column for the Sunday *New York Herald Tribune* about coffins of young servicemen arriving at an airbase in California. I could never find the column and I asked Breslin about it, but he had forgotten he even wrote it. But it stuck with me. Coffins coming out of the cargo holds of airplanes. That's all I needed to know about the Vietnam war. It was another travesty of democracy.

My next great memory of Breslin was in the New York miraculous year of 1969. My terrible Mets were World Champions. So were my Jets and so were my Knicks. And an American landed on the moon. And to top it off, Norman Mailer and Jimmy Breslin, respectively, ran for mayor of the City of New York and City Council president.

The chaos they caused was fucking great! What did Thomas Jefferson say? "I hold it that a little rebellion now and then is a good thing."

The august press thought it was a disgrace, but I thought it was hilarious. *Go get them!* I thought. My future friend and mentor, Joe Flaherty of the *Village Voice*, was their campaign manager and wrote a wonderful book, still germane today, called *Managing Mailer.* Of course, there was no managing Mailer or Breslin. Mailer and Breslin lost, of course, but they made people think, which, I think, is the main job of writers.

DESTROYING NIXON WITH A VERY IRISH BOOK

The United States of America at that time began to morph into the swamp of democracy that we are still suffering through today. Before Trump, there was Nixon, a gutter rat of the first magnitude.

"It was as graceless at the end as it was at the start."

That's Breslin's first sentence, first paragraph, of *How the Good Guys Finally Won.*[40]

In this time of Trump I went to my bookshelves and pulled down a very old copy of Jimmy Breslin's *How the Good Guys Finally Won: Notes from an Impeachment Summer*, which was published in 1975. As I flipped through the first few pages I realized that this was a copy that Breslin had autographed for me. The inscription reads: "June 19, 1996. For Dermot McEvoy—Thanx for appreciating my personal favorite. Jimmy Breslin."

Man, Breslin's "personal favorite."

"For a little island, it has caused so much pain," is Breslin's description of Ireland. *Good Guys* is a very Irish book. Its heroes are its writer, Breslin, and Massachusetts Congressman Thomas P. (Tip) O'Neill, who is described in the flap copy as being from "the wrong side of Cambridge," meaning the side that didn't contain Harvard University.

"He comes with the full blood of Cork City in his face," wrote Breslin of O'Neill. "O'Neill is a grandson of the Great Hunger and in their pursuit of the American Dream the O'Neills first investment was in 'the Irish stock market—cemetery plots.'"

Being Irish, Breslin was a great believer in Original Sin and the workings of the Catholic Church. "Into the second-floor offices of the Special Counsel to the Chairman of the House Judiciary Committee came thirty typists. Most of them had been picked because they were graduates of Catholic high schools. They were trained by nuns to believe in causes, and now they were to work on another cause, the greatest search for justice in the nation's history."

O'Neill's Irish Catholicism, Breslin believes, had a lot to do with the decency that emanated from O'Neill: "In a time of lies and fear and weakness and hypocrisy, in a time when evil was matched against evil and the results were pronounced as good, O'Neill provided a few shafts of sunlight, of charm and humor and mature compassion. Nobody ever said you have to torture life to produce history."

IT MAY BE TRAGEDY, BUT YOU CAN STILL LAUGH

Breslin's book is very serious and thoughtful—a textbook on how political power works—but it is ripe with humor, some of it laugh-out-loud funny. The Irish, well aware that life is tragedy, have learned to laugh through famine and revolution and this black humor is how Breslin and O'Neill viewed the sewer of Watergate.

O'Neill, who said "money is the mothers' milk of politics," tells a very funny story about his friend John F. Kennedy raising money for his run for president in 1960. Tip is collecting money all around the room and ends up in a closet with the future president. "Now I have twelve thousand in cash and seventeen thousand in checks, what do you want me to do with it?" O'Neill asked Kennedy. "Give the checks to Kenny

O'Donnell," said JFK. "I'll take the cash." Now you know how millionaires stay millionaires.

There is also this priceless story about Nixon pitying himself and threatening suicide. "Early in the going, Nixon is supposed to have mentioned something about committing suicide. And [Chief-of-Staff Alexander] Haig supposedly said, 'That might be an idea worth considering.' And Nixon didn't speak to Haig for about a week."

Even the story about how O'Neill knew early on that Nixon had the White House bugged is funny. It happened at a dinner the night the Vietnam War ended. "As [Nixon's] saying this, he first has raised his voice. Then I see he's looking upward, at the chandelier or whatever was there. . . . Now I see he's not only looking up, but he's pointing with his finger, as if he's talking to somebody up there. And I say to myself, you've got to be kidding. He has this place bugged."

Breslin showed his belief in the American democracy and how the country survived Nixon. I just wish Jimmy Breslin was here in the time of Donald John Trump. The columns would write themselves.

TAKING ON TRUMP OVER THE "CENTRAL PARK FIVE"

Speaking of Trump, he and Breslin have met in battle before. Back in 1989 when five black kids were accused of raping and leaving for dead a young woman in Central Park, Donald Trump thought it his civic duty to take out newspaper ads—while anxiously waiting for the young woman to become a corpse—and requested the death penalty for the five boys. No homicide had been committed yet, but that didn't bother Trump. It may have been our first notification of how much of a bigot Trump was.

Breslin wrote a column on May 2, 1989 for *Newsday* called "Violent Language, Between You and I" and called out Trump for what he was then and what he is today—a moral coward.

"[O]ne recoiled, but was hardly surprised to find in the newspapers this morning a full-page advertisement by 'Between You and I' Trump in the insolent, cruel words one would expect of him for, of course, lack of knowledge of a language always breeds words of thuggery. The ad for the first time reveals all the rest of the things that anybody would want to know about Donald Trump. In his ad, which ran in all four of the city's newspapers, 'Between You and I' Trump practically called for the death of the teenagers arrested for the rape and attack on the 28-year-old jogger in Central Park."

"Outside the courthouse," Breslin went on to warn, "beware always of the loud-mouth taking advantage of the situation and appealing to a crowd's meanest nature."

In his ad Trump wrote, "Mayor Koch has stated that hate and rancor should be removed from our hearts. I do not think so. I want to hate these muggers and murderers. They should be forced to suffer and, when they kill, they should be executed for their crimes. . . . Yes, Mayor Koch, I want to hate these murderers and I always will. I am not looking to psychoanalyze them or understand them, I am looking to punish them. . . . I no longer want to understand their anger. I want them to understand our anger. I want them to be afraid."

Tough guy, that Donald John Trump, especially with other people's lives.

"Such violent language sounds," Breslin correctly guessed, "as if it were coming from someone who walks around with bodyguards."

Then Breslin let the media have it—and he was right on. A quarter of a century later they would take a draft-dodging, serial misogynist, give him free coverage on TV, and turn him into the forty-fifth president of the United States: "The curious thing about 'Between You and I' Trump," Breslin warned, "is not that he destroyed himself yesterday, for all demagogues ultimately do that, but why he became so immensely popular with the one group of people who are supposed to be the search-lights and loudspeakers that alert the public to the realities of such a person. That would be those who work in the news business. Even the most unhostile of eyes cannot say that his buildings are not ugly. Yet all news stories say 'imaginative' when common sense shouts 'arrogant.' Always, the television and newspapers talk of his financial brilliance, when anybody in the street knows that most of 'Between You and I' Trump's profits come from crap games and slot machines in Atlantic City, the bulk of that, the slot machines, coming from old people who go down there with their Social Security checks."

Breslin went on to say "the news business today is so utterly dishonest that the people are below taking bribes. Instead, Trump buys them with a smile, a phone call or a display of wealth that so excites these poor fools that they cannot wait to herald his brilliance."

By the way, the so-called Central Park Five (now known as the Exonerated Five) were innocent—which I'm sure didn't bother Donald Trump in the least.

SON OF SAM: "HELLO FROM THE GUTTERS OF N.Y.C."

The big movie the summer of 1977 was *Saturday Night Fever* starring John Travolta. The big song from the movie was the Bee-Gees "Stayin' Alive." For many young New Yorkers in love that summer it was not to be, for this was the Summer of Sam and Sam's hunting grounds were the outer boroughs of the City of New York where *SNF* took place.

On May 30, 1977, Breslin received a letter which began, in the best Jack-the-Ripper manner: "Hello from the gutters of N.Y.C. which are filled with dog manure, vomit, stale wine, urine and blood." You had to hand it to Sam, he had flair—and Breslin had found a demented friend that would make his column the most read in the city.

Sam went on to state that he was a fan of Breslin's and read every column and found them "quite informative." He referred to his first victim, Donna Lauria, and the upcoming first anniversary of the attack. Ominously, he asked, "What will you have for July 29?"

He went on to write, "Please inform all the detectives working the slaying to remain." He signed it "Son of Sam." Oddly enough, he said "I don't care for publicity," but he was obviously lying.

County Kerry-born Deputy Inspector Matthew Dowd, the man running the investigation called "Operation Omega," told Breslin to print the letter, saying, "He'll come in through you."

Breslin was very impressed by the writing. "The cadence of what he was writing was sensational," Breslin later said, according to John Hockenberry of NBC News. "The guy could have a column and do me out of a job. He can really capture you, compel you to read. He's terrific."[41]

The Irish played a big part in the apprehension of David Berkowitz, AKA Son of Sam. Berkowitz seemed obsessed with Breslin. He sent him two letters and used his neighborhood as a hunting ground. Breslin was so concerned with Berkowitz that he moved his family out of his Forest Hills home. Years later, Breslin, with a shrug, confided to me that he thought he was being stalked by Berkowitz.

Capturing the Son of Sam came down to luck. On his last attack, Berkowitz's car was ticketed because it was too close to a fire hydrant. A local woman, Cacilia Davis, walking her dog, saw Berkowitz return to the car with his arm held stiffly by his side, holding the gun he had just used. He stared her down. Disconcerted, she took off for home and heard shots as Berkowitz fired after her. Terrified, she did not report the incident until four days later. When the police pulled the tickets, it led them to Yonkers and David Berkowitz. Unlike his terror, his surrender did not end with a bang, but rather a whimper. He was arrested on August 10 outside his apartment without incident. New York's summer of fear and agony was over.

New York was lucky to have a couple of Irishmen, Jimmy Breslin and Timothy Dowd, around in the summer of '77. Heroically, they rose up to defend their city while the snake named Son of Sam slithered in its sewers.

ALWAYS THE FIGHTER

Journalist Peter Finley Dunne famously wrote, "Comfort the afflicted, afflict the comfortable." It should be chiseled on Jimmy Breslin's gravestone, for he was the defender of the poor and the powerless.

In the last fifty years of his life, Breslin was in on every major story. He won a Pulitzer Prize for his coverage of the AIDS crisis and when others buckled under the racist mayoralty of Rudy Giuliani, Breslin was there to give it out, calling the fascist-in-training "Young Mussolini . . . with a face like a cadaver"—a description accurate to this day.

He also stuck up for the little guy—in one case a little woman named Cibella Borges, who was sworn in as a police officer in 1981. In the case of Borges, Breslin had to take on his "own people"—Irish Catholics. "I used to write columns and make fun of them," he told me years ago. "They've got big schools, but they don't produce anybody who writes. They produce a lot of insurance agents and corporation lawyers and police. They write tickets instead of stories. They've taken a great heritage and not done anything with it over here. They also associate me with the blacks. They just see me and say, 'those are his friends.'"

"At four-foot-eleven and ninety-five pounds," Breslin wrote of Borges, "she was the smallest police officer in the department's history. She also spoke Spanish in a city where there are far more Hispanics than there are citizens with Irish names, although the police department is commanded almost entirely by middle-aged Irish Catholics."

Officer Borges's mortal sin was that she once, before she was a police officer, posed nude for a girlie magazine. Of course, all the holy Irish Catholics of the NYPD thought this scandalous and terminated her. Breslin to the rescue.

"Her photographer spent many months," he wrote in a column called "Por Unas Horas," "showing the pictures around town to editors who work in the city's literary underground. Finally, he was able to sell them to a magazine named *Beaver*, 'which is a publication read with one hand.'"[42]

Tongue firmly still in cheek, Breslin continued:

> The police department should have been proud of the pictures, as they prove that at least one member of the force is in marvelous physical condition; most officers are in such deplorable shape that if called upon to pose for pictures, they would first put on overcoats.
>
> Yet Cibella was in trouble. As a Hispanic, she could not invoke the rules of the Irish-dominated force: the surest way an Irish cop explains away most offenses, and particularly sex offenses, is to claim alcoholism. Misuse of alcohol is acceptable to the Irish; misuse of the body calls for condemnation to a chamber of Hell. If born Irish, Cibella would have walked into the hearing and said, "I drink too much and I don't know what I'm doing. In fact, I'm thirsty right now."

Breslin went on to write that "these aging Irish Catholics who run the police department are frightened of sex, which is at best the Act of Darkness, and becomes dangerous when it is being committed by some dirty naked Puerto Rican. The Devil in the squad room."

The Patrolman's Benevolent Association was so annoyed at Breslin that they took a sixteen-thousand-dollar ad out in Breslin's paper, the *Daily News*, to protest Breslin's writings. Breslin commented that the PBA was "guilty of premature semicolons" and chided them for spending sixteen grand on an ad when they should have been defending one of their members, Ms. Borges.

Borges sued the NYPD and, in 1985, a judge overturned the ruling, reinstating her with eighty thousand dollars in back pay. She retired in 2002 with the rank of detective sergeant. Mark another one up for the good guys.

I MISS THE PRICKLY BRESLIN

Breslin was not all sweetness and light. When he wanted something he could romance you and spend hours with you in his apartment just above Lincoln Center on lower

Columbus Avenue. But if you needed something, say a quote, the phone could slam down with unceremonious finality. In the HBO documentary on Breslin and Hamill, there is a whole segment dedicated to being hung up on by Breslin. I guess I made the club.

But after all is said and done, I really miss Breslin and his characters based on real-life rogues. I miss Marvin-the-Torch, the happy arsonist, Fat Thomas, the degenerate gambler, Klein-the-Lawyer, who put the sleaze in lawyer, and Jerry-the-Booster, who could clean out the inventory of a department store under his coat in fifteen minutes. I miss that he was there the night Bobby Kennedy was shot in Los Angeles and how he could get through a friend's murder and still write it up. And, above all, I miss the laughter and how he could needle the Irish and, basically, drive them insane.

But Breslin's special gift was that he helped New Yorkers cope. He helped us through assassinations and terrible politicians. He helped us through senseless wars and guided us through the terrible days after 9/11. He was almost a holy shepherd guiding his New Yorkers—whether they liked it or not.

And it should not be forgotten that he was a pretty good author of both fiction and nonfiction. His novel *World Without End, Amen*'s first hundred pages contain maybe the best stuff ever written about the Irish in New York. All in all, besides his newspaper columns, Breslin wrote seventeen books.

Yeah, I really miss Jimmy Breslin, a great Irish New York talent.

CHAPTER SEVEN

PETE HAMILL

THE HEART AND CONSCIENCE OF REAL IRISH NEW YORK

The one thing that strikes you about Pete Hamill when you read his writings or get to know him personally is his profound sense of decency. It had to come from his parents, Billy Hamill and Anne Devlin. Anne was born in New York but returned to Belfast as a child. "Once [my grandfather] had his second child," Hamill told me, "my mother and her brother, he decided he couldn't live in Belfast as a Catholic. He had seen the world and he wanted to live—where else would you live?—in New York where nobody is going to say, 'what are you?'; 'what church do you go to?' So he came to New York when my mother was a little girl. She was five when he got killed in an accident falling off a ship in Brooklyn." Young Anne returned to Belfast to be brought up by relatives. She would return to New York in 1929 with an omen ringing in her ears—it was the day the stock market crashed.

His father Billy was born in Belfast and was a member of Sinn Féin. After a British soldier was blown up, according to Pete, "he went on the lam to Liverpool, and from Liverpool he came here." Soon after arriving in America, Billy lost a leg in a football accident. Despite his handicap, he worked hard to support his wife and seven children. In 1933, Anne and Billy would meet, and they married the next year. Pete was born in 1935.

Mother Anne had a great influence on the way the young Hamill learned to think. "I remember once we went to Times Square from Brooklyn," Hamill told me, "because my brother Tom and I loved going to visit the *Normandie* [sunk in the North River by fire in 1942], which was on its side. Each time we got there, there was less of it because they were dismantling it. We were on our way there from Times Square and we passed what we called in those days a 'bum'—he would now be called homeless—and he had a cup and he was begging, and my brother Tommy and I made some remarks about a 'bum.' And I must have been nine and Tommy was seven and she got furious and said, 'don't you ever look down on anybody unless you're giving them a hand to get up.' I don't think she was a saint. I think it was that whole generation of Irishmen and Jews and Italians and everybody in this town who felt you don't look down on people. Help them because if you don't help them who the fuck is going to help them? And it stayed with me all my life."

THE WRITER AS *MENSCH*

In contrast to Breslin you have Hamill, a *mensch* of a man, as they say at the corner saloon. Like many of the people they wrote about, both Breslin and Hamill came out of poverty, but Hamill was not tainted by it. His brother Denis, also a writer, perhaps put it best, "Poverty was not a sin." Pete is honest in his progress as a man. His relationship with Robert Kennedy was remarkable and, in a way, tragic because he sent him a letter that convinced Kennedy to run for president. He was there when RFK was murdered and said he made a "terrible mistake as a journalist."

"Pete's a complicated man as well," said Steve McCarthy, one of the director/producers of the HBO documentary *Breslin and Hamill: Deadline Artists*.

"His stories about stickball and bars in Park Slope reminded me of my own childhood in Bay Ridge," McCarthy told me when the documentary premiered. "We weren't wealthy but had food to eat and clean clothes. And, our parents valued education. Pete's relationship with RFK had a major conflict in it. He, like many progressive Irish-Americans, fell in love with the Kennedys. They saw that this dynasty proved the Irish made it in America. They also saw how they didn't forget where they came from. Instead of kicking the next guy coming up the ladder they extended a hand to help bring them up. The fact that both Pete and Jimmy were right there when RFK was shot is amazing. It makes for one of the most interesting parts of the film."

JIMMY WECHSLER GIVES HAMILL A BREAK

Until he was twenty-five, Hamill made his living as a graphic artist. He wrote a letter to James Wechsler, editor of the *New York Post*, lamenting the lack of "working class" journalists at the paper. Wechsler invited Hamill to come in for a tryout—and the rest is history.

Hamill knows that in today's world he couldn't get inside the front door without the sheepskin. "I think that goes back to this immigrant mentality," he told me, "that this is America and you can do anything. And I believed it! Today, in my case, with two years of high school, it's not that you'd wouldn't get to the editor, you'd never get past the personnel directors, who are making decisions based on resumes, which is insane. Jimmy Wechsler was a great man. He made my life possible."

By the mid-'60s he was a columnist and that led to him writing books. His first novel was A *Killing for Christ* about an assassination plot on the pope. He soon had a book of his collected columns called *Irrational Ravings*. Ironically, the title was suggested by then–vice president and media basher and Nixon hatchet man Spiro T. ("nolo contendre") Agnew, who had held up a Hamill column and exclaimed, "Listen to these irrational ravings!" Thanks, Spiro.

NEW YORK IS THE STAR OF HAMILL'S BOOKS

Many of Hamill's novels have New York at the center of the plot. *Forever, Snow in August, North River*, and *Tabloid City* are all located in New York. Once again, Anne Devlin was the great influence. "I think it goes back to the way I grew up," said Hamill. "My father couldn't move around New York because he only had one leg. So we knew New York—when I say New York I mean Manhattan because we were living in Brooklyn—we knew because our mother took us by the hand. When I say 'we' I mean me and my brother Tommy. She would take these two kids and show them and explain what Trinity Church was and that there were people called 'Protestants,'" said Hamill with a laugh. "She never made comments making fun of anybody like that. So she would take us around to Chinatown and the west side piers because her father had worked for the Cunard Lines."

I asked him about his urge to write fiction. "Before me and Jimmy [Breslin] there was very little tradition of American journalists writing novels. The instinct to make fiction was always there, even after I started to have some successes at journalism."

He also has written nonfiction books that go in different directions, *Why Sinatra Matters* about Old Blue Eyes and *A Drinking Life*, a memoir of the young Hamill and his battle with drink. *A Drinking Life* has become an inspiration to many battling alcoholism and the books tells us a lot about the young Hamill and the maturation process that went into Pete's life.

A Drinking Life is autobiography from afar because it traces Hamill's life only until the time of his great alcoholic quenching, stopping in 1973. "It's the kind of book about drinking that you can give a friend with the problem," Hamill told me when I interviewed him for *Publishers Weekly* when the book came out. "It's not saying: 'For Chrissakes why don't you get with the program?' Here's a guy talking honestly about it, as straight as he can, about facing your life. How do you want to live? Do you want to get old, or do you want to die?'"

"One of the things I didn't want to do with the book," Hamill continued, "was to make it into a sermon. I was saying, 'this is how you begin to get into the culture of drinking.' Because I think it is, in a sociological sense, a culture. What I have come to learn is that you can't solve something like a drinking problem or a drug problem without examining the entire life."

Hamill stopped drinking on his own. For him, there was no Betty Ford Clinic, AA meetings or, as the Irish put it, "whiskey school." "Somehow I knew that if I went to encounter groups, or to 12-steps, or to a shrink, or whatever, no matter what, *I* had to do it. It's all up to you in the end, it's your will that's involved and our determination. It wasn't a conscious thing: 'I will not go to AA.' I just said I'm going to stop.

"And I then began to use what I had," he continued, "I was a writer. I began to keep a journal in which I tried to analyze the problem, which was the equivalent of standing up in front of a group. There were things I couldn't figure out, or I thought I'd figured out, and didn't realize until much later that I was wrong. But it ended up a benefit. I ended up kicking this thing.

"After the first year," Hamill emphasized, "you get a point where you say, 'Jesus Christ, I can't even think about doing it again.' The first year was far and away the hardest, the first six months in particular."

Hamill, begrudgingly, even gives thanks to Lord Mountbatten—of all people—in inspiring him to stay on the wagon. "I remember a party in London where the guest of honor was Lord Mountbatten and the only other Irish person in the place was Edna O'Brien. It was one of these long, formal dinner tables with Mountbatten in the middle. And Mountbatten starts telling jokes. He's one of the most boorish people I've ever met. And he starts to tell Irish jokes. And he starts to tell Irish *drunk* jokes. And at one point I lean back like this, and Edna leans back like this and looks at me and we laughed. He had no idea. To him I was a Yank and Edna O'Brien was someone who lived in London. But I did have a feeling: I'll never give these bastards the satisfaction of getting drunk in front of them."

I asked him if he sees any connection between writing and drinking. "I think newspaper writers and drunks share a similar need for the instant reward. You're attracted to the newspaper because your story will be in the paper tomorrow. Sometimes that night. You finish, you go to the bar, the first edition comes in, and there it is. You get the instant kickback. You get the same thing with drinking."

"My feeling was that if I was going to be any kind of a writer, it was going to take me a long time. I'd probably have to wait until my fifties to write my best stuff. Maybe sixties. But I couldn't do it unless I could remember. Writers are rememberers or they're nothing. And that remembering means remembering the pain and the grief and lousiness along with all the joys and triumphs and everything else.'

HAMILL—IRISH LADIES' MAN

Steve McCarthy and his partners in *Breslin and Hamill: Deadline Artists* dared to go where many fear to tread—Pete Hamill's famous love life. He's had dalliances with Jacqueline Onassis and Shirley MacLaine. (For the record, I once saw Pete in the Lion's Head with Mary Tyler Moore—not bad for a kid from Park Slope, Brooklyn!) So, how did McCarthy do it? "As talented and handsome as Pete is, he is also modest. He did not boast about the glamorous women he went out with. He actually didn't tell us much. When we asked him if he loved Jackie Onassis he replied: 'I'd really agree with Garcia Marquez who said once, that everybody's got three lives—a public life, a private life, and a secret life. Private life is by invitation only. A secret life is nobody's business.'"

One of the highlights of the film is Breslin commenting on the love life of Hamill in a column, no less. "One of the funniest parts of the film," McCarthy told me, "was when Jimmy wrote a column about Pete going out with Jackie O and Shirley MacLaine at the same time. Shirley hit the roof, Jackie O laughed, and Pete was pissed off. He called Jimmy about it and Jimmy said, "*I needed it*" —meaning he needed something for a column that day." Another funny Breslin-Hamill encounter was when Breslin said that the Son of Sam wrote so well he thought "Hamill wrote it!"

With Breslin and Joe Flaherty now gone, we are lucky to have Pete Hamill still with us and reminding us that we should all reach for the decency that is the foundation of civilization. It can be found easily in every Hamill book.

CHAPTER EIGHT
JOE FLAHERTY

A REAL *IRISH NEW YORK WORKING-CLASS WRITER BLESSED WITH TALENT, WIT, COMPASSION*

The term joie de vivre must have been invented for Joe Flaherty. Seldom has a man so loved life. He loved writing and he especially loved his children Liam and Siobhan and his wife Jeanine. He also loved racehorses, prize-fighters, Willie Mays, the camaraderie of the saloon, and most of all he loved to laugh. From 1966 until his death in 1983 he graced the pages of the *Village Voice* and other publications bringing us a unique perspective on the craziness that was New York in those days.

I first came across Joe when I was in high school and reading the *Village Voice* when it hit the street in Sheridan Square on Wednesday mornings. He was exactly what I was looking for. He was not Breslin or Hamill, but a guy who actually came out of an *On the Waterfront* background working for ILA Local 1268 of the Grain Handlers' Association. He made fun of everything I made fun of—the Church (his comment to me on the late Francis Cardinal Spellman was right on—"He died of a poisoned altar boy!"), our fellow Irish Americans (once while we were watching the St. Patrick's Day Parade on TV at the Lion's Head he observed, "We obviously save our rhythm for the sheets, not the streets!"), the absolute stupidity of amoral politicians, and the conservative politics of the Irish—he even took on the nuns! Above all, he had a terrific sense of Irish justice. And he made me laugh out loud with a prose so stinging and original that it's still a joy to go back and read it after all these years.

SON OF BROOKLYN

The lowdown on Joe Flaherty was written by himself in the author's preface of *Chez Joey*, his collection of pieces. "I was born in 1936 in Brooklyn," he wrote, "the third son (of four) to John Flaherty of the County Galway ('herring-chokers') and Maggie Casey of the County Tipperary ('stone-throwers')."[43] His father "worked the docks for a living" but was also the head of his union. His refusal to knuckle under to the mob resulted in his murder. They would fish John Flaherty out of the Gowanus Canal when Joe was nine.

To put it mildly he was not inundated with Irish culture as a child. "Culture was a languid malady of the leisure class," he wrote. "I would like to report that as boys we read Yeats and Joyce in my home, but it was more like the *Daily News* and the Catholic paper, the Brooklyn *Tablet*. (The latter was our invaluable guide to what we supposed were horny movies. The Legion of Decency once condemned a Betty Grable–Dan Dailey opus because they were contemplating divorce. In retrospect we must have been the original *Deep Throat* for swallowing such fantasies.)"

And like a lot of ethnic New York children whose playgrounds were the gutters of the neighborhood, he remembered those days with joy. "Relaxation for the old-timers came on summer nights when they would sit in their undershirts on stoops drinking tap beer from tin buckets obtained from the 'beer garden,' while their sons played stickball in the streets. Once again, if you were to substitute porch for stoop, lemonade for suds, and baseball for stickball, the specter of the small town rises."

Joe was a rowdy scholar. "And when on my first day of school, a nun spied my colossus of a dome and said, 'I'll call this one Big Head with Nothing in It,' I realized my tenure would be more slugging than spiritual." His time at St. John's Prep would also be short. "Thankfully for both sides," he recalled, "St. John's demanded academic standards I couldn't or wouldn't approach. To this day the thought of solving an algebra problem or conjugating a French verb is enough to send me to a saloon for a week. So with the delicacy of government change in a banana republic (they ordered, I fled), the good fathers and I parted company."

On to the William E. Grady Vocational High School, where much of his time was spent cutting classes and sneaking into movies, not unlike what his contemporary George Carlin was experiencing uptown. "Our days were spent in those wondrous dark balconies of New York movie houses, to be followed by a gourmet lunch at Grant's on Forty-second Street of hot dogs (still the best in the city) and a cherry smash (instant diabetes). The expense for the day was marginal, since we rarely paid for the movie."

He would get kicked out of Grady Vocational too, becoming in the process a disgrace to the Irish race. "But all this only shortly forestalled the doom and disgrace I was about to heap upon my mother," he remembered. "She was advised that I should be removed from school (her disgrace, my reprieve). It was a teary scene. My mother cried, when my Irish guidance counselor said I had shamed her, my dead father, and—most important—the Irish, a charge that has chased me through the years. I believe his conclusion was that I was acting like an Italian."

His ejection from high school began a round of odd jobs that is staggering. His first was as a squad boy on the floor of the New York Stock Exchange. While horsing around he managed to send GM stock skyrocketing. Corporate America's revenge would be swift. "I was fired immediately and walked to the subway hugging the building to avoid being flattened by the leapers."

He was also a helper on a laundry truck, worked in an airplane parts factory, and was a candy packer in an A&P factory. He decided to try his luck out in sunny California, where he "went from selling my blood for cash to selling shoes for cash. (Knowledge accrued: Many English women don't wear panties.) Ever onward and upward, I became a female placement counselor in an unemployment agency, a job that combined the spiritual qualities of a father confessor and the horniness of a Freudian counselor." After two years in the Army, Flaherty finally settled into the "family business" back in Brooklyn—a grain trimmer on the waterfront.

ENTER SPILLANE, O'NEILL, AND FITZGERALD

Flaherty's first literary influence was Mickey Spillane, of all people. "There was no doubt about it—I wanted to become a writer. The plays of Eugene O'Neill piqued my Irish gloom, and I wrote boozy tragedies of dinosaur proportions."

"But it was Fitzgerald who haunted me," he states, "especially *The Great Gatsby*. The delicacy of the blue lawns of Long Island was a three-sewer clout away from my Brooklyn streets, but he was my main man. After *Gatsby*, I just had to be a writer. But much to my dismay I discovered (as usual) that I lacked discipline, and my style was not dashing and new but bowed to the secondhand shops of literature. In short, I had no voice of my own."

He worked the grain ships by day while writing for the local Brooklyn neighbor-hood newspaper, the *Park Slope News*, by night. One-night Mayor John Lindsay was in the neighborhood trying to get a referendum passed on a Civilian Review Board of the police. Lindsay was berated by the crowd, which inflamed Flaherty: "He wasn't allowed to speak. Taunts and litanies of 'nigger lover' fractured his every sentence," he recalled in *Chez Joey*. "One fat guy was the biggest offender, and I told him to shut the fuck up and let the mayor speak. The loudmouth weighed my strange makeup, a beard (he could cream such a fairy), and my longshore rig (maybe not). He acqui-esced, and the mayor of New York gave me a grateful nod. Already I was recognized in high places."

He stayed up all night and wrote the altercation this way: "He was a big kid but not like his ancestors who worked the docks or the ones who wore shamrock-embroidered trunks under the Garden lights on long ago Friday nights. He had the weight, but it was going nowhere. His backside looked like a giant teardrop, probably from sitting too long on stools in the Knights of Columbus drinking 10-cent beer with his own kind to the tune of 'The Ballad of the Green Beret.' . . . A guy wearing work clothes and sporting a beard turned to him and told him to shut up and give the mayor a chance to speak. [Another] guy in tweeds muttered something, and the beard told him that there should be an ethical review board to examine his lack of manners. The tweed eyed the size of the guy and decided to shut up. Right away you knew this was one Hibernian who wouldn't have gone one round in the Garden. Lindsay looked gratefully at his ally and began to speak again." Of course, the guy in the work clothes and beard was none other than Joe Flaherty himself.

He sent it to the *Park Slope News*, who found it much too liberal for their reader-ship. Luckily for Flaherty, a young staff member named Jack Deacy, a future colum-nist for the *Daily News*, took his piece, put a cover letter on it, and sent it to Dan Wolf at the *Village Voice* in the Sodom and Gomorrah known as Greenwich Village. On October 27, 1966, a banner shouting "Why Has the Fun Fled the Fun City?" made the front page of the *Voice*, and a writing career was born.

After finally learning his piece had run, Flaherty descended on the Sheridan Square office of the *Voice*, to meet Wolf. The receptionist took one look at Joe in his dockworker clothes and said that Wolf was away and wouldn't be returning any time soon. When he said who he was they were overjoyed that they had found the elusive Joe Flaherty, a writing star in the making.

"The tracks. The ring. The movies. The Church. The bars," wrote Kevin Michael McAuliffe in *The Great American Newspaper: The Rise and Fall of the* Village Voice. "That was where Joe Flaherty came from. That was what he knew. That was how he wrote, in an up-front, no bullshit, tough guy shorthand full of working-class wise-cracks. He was a raconteur of rum and Romanism, a chronicler of Irish lowlife, a dispenser of dockworker and detective-novel wisdom, and he had no pretensions about being anywhere else. . . . His *macho* was undeniable, but in an old-fashioned, romantic, positive sort of way, and his self-deprecation about his own manhood bordered on the hilarious. His politics were left of center, but with a small *l*, because, unlike so many others at the *Voice* who talked about the working class, Joe Flaherty *was* working-class. He had been there, and he never forgot it."

"He was probably one of the last writers," wrote Patrick Fenton in a *New York Times* Op-Ed entitled "What Flaherty Was," "to come out of the world of tenements and factories and to make it in this computer age as a newspaperman."

For his next assignment, Wolf suggested that Flaherty go to the Police Benevolent Society's victory party celebrating the defeat of the CBR referendum. Things did not go well. "I asked an off-duty cop his thoughts on this victorious evening," he recalled in *Chez Joey*, "and instead, he gave me his thoughts on my sexual proclivities." It turned into a fistfight with someone yelling, "Jesus, a beatnik is killing a cop!"

THE MAILER-BRESLIN-FLAHERTY MÉNAGE À TROIS

Flaherty's next great experiment was "managing" the Mailer-Breslin ticket in 1969, an amazing year for New York—the Jets won the Super Bowl, man would land on the moon, the Mets would win the World Series, and the Knicks were on their way to their first World Championship. The Mailer-Breslin venture into city politics only added spice to the delicious stew the Big Apple was brewing that fateful year. And there was something in the air that might help Mailer-Breslin. "There was a jaunty feeling of 'fuckyouism' running throughout the town," Flaherty wrote in his memoir of the campaign, *Managing Mailer*, "a feeling that was essential to a Mailer-Breslin ticket."

Mailer was running for mayor and Breslin was his running mate aiming at City Council president. Between the three of them there was enough daily ego, booze, cigarettes, and testosterone to kill an elephant.

The chaos started immediately. "I arrived at Mailer's house," Flaherty wrote in *Managing Mailer*, "and found a number of other writers, including myself, taking notes, all having purple wet dreams about next year's National Book Award for Arts and Letters. . . . Like all such evenings attended by polemicists, it resembled the building of the Tower of Babel. Right winger Noel Parmentel wanted Mailer to run alone in an attempt to appeal to the working class. Another group was pushing for a Black Panther for comptroller, and still another wanted a woman on the ticket to run on the platform of female rights. Along about now I was wishing that Carmine DeSapio would enter the room and restore some decent totalitarian clubhouse order."

Jimmy was not amused. "Breslin apparently had had enough of the spirituality," Flaherty wrote, "the bickering, and the skirting of what he thought were the real issues. He exploded into a monologue that ran second only to Molly Bloom's. 'Norman, stop the fuckin' Mickey Mouse shit. There's no issues in this town. Leave that Mickey Mouse shit to those other clowns. Just get on TV and look at the camera and say, 'All these other guys are full of shit.' So what if they blip you out. People will be able to read your lips. Every asshole sitting on a barstool in Brooklyn and Queens will fall on the floor laughing and run out and vote for you. Fuck issues—this city is lost.'"

The big idea was to make New York City the fifty-first state. Why should hardworking New Yorkers be subsidizing those deadbeats upstate? Sure, if it wasn't for New York City felons and the state prison system there would be no employment north of Albany! Oddly enough, the idea of the city of New York as a state was not a new idea. It was enthusiastically broached by none other than George Washington ("Honest Graft") Plunkitt. He waxed philosophically about making New York City a state: "The time is comin' and though I'm no youngster, I may see it, when New York City will break away from the State and become a state itself."[44]

"Say," Plunkitt wrote, "I don't wish I was a poet, for if I was, I guess I'd be livin' in a garret on no dollars a week instead of runnin' a great contractin' and transportation business which is doin' pretty well, thank you; but, honest, now, the notion takes me sometimes to yell poetry of the red-hot-hail-glorious-land kind when I think of New York City as a state by itself."

At least Mailer-Breslin-Flaherty were in good, interesting company with old Plunkitt.

Managing Mailer—Christopher Lehmann-Haupt, in a review in the *New York Times*, called it "a hugely entertaining account of men and windmills"[45]—gives a fascinating, hilarious history of the campaign. It is a book that should still be taught in political science classes because it is just as pertinent to New York City today as it was in 1969. Flaherty's descriptions of the candidates and their foibles are delicious:

Democratic candidate Mario Procaccino: "the one most preposterous candidate of my time in my city."

Bronx Borough President Herman Badillo, who would become the first Puerto Rican elected to congress: "His biggest problem was his personality. He possessed none of his Latin brothers' fire and life, and indeed, in his dark Petrocelli suits he looked wooden—a Puerto Rican Robert Goulet." Flaherty also noted that he was "eternally starched . . . with a manicured anchovy of a mustache on his upper lip."

Former Mayor Robert F. Wagner Jr., trying for a comeback after ruling the city for twelve years, was a "municipal Lazarus." Flaherty also handicapped the candidates as if this was a horserace. He referred to Wagner as a "twelve-year-old gelding"

Mailer himself was "a satanic Will Rogers."

In the winter of '69 a huge blizzard landlocked the borough of Queens, which was why Mayor Lindsay was in such trouble. Every candidate was asked what he would do with the snow if there was another blizzard? One persistent questioner maddened Mailer until he finally said, "I'd piss on it."

Both Mailer and Breslin hit the college circuit around New York, and things did not go smoothly. Breslin had his problems with the young feminists and Mailer also had his problems. "Mailer wasn't overly impressed with the student body [of Brooklyn College]," wrote Flaherty. "'The problem with these kids is that they would rather jerk off at a beautiful thought than have a dubious fuck with a mean woman.'"

There was also that great evening at P.S. 41 on West 11th Street in the Village where both Mailer and Breslin showed up to speak. I was in attendance and the auditorium was packed. Breslin's voice was shot and he had to stop speaking. Mailer took over and did his shtick. Near the end of Mailer's talk the stage was rushed by some crazies who would not let Mailer finish. The great Mailer saw red! "The CIA," he shouted, "has infiltrated the Motherfuckers!" I was laughing so hard I fell in the aisle.

Of course, Mailer-Breslin did not finish in the money. With Procaccino and state senator John Marchi splitting the conservative vote, John Lindsay, the Liberal and Independent candidate, squeezed in for a second term. Flaherty had learned his lesson. "But the voting booth is no bright big top," he wrote. "It is a dark confessional with a curtain to muffle the blackest intents of the soul."

A MAN FOR ALL WRITING SEASONS

I remember reading *Managing Mailer* on the subway on my way back from college. And Flaherty's pieces in the *Voice*! His imagery was just outstanding. He even found redeeming social value in the less-than-Hollywood-beautiful looks of Howard Cosell. "Cosell's mug has something," he wrote. "It slopes downward like a ski slope for Lilliputians. It's the kind of face you'd be likely to see in an old *Batman* episode: there are curves of high camp in the profile. And perhaps that is one of the reasons Cosell is the hottest thing in sports broadcasting."[46]

In the same profile of Cosell, Flaherty shows his whimsical sense of humor while riding in a cab with Cosell. It seems the cab driver has just been circumcised that very day: "For about ten blocks Cosell sits *shiva* in deference to the driver's loss, and, as we debark, Cosell has added another lifetime fan. . . . Much to the cabdriver's credit, he didn't blame the bris on Mayor Lindsay. Another Cosell first."

Flaherty had a great range too. He could write about Willie Mays one day and Governor George Wallace the next. He attended a George Wallace rally at Madison Square Garden when Wallace ran for president in 1968 and it wasn't so much about Wallace, but the Wallace followers:

> Then they brought on Wallace. For about fifteen minutes the Garden exploded with clapping, whistling, foot stamping, and shouting. . . . There were the Italians who had left their sanctuaries in Bay Ridge and Staten Island with the Blessed Mother standing sentry on their lawns. There were the young Irish kids who shot baskets at netless hoops on the blacktop schoolyards of Our Lady of Something or Another. . . . And . . . the innocent, untouchable girls of our boyhood. Their faces now prematurely old with hate and their legs grown heavy with too many children. The same girls you tried to maneuver against banisters with their mothers a flight away. . . . As they left the Garden, they performed the most primitive ritual of the evening. They gathered in groups, as they made their way toward their homes, like men in a time when fire was not yet discovered, gathered to protect themselves against the eternal black night they live in.[47]

He was also one of the few who would not pile onto world-class bully Sonny Liston when the boxer died. "Well," he wrote, "the reader may justifiably say that the back of the hand is the only tribute a blackguard deserves. After all, the man was busted twenty times. He was a union goon, ran with the mob, cracked heads with the same niftiness a short-order cook prepared 'two over light.' . . . In short, Sonny was a badass nigger.

"Was he the bastard everyone says he was? To many, yes. To others, such as Claude Brown [author of *Manchild in the Promised Land*], he was the only man alive who could have quelled the Watts riots. I'm not pleading for his life-style—a bastard maybe, or, perhaps more fair, he did bastardly deeds. But he should be judged in context. He was better than the sport he practiced and the men who rule it. . . . And he was a lot better than the hucksters for sport who now so cavalierly dismiss his life."

And, of course, he was a Swiftian satirist also. Merle Miller commented on the problems of homosexuals. He was followed by Andrew Sarris commenting on the problems of heterosexuals. But what about the problems of asexuals? Soon the *Voice* had an article called "Asexuals Have Problems, Too."

In one of the great literary pranks, Flaherty, under the pen name of "Harold Nederland," leaped out of the asexual closet. The *Voice* in those days was filled with pieces about women's liberation, gay liberation, and every kind of sexual orientation. Yet nothing appeared about the poor asexual until Flaherty intervened. "But what about us asexuals?" Harold asked. "They must think it's a big thing to confess how many broads they've laid or boys they've buggered. Where is the man or woman with the courage to say the whole sexual business leaves them feeling like a limp noodle?" Then Harold takes a poke at Flaherty, "But not in the *Voice* where that boorish Joe Flaherty writes metaphors with his prick rather than his brain."

Then Harold ends up with a bang, "And God, the agony of the Thanksgiving dinner when someone says, 'Pass the mashed potatoes to *it*.'"

The column received numerous letters of praise. And one *Voice* reader even volunteered to write a weekly column entitled, "Asexual Consciousness Raising."

WAITING FOR FLAHERTY

Samuel Beckett had his Godot, I had Joe Flaherty. I had been reading Joe since high school and the highlight of my week was when the *Voice* came out on Wednesday morning. It was the best fifteen cents I would spend all week.

After the IRS closed the Lion's Head for unpaid taxes, Flaherty wrote a column called "Three Nights Without the Lion's Roar." It was a story of Saturday-night debauchery that ended with folksinger Liam Clancy and the house Mohawk Indian,

Shannon Two-Feathers, checking themselves into St. Vincent's Hospital for "the cure." It was a rip-roaring piece and I just had to meet Flaherty.

It was the spring of 1973 and I was about to graduate from Hunter College. I would drop into the Lion's Head, two blocks from my apartment, hoping to spy the great Flaherty. I struck out a few times, but one rainy day I descended the steps and there he was, reading the *New York Times* as he leaned against the back bar. The place was nearly empty, with only Flaherty, me, the barman, and two guys who looked like construction workers sitting at the top of the bar. I kept looking at Joe, too intimidated to even say hello. The two guys at the top of the bar were very animated in their conversation. Flaherty was ready to go. He slowly and meticulously folded the broadsheet and tucked it under his arm as he headed for the door. One of the guys at that very moment said, "Then, this Irish asshole says to me . . ." Joe didn't miss a beat as he went by him. "Don't be redundant!" he said as he exited. I was laughing so hard I fell off my stool. And I was totally in love.

I went to work for Doubleday as publicist and started to hang out at the Head, as the regulars called it, at cocktail hour. It was a real writers, bar. Soon the cocktail hour was filled with people like novelist David Markson, poet Joel Oppenheimer, literary agent Knox Burger, and, of course, Joe Flaherty. We became friendly and I soon was introduced to Jeanine Johnson, who soon became his wife. I even tried, unsuccessfully, to work out a book deal for him at Doubleday. Him being a writer and me being a book publicist, we had a lot in common. He had some of the funniest author media horror stories I ever heard.

There was a "comic" named Joey Adams, who had a column in the *New York Post* and a radio show on WEVD. I never thought he was remotely funny. He taped the show in the afternoon, and he treated his guests like garbage. Joe goes up to do an interview for *Chez Joey*. Adams had no clue who he was and treated him rudely. He finally starts the interview and says to Flaherty, "Joe, your book, *Chez Joey*, could be the story of my life." To which Flaherty replied, "I don't write tragedies." And it went right over Adams's dense head.

Another time he was going to do a live interview with Long John Nebel, who had a talk show on WMCA radio that started at midnight. The book was *Fogarty & Company* about a working-class Irish guy not unsimilar to Flaherty. Joe had a few drinks at the Lion's Head with his friend Tommy Butler, then Butler drove him uptown for the interview. Tommy got him there just in time for the interview and sat in his car listening to the beginning of the show. Nebel introduces Flaherty and his first questions was, "What do the Irish want?" Flaherty's reply was swift and direct, "They don't know what the fuck they want!" End of interview. Joe went downstairs, jumped in the car, and both Flaherty and Butler returned to a proper setting, the Lion's Head.

His knowledge of the Village was great. There were two fishmongers on Bleecker Street between 6th and 7th Avenue. He advised all which one was good for taking book on sports and which one was good to buy fish in. One Saturday morning at Jimmy Day's saloon in Sheridan Square the gang was still recovering from drinking all Friday night when Joe, out doing his errands, happened to walk by. He came in to survey the wreckage. One guy, whacked out of his mind, tearfully starts telling him about an article that was in the *New York Times Magazine* the previous week about how some scientists had turned baboons into alcoholics. "Don't worry about me," Joe said, "I don't fuck around with those banana daiquiris!"

When Joe died, the headline in the *New York Times* obituary read: "Joe Flaherty, Writer and Newspaperman Noted for His Humor." I think Joe would have liked that.

LIFE IS UNFAIR

John F. Kennedy once famously commented that "Life is unfair." It was especially unfair to Joe Flaherty. By 1983 things were looking up for Flaherty. He had a new novel coming out called *Tin Wife*, and he was about to go to work at the *New York Times* as a reporter in the sports department. The only thing wrong was that he had this persistent pain in his hip. He went to many doctors and the cause remained mysterious. Finally, one doctor discovered what it was—advanced prostate cancer. After surgery Joe was doing fine. I remember meeting him on the street and he asked me to accompany him to the Off-Track Betting (OTB) down on Varick and King Streets.

It was the last time I saw him walking. Soon after the cancer ate into his spinal cord and crippled him. I would spend a lot of time with him that summer. When his wife Jeanine was away at work, friends would come in and sit with him. If you didn't know he was a sick man, you'd never guess it. The phone never stopped ringing as people called, many asking him to come on their radio shows. Joe wasn't up to it, but he had these two huge Rolodexes and he would pluck a name for the guy at the radio station. We would watch the Mets and talk and when Jeanine came home I would leave.

On October 26, Joe passed away at home. I had seen him days before when I went to pick up the manuscript for *Tin Wife* so it could be reviewed in *Publishers Weekly*. I knew the end was near, but it still came as a shock. I went to the Lion's Head, but I couldn't take the wholesale grief. I went to a bar I never went to and had a whiskey and a cry. Joe was all of forty-seven years old.

On November 18, Jeanine organized a memorial service at the New School. It was not morose, but jolly. As you walked in, piano players were hashing out tunes from *Guys and Dolls*, like "Fugue for Tinhorns": I got the horse right here, the name is Paul Revere.

Joe would have loved it.

The speakers included Norman Mailer, Wilfrid Sheed, Ross Wetzsteon, Joel Oppenheimer, Vic Ziegel, John and Julienne Scanlon, and Mayor Edward I. Koch. This was one afternoon when the Lion's Head would indeed be empty. Koch came out and talked about Joe and the other writers at the Lion's Head. Koch said it was true that writers leaned over their typewriters and waited for the muse to arrive. You might have to wait all day. And when it finally arrived in the middle of the afternoon the muse had this advice—"Go to the Lion's Head!"

It was absolutely true, and everyone laughed. And Joe would have laughed too.

On the memorial program, Jeanine wrote that "Joe was entirely self-wrought, an extraordinary man with firmly grounded values who cut his own groove. With high style, surpassing wit, uncommon good sense, courage, generosity and grace, this self-described romantic, this verbal dandy, this apostle of laughter ("Diversion was always my sport," he said), set a possible standard of human conduct. In his time, Joe captured corners of a multitude of lives. He will always live there. Remember with me now the pure joy of having had his love and the pleasure and privilege of his company."

A few weeks after Joe passed away, I had this vivid ten-second dream. I was all alone at the bar of the Lion's Head and Joe came through the door. "I thought you were dead," I said to him.

"Nah," he replied, "I was only fuckin' with ya!" And with that, the dream ended.

In Edwin O'Connor's *The Last Hurrah*, the mayor on his deathbed looks at Ditto and says, "How in the world do you thank a man for a million laughs?"

I feel the same way about Joe Flaherty. I grieved for him in 1983 and I grieve for him today. I am proud to call him my friend and mentor. God bless, Joe. I still miss you every day.

CHAPTER NINE

FRANK McCOURT AND THE MAKING OF *ANGELA'S ASHES*

THE PULITZER PRIZE–WINNING MEMOIR TAKES PLACE IN LIMERICK CITY, BUT IT WAS WRITTEN AND DISCOVERED IN REAL IRISH NEW YORK

Who can forget that first page of *Angela's Ashes*?

"It was, of course, a miserable childhood: the happy childhood is hardly worth your while. Worse than the ordinary miserable childhood is the miserable Irish childhood, and worse yet is the miserable Irish Catholic childhood."[48]

It could be said that *Angela's Ashes* was conceived and delivered by an Irish saloon down on Christopher Street called the Lion's Head.

I was first introduced to Frank McCourt at the Lion's Head by bartender Mike Reardon in 1975. At the time Frank was a teacher at Stuyvesant High, a school noted for its brainy students. Frank was very soft-spoken, and it never occurred to me that he was the brother of the brash, rambunctious Malachy, who at that time was causing havoc with his radio show on WMCA Radio and his saloon, the Bells of Hell, up on 13th Street. I saw a lot of Frank in the latter part of the 1970s because he was also a friend of my friend, the writer Ralph Tyler, whose son Mike was a student of Frank's at Stuyvesant.

The Lion's Head was known as a "writers' bar." It may have had something to do with the fact it was right next door to the old office of the *Village Voice*. Writers would get their meager checks from the *Voice* and walk right into the Head, as it was affectionately called, cash it, and then drink it.

Voice writers like Joe Flaherty found the Head to be a second home. On any given day or night there might be Pete Hamill at the bar, slinging whiskeys along with the likes of poet Joel Oppenheimer or novelist David Markson. At cocktail hour super literary agent Knox Burger would bring his writers around. One day it might be Martin Cruz Smith who wrote the mega-bestseller *Gorky Park* or Vincent Patrick, author of *The Pope of Greenwich Village*. Dinnertime might bring in Norman Mailer or playwright Lanford Wilson. If you were lucky, the literary talk might be serenaded by the Clancy Brothers.

Writers soon began to bring jackets of their books and scotch tape them to the wall. Al Koblin, one of the partners who owned the Head, started putting them up on the wall in frames. I remember the first one was Fred Exley's *Pages from a Cold Island*, his follow-up to his renowned *A Fan's Notes*. Pretty soon the back wall was full, and the jackets were creeping to every available space in the joint. I remember Frank enviously looking at that beautiful wall, a glassy, gorgeous mosaic of books, and saying to me, "Someday."

The Head would play two important roles in the creation of *Angela's Ashes*. First, Frank would meet his wife, Ellen Frey, there in December 1989. She would be the catalyst that brought forth the book. "I really think Ellen was the real muse and genius of all this," said writer Mary Breasted to me, "creating an atmosphere of ease and happiness for Frank that just put him into the exact right mood to get his book done."

"In October 1994," wrote Jim Dwyer in the *New York Times* at the time of Frank's death in 2009, "two months after they were married, he began *Angela's Ashes*, rising early, sitting with a board across his lap, writing longhand. 'He'd bring me coffee in bed in the morning—he liked to say he was the perfect husband—and then he would read me the work from the day before,' Ellen said."[49]

The second major event in the birth of *Angela's Ashes* was his friendship with Mary Breasted, who was also known to belly up to the bar at the Head.

MARY BREASTED IS ASKED TO TAKE A LOOK

"It seems to me that I always knew who Frank McCourt was from the first or second year I made it into the Lion's Head," Mary Breasted told me. "I lived up the street from the Head in 1968–1969, and I was writing for the *Voice*, so the Head was my local restaurant and pub, anyway.

"My first memory of Frank," she continued, "was probably after I'd gone to work for the *New York Times* as a general assignment reporter under City Editor Crazy Arthur Gelb. It was on a night when I was standing with the guys by the bar doing that fast talk we all liked to do in the evening when we had finished work, gossip and rants and one-liners about our idiot editors or our even greater idiot political representatives. We would get, or I would get, more and more outrageous as the night wore on, and I seem to remember that on that particular night when I was being shocking, probably loudly denouncing my bosses, I noticed Frank just leaning against the wall with maybe a beer in his hand looking at me with his amused sizing-us-up expression. 'That's Frank McCourt,' one of the guys said. 'He's a school teacher. But watch out for him. He's writing a book. He could put you in it.'"

"But Frank and I hardly ever talked to each other in those days," continued Breasted. "He was quieter than most of the Lion's Head wits, at least that I can remember from the 1970s. I really only got to know Frank and to begin to pay attention to the way he talked after I met Ted Smyth, the young Irish diplomat. . . . Anyway, in November 1978, I fell under the spell of Irishry, chiefly represented by Ted, but Ted was at the center of a circle of funny, smart, fast-talking men that included Terry Moran and Malachy and Frank. So, from then on, I saw the McCourts quite often. It took a while for me to realize that the most literary one of them was Frank because Malachy was so entertaining and usually hogged the stage in our circle."

It was at a party after Mary and Ted married in 1981 that Breasted discovered Frank McCourt's magic: "We were at a party in the posh Upper East Side apartment of the Irish Consul General Sean O'Huiggin and his lovely proper and proud former TV presenter wife, Bernadette. Frank and Malachy were there. They seemed a little restless in the elegant setting. Frank asked Bernadette where someone was. 'He's in the library,' Bernadette said. 'Down the hall. It's the room with all the books.'

"Frank used to repeat this remark pursing his lips like a snooty Dublin matron," recalled Breasted. "It tickled him that anyone would have to tell him, a Stuyvesant English teacher, the library was the room with all the books.

It must have been because of Bernadette's innocent helpful remark that a bit later at this same gathering Frank got launched into his tale about the coin-operated bath heater in his Dublin bedsit from his Trinity College grad school days. He set it up quite deftly, telling how poor he was then, how hard done by his professor, Brendan Kennelly, and how overburdened he was by needy undergrads. The fact that he had also then still been married to his [first] wife back in the states was very lightly touched upon. He said this bath incident happened on a Sunday, time for his weekly soaking. The heater required a large coin, maybe only about three-pence worth but precious to him in his near penniless state.

No sooner had he drawn this wonderful hot bath than his doorbell rang. He ran downstairs to find one of the needy undergrads standing there looking more needy than ever. He told her to come on in. "I was just after takin' a bath," he told her. "Would you mind if I went ahead with it? You can wait for me in my bedsit. I don't want to waste the hot water." He got into the bath, he said, and the needy undergrad came into the bathroom and offered to scrub him off, and then something came up and she ended up in the bath with him and from there in the towel with him, and things progressed to the bed. She couldn't stay much longer after that, and thank goodness, because wouldn't you know it, another female seeker of good advice showed up on his doorstep soon after-wards, and he invited her up, and again he told her he was just after takin' a bath, "Would you mind if I went ahead?" I think at this point one of us cheekily asked, "Wasn't the water getting a bit tepid?"

Frank ignored the question. He had an audience of at least five women, the prim Bernadette among them, and also Marcia Rock (then married to Terry Moran), myself, and two others. His story continued through the seduction of the second doorstep waif and then on to a third, each of these encouraged to scrub him off in the bath and see what came up. I remember relishing Frank's demeanor through all this, his put-on expression of boyish innocence, and I took note of the women all looking at him with not just amusement for the fun of his tale, but also wonderment at a man who could take care of three needy women on one Dublin afternoon.

This man is a brilliant storyteller, I thought. *He should be writing books.* From then on, I began telling him: write it down, Frank.

And more than ten years later, Frank asked Breasted if she would mind taking a look at what he'd written so far.

HANDING OFF TO MOLLY FRIEDRICH

"It arrived in a brown envelope," Breasted recalled. "I remember I waited to open it until the kids were asleep. I brought it to bed with me, a little apprehensive. Ted and I were very fond of Frank. What if I didn't like his book? Ted fell asleep, and I thought I would soon be asleep, too. But of course I stayed up half the night reading. I knew what I had in my hands. It was a work of lyric and comic genius. Frank had the instincts of a poet, never to say too much, never to tell you what you should be feeling, just to give you the evidence, the taste and smell and sound of it all. And he had that transcendent humor which made the terrible story bearable and the teller completely loveable. Putting the tale into the voice of a child but also the man remembering the child was the real art of it."

The next morning Breasted rendered the verdict to McCourt. "I called Frank as soon as I had got the kids to school. I told him what I thought. 'Do you have an agent, Frank?' 'No,' he said." Luckily, Breasted had a "a friend down the road."

Mary's editor at the time, the eminent Aaron Asher of Harper & Row (also editor to Saul Bellow, Philip Roth, and Milan Kundera), had told her agent, Dan Green, that "Irish books don't sell," and indeed, Green faced fifteen rejections before he sold her Irish novel. Mary decided this ordeal would make it hard for him to look fondly at Frank's manuscript.

Breasted's friend down the road was literary agent Molly Friedrich. "I knew Molly had sold a fine memoir by an unknown woman writer Esmeralda Santiago, called *When I was Puerto Rican*. It was doing splendidly. But I didn't know Molly all that well. Her daughter Julia had been babysitting our children sometimes. Julia was in ninth grade at their school, so I saw her often. During the week, I told her I had a manuscript that I thought was really good and I might want to show it to her mom. Did she think Molly would mind? 'Just bring it to her, Mary. Bring it to her. She stays home on Fridays.'" When Breasted showed up at Friedrich's doorstep "Molly gave me a pained look."

"A memoir by an unknown writer set in Ireland in the 1930s?" she said. "Tell him I might not get back to him very fast."

"Just read the first five pages, Molly. Read the first five pages," I said.

She called me Monday morning: "Mary, how do I reach Frank?" Her voice sounded as though she had just come from the scene of a terrible accident. "Oh, my God, this book!"

ASHES COMES TO MOLLY FRIEDRICH IN A TIME OF TRAGEDY

It is ironic that *Angela's Ashes*, a book about the tragedies of life, came to literary agent Molly Friedrich in a time of personal tragedy. Molly's father, Otto Friedrich— journalist, writer, historian, author of fourteen books, and one of the great American intellectuals of the twentieth century—passed away just as *Angela's Ashes* came into her life.

"My father, Otto Friedrich," Molly told me, "died at age sixty-six on April 26th, 1995. He'd gone into the hospital that Easter Sunday because he wasn't able to handle the pain. Like so many men of his generation, he'd assumed that his pain was the pain of creaky aging, poor health habits, you know, drinking and smoking throughout his adulthood finally catching up with him. Within about an hour of his arrival in the hospital, the doctors had located cancer throughout his body. He died a few days later. I was very close to him and also perhaps imprudently represented him as his agent. We were all of us in deep, abiding shock and he'd left his estate in complete chaos. Hating the stock market, he'd opened more than thirty accounts, he even had war bonds, for crying out loud! My strongest memory of my mother at that time—who died, also youngish, fewer than eighteen months later—was her shifting bills and insurance claims from one end of the dining room table to the other, paralyzed and grief-stricken."

Enter Mary Breasted and a tattered "partial" manuscript.

Molly continued:

Anyway, it was into this chaos and sadness and shock that my friend Mary Breasted walked into my kitchen in Mount Kisco, New York. She lived just around the corner and we had an easy, casual kind of friendship, dropping by unannounced was not unusual. She was carrying an envelope in her hands as she emerged from the car. I honestly thought she'd arrived to give me a hug, but no, she was determined to get me to read her friend Frank's partial manuscript. I stared at her and said, "Mary, do you realize that my father died just two days ago?" She had realized this and yes, she was terribly sorry to hear that, but wouldn't I please read her friend Frank's manuscript?

I was livid and pissed off and astonished by the depths of her tone-deafness, at her importunate, nearly messianic determination to get Frank's manuscript read. I remember asking her what the book was about, and whether anyone had ever heard of this guy?

This was all of course, in 1995, way before the blandishments of poorly written blogs passing themselves off as publishable books, before the over-used words like brands and platforms had invaded our industry. Still, her answers were truly dispiriting—siblings had died, he'd returned to Ireland to starve with other siblings, etc. Mary did, of course, become positively rhapsodic about the writing but I was only half-listening, I was just too cross with her insensitivity to my own overshadowing grief. I had already received over four hundred condolence notes from writers and editors who'd known my father and I'd been elected by my family to plan a memorial service.

To get Mary to stop muttering about the wonders of this manuscript, I just rudely took it from her hands and left her standing in the driveway. I brought the manuscript into my kitchen and then became even angrier. It was single-spaced, 125 dense-looking pages on onionskin typing paper. Because it had been typed on some ancient machine, all the 'o's had been punched out, the pages looked like an angry crow had pecked at them. So I left it in my kitchen for two whole days, sitting under a large, rectangular can of Berio Olive oil. When I realized that the first page had a ring of greasy olive oil on it, I decided to take it upstairs to my bedroom, where all my most consequential reading happens.

Not surprisingly after nearly a quarter century, Mary Breasted's memory of the delivery of the sacred manuscript is a little different:

I also have no memory of my having known at the time that Molly's father had just died. I know I read the obituary in the paper and then spoke to her about it and of course expressed huge sympathy. The obit ran that day, but I think I would have remembered then being aware of it as I approached her house with Frank's brown envelope. I think I didn't see the obit page until later, but Molly could well be remembering this more fulsomely than I. Anyway, I was surprised to read about myself being such a total creep in a scene I don't remember. What I remember about the encounter was that I had briefly told her the barest minimum of Frank's story over the phone and that our conversation on the doorstep was very succinct. Molly stood in the open door, and I handed her the envelope. Maybe I praised the writing, but I thought I just urged her to read the first five pages as I was backing out of the door she was trying to close.

Molly Friedrich continued:

I do remember, quite vividly, my experience of reading that first page! When I got to that fourth paragraph, "Above all—we were wet." I put the parchment-like page down in my lap and just started shaking, it was so transparently obvious that I had stumbled, kicking and screaming in low-grade resentment, onto a truly great piece of writing. I had no idea if the writing could be sustained at such perfect pitch, but I was vibrating with the thrill of a possible great discovery. It was finally here, a non-posthumous classic, waiting to be born! I kept reading, savoring every word, slowly turning over each crackling page, with the little punched out 'o's' all over my quilt.

Of course, I called Frank the next morning and got Ellen on the phone instead. I was babbling incoherently about the wonders of this partial memoir, while Ellen laughed her great, gulping guffaw, saying, "Well, Molly, great! We love it, too!"

We met, Frank and I, just a day later, I wasn't about to let another patch of moss grow under my feet, I was too hysterical. *Now* I understood the gleam in Mary Breasted's eye. Frank wanted to know how I might sell it, I told him I had no clue but sell it, I would.

JONATHAN SWIFT'S BIRTHDAY AND A "ROGUE CATHOLIC" EDITOR

Friedrich continued:

As I was reading, I had been brooding about how to sell this manuscript. Frank was sixty-six years old, perhaps sixty-eight—not ancient but not a young new writer. He was completely unknown within the publishing community. He had also only written a plump third of the manuscript, and who actually knew if he'd deliver once under contract? I asked him when he thought he might finish the draft and he looked at me, smiled and said, "On Jonathan Swift's birthday." Huh? Well, he explained, that's November 30. So two-thirds of the book would be written in just six months! "Maybe," I thought, darkly. "We'll see." All of these terrible negatives were floating about my head as I met with Frank. I didn't want to oversell either myself or the skittish publishing community. I explained to him that it might be wisest to submit to one editor at a time. He was deeply trusting and affable, whatever I thought a good idea was clearly fine with him.

I decided to choose Nan Graham, a senior editor at Scribner's. I hadn't seen her in years but during various gossipy lunches with other editors, I'd remembered two seemingly useless bits of information about her. The first was that Nan had recently converted to Catholicism. The second was that, although not married at the time, she was either pregnant or had just had her first child. To my way of thinking, this sort of rogue Catholic, also a deeply literary reader with a fair amount of staying power, made Nan the perfect first choice for submission. So I called her up on a Thursday and after desultorily chatting with her, I asked her when she'd last heard from me. "Well, Molly, it's been years." I then asked her, without describing a single moment of the memoir, if she was interested in reading her first non-posthumous classic? I reminded her that this would be an exclusive submission and that this was a prize-winner if ever there *was* one, and that I never bugged her with slipshod submissions, I so valued her time. If nothing else, my job was to make her genuinely curious. I explained that I had never ever described a manuscript as a prize-winner before, I was honestly too humble for such over-selling.

Nan read the memoir over that weekend and of course, flipped out. Instead of making an offer, she urged me to bring Frank into their offices, they wanted to meet him. Frank showed up in a white suit, I do remember that. When you describe a writer in a white suit, you of course think of Tom Wolfe, but Frank's white suit was worlds away from Mr. Wolfe's fine linens, it was more of the Wrangler family, a rugged, somewhat ill-fitting jeans suit. Anyway, Nan and Susan Moldow and Pat Eisemann all fell into a direct swoon over Frank, and

why not? He was charming and literate, with the gift of easy gab, either from his
Irish bones or from having stood for twenty-seven years in front of classrooms.
Nan offered $125,000 for US and Canadian rights and the rest is literary his-
tory. The book was sold all over the world, translated into over twenty-five lan-
guages, it won a Pulitzer and marvelous reviews.

AN OVERNIGHT SUCCESS AT SIXTY-SIX

The good news is that at the age of sixty-six Frank McCourt was published to acclaim.
He finally had money for the first time in his life and he could actually enjoy life.
Friedrich recalled:

At a writers' conference in Southampton, Long Island, I had asked Frank
whether he had any regrets. By then his cancer was in full if stealthy bloom. He
looked at me and said, "Well, my only regret is that I didn't get started writing
sooner." For a man his age to finish a perfect memoir in just six months. And
then to write two more, along with an illustrated children's book? While touring the world and having the time of his life, navigating all the demands upon
his time? That was an awful lot to have accomplished.

At one point, when his touring became so relentless and when he was having trouble ever turning any request away, Ellen had confronted him and asked,
"Frank, are you a writer or a one-book wonder? Do you want to become an
after-dinner mint or be remembered as a serious writer?" Something like that,
anyway!

And the joke among the New York Irish writing community was that Frank was a
"Blurb Machine." Blurbs—usually one sentence of praise from a famous person for a
new book to be posted prominently on the cover—somehow became a publishers'
obsession, and Frank was always happy to accommodate his friends, including me. I
gave Frank the sobriquet of "Blessed Frank McCourt" because of his blurb genius.

"Publishing parties simply don't happen these days," said Molly Friedrich, "but
back then, there was a robust feeling shared by all of us that something ought to be
done to celebrate this marvelous book! I cannot remember how we all ended up in
some grand building owned by NYU, but the place was packed, the champagne and

Guinness flowed, it was truly celebratory. Most meaningful was the fact that it was the first time in seventeen years that Alfie, Michael, Malachy, and Frank were together in the same room! Everyone there was aware of this, it was a singularly powerful moment. The four brothers didn't know where to put their words or their collective hearts and so they got up to the podium and began singing, all four of them. Felt like a deeply healing moment and to quote from the great Ludvig Bemelmans, 'Not a single eye was dry.'"

THE BEGRUDGERS LOSE OUT TO THE PULITZER

Irish Alzheimer's, it is said, is when they forget everything except the grudges. And a close Irish relative of the grudge is the begrudger. Frank McCourt and *Angela's Ashes* would have their share.

It was not always smooth sailing—on both sides of the Atlantic. "Yeah," confessed Friedrich, "it was a bestseller in Ireland, and yeah, the Irish were 'difficult.' Also perhaps jealous of his high and mighty success. But at the old Leamy School, ("stock your mind, McCourt, stock your mind!") there is a wonderful sculpture of Frank's head sitting outside the front doors, so he's also been honored in all Limerick."

Breasted remembered: "Frank and Ellen were at the 1996 Frankfurt Book Fair, and I was there promoting the German edition of my Irish novel. Frank's reading was packed and standing room only in the back. I got a seat near Ellen. Frank told his fans he was going to do something for me in thanks for my help. 'This song is dedicated to Mary,' he said. He proceeded to sing *The Rose of Tralee* on stage with all his pious party piece gestures. To me that was almost as satisfying as the day he won the Pulitzer Prize."

After that show of gratitude, Breasted did not take criticism of McCourt easily. Breasted's love of McCourt would have her coming out fighting to uphold Frank's reputation as a great writer:

Frank's success did make me feel validated in my literary judgment, and I felt protective of his reputation at times, when I heard the sour grapes comments of some Irish intellectuals, who would dismiss his book as "pastiche" and call him sneeringly "a good raconteur."

Ulick O'Connor and Anthony Cronin, for instance, were dejectedly hanging around the bookstore outside where Frank's huge crowd had gone in to hear his reading in Frankfurt in October 1996, looking at the huge pile of *Angela's Ashes* near their own tiny piles, and I heard Ulick say, "I hear it's just a bit of a pastiche." Cronin, author of a really good memoir about Brendan Behan, Patrick Kavanagh and Flan O'Brian and their drinking buddies called *Dead As Doornails*, really should have known better. But Ulick, who wrote unendurable Noh plays and was a total snob without the brains to justify the height of his nose, would never know better. What really irked Ulick was the way Frank's fans thundered toward the same room where Ulick's tiny audience had come tottering out like bewildered Spanish dowagers who might have strayed onto the wrong Pamplona Street before the running of the bulls.

MARY BREASTED VS. *TNYTBR*

Mary Breasted would also take her fight to the Old Gray Lady's *Book Review*:

I did stick my neck out once with feeling after the *New York Times* ran Dennis Donahue's lousy review of *Angela's Ashes* on the cover of the *Book Review*. I knew Donahue's stuff. I had read his reviews of contemporary Irish books in Dublin newspapers, and I'd heard him expound upon James Joyce at the Joyce Symposium in 1982 there. He was brilliant on Joyce, but he was a coward on living writers. He wasn't going to hazard praise for writers whose reputations had not been established. . . . Donohue's own memoir, *Warrenpoint*, published in 1990, had sunk like a stone. I had tried to read it at the time. It was full of pretentious references to arcane philosophers or other bits of Donahue's remembered classical education dropped in without any sense of their usefulness or relevance to his narrative. . . .

I was so annoyed that I rang Charles McGrath who was then the *Book Review* editor. I told him he should have known better than to pick Dennis Donahue to review *Angela's Ashes*, that Donahue was still smarting from the non-success of his own memoir, that I knew his stuff, and he would never have the courage to praise a writer whose reputation had not been established. He never praised living writers. I said that the *Times* often made the mistake of picking someone in the same field to review a book about which the reviewer might be ruinously envious or at least not objective. McGrath was of course not pleased with me.

When Frank won the Pulitzer after the encounter with Chip McGrath, I did feel vindicated. Because Frank's style was so accessible and his book became so popular, the "academy" in Ireland was loath to embrace it. But the next generation of Dennis Donahues will find ways to bring it into the canon. Ellen no doubt knows better than the rest of us what Frank would think about all this reputation business. I like to imagine he's telling his friends in the afterlife that I don't believe in; his work is in every library in the English-speaking world. "You know what the library is, don't you, the building with all the books."

Molly Friedrich said, "It was a great honor to know Frank and to have been his agent for the full length of an extraordinary journey." But she remembered not only the joy of getting Ashes into print, but the personal tragedy of her own life that still goes along with it. "As I mentioned, my mother also died, actually within a month of the hard-cover publication of Angela's Ashes. So ashes, those of my own parents, they form a quite perfect bookend to this first book's publication."

ON THE WALL AT LAST

The Lion's Head closed on October 12, 1996. Months before its demise Frank McCourt's Angela's Ashes became the last book by a regular to mount the authors' wall.

"Frank was very proud of just that moment," Ellen McCourt told me. "It was 'like winning the Noble Prize,' he said."

'Tis.

PART FIVE

HOLY MOTHER CHURCH AND *REAL* IRISH CATHOLIC NEW YORK

IRISH NEW YORK HAS HAD ITS SHARE OF COLORFUL YET PIOUS CATHOLIC ICONS

The archbishop of New York has always been an Irish Catholic. Look at the names over the last century and a half: Hughes, McCloskey, Corrigan, Farley, Hayes, Spellman, Cooke, O'Connor, Egan, right up to the present archbishop, Timothy Cardinal Dolan.

There are two reasons for this: 1) Archbishop John Joseph Hughes; 2) the Great Irish Famine of the 1840s. Hughes, known famously as "Dagger John," became archbishop of New York in 1842 and was elevated to archbishop in 1850, as the rising tide of Irish escaped the famine and landed on the East Coast of the United States, hitting Boston, Philadelphia, Baltimore, and especially New York.

Hughes in the 1840s had stood up to the Know-Nothings, the Trumpsters of their day, when they were thinking about burning down Catholic churches in New York for sport. He established his own Catholic infrastructure which included schools, hospitals, orphanages, and St. John's College which is known today as Fordham University. New York Catholics would no longer be reading the King James version of the Bible in city schools. He also started to build St. Patrick's Cathedral. Dagger John may have been more politician than spiritual leader, but he planted his giant Irish imprint on New York, and it exists 180 years later.

The Irish weren't the only Catholics in New York. There were also the likes of Elizabeth Ann Seton, who was born in New York City in 1774 and would go on to form the Sisters of Charity religious order which would have a great influence in Hughes's schools and hospitals. Mother Seton died in Maryland in 1821 at age forty-six. She was canonized by Pope Paul VI in 1975.

Frances Xavier Cabrini was born in Italy in 1850 and arrived in New York in 1889, just as the Italians, like the Irish forty years before, were beginning to inundate the city. Mother Cabrini was instrumental in supporting these Italian immigrants, opening schools, orphanages, and hospitals to care for her fellow countrymen. She would move on to Chicago and continue her good works, dying there in 1917. She was canonized by Pope Pius XII in 1946.

But New York was always dominated by the Irish. In this section we will deal with "Dagger John" Hughes; socialist Dorothy Day, who may someday become a saint; Father Mychal Judge, chaplain of the FDNY and a man many believe was a saint; and NYPD Officer Steven McDonald, a man who forgave the boy who destroyed his life. They're all here in Real Irish Catholic New York.

CHAPTER ONE

"DAGGER JOHN"

ARCHBISHOP JOHN HUGHES STOOD UP TO THE KNOW-NOTHINGS AND BUILT THE INFRASTRUCTURE THAT MADE THE ARCHDIOCESE OF NEW YORK THE MOST POWERFUL IN THE COUNTRY

I f he was alive today, Archbishop "Dagger John" Hughes—Irish immigrant—would come out punching against Donald John Trump, and he would not only enjoy the fight—he would win.

Archbishop John Joseph Hughes of New York led a colorful, albeit, untidy life and a century and a half after his death, he is still revered by Catholics—especially Irish Catholics—for his stand against nativism in the time of the Know-Nothings.

Hughes's feistiness may be attributed to the fact that he was born in Annaloghan, County Tyrone, on June 24, 1797 just a year before the United Irishmen launched their revolution in the "Year of the French" to rid Ireland of its English hegemony. He was proud of being Irish and commented "that to me no derivation of life could be more highly appreciated than that which has descended to me from my Irish ancestry."

Hughes's quarter-century as archbishop of New York involved every important Irish event of that epoch—standing up to the nativists, the establishment of Fordham University, the Irish participation during the Mexican War, the influx of Irish during the Great Famine, the building of the new St. Patrick's Cathedral, becoming President Lincoln's European emissary during the Civil War and, finally, his response to the Irish-led Civil War riots of 1863—just to name a few.

A HUMBLE BEGINNING IN TYRONE

Hughes was born to a farming family in Tyrone. They were neither rich nor poor, just working farmers. In a good crop year all was well, and in a bad crop year, things could be fearsome. The bad years outnumbered the good years, and with the limitations of being Catholics in Protestant Ulster, it was decided that the family would move—in shifts—to America.

Sailing from Belfast, Hughes arrived in America in 1817. His father was up in Pennsylvania, but Hughes, looking for work and education, ended up in Catholic Baltimore. Back in Tyrone, Hughes had worked as a landscaper and this skill helped him land a job where he first came into contact with black slaves working the land. It would be noted by John Loughery in *Dagger John: Archbishop John Hughes and the Making of Irish America* that Hughes was the "superintendent of a slave plantation in his youth."[50] It would not last long and he was eventually fired from the landscaping job.

Hughes ached for higher education and hoped to find it at Mount Saint Mary's College in Emmitsburg, Maryland in 1819. Mount Saint Mary's was run by a crusty French cleric named John Dubois and their remarkable relationship would stretch over two decades, ending in New York.

Hughes tried to enroll as a student, but Dubois would only hire him as a gardener and groundskeeper for the school. Hughes was humiliated, but he kept trying. And it would literally take a saint, Elizabeth Seton, the founder of the Sisters of Charity also situated in Emmitsburg, to gain him entrance. She spoke with Dubois and Hughes, still doing his gardening duties, was finally admitted in 1820. Loughery, in his biography of Hughes, wrote that "Dubois treated him like an unwanted stepchild." Hughes's long Irish memory would make note of this.

Hughes, working tirelessly at Mount Saint Mary's, was finally ordained a priest on October 15, 1826 at the age of twenty-nine. He was assigned to Saint Joseph's Church in Philadelphia.

It was in Philadelphia that Hughes earned his reputation as a polemic. He would fight in the newspapers, defending Catholics against Protestant bigotry. Sometimes he wrote under his own name and sometimes under the pseudonym "Cranmer." The result was a higher profile for one John Joseph Hughes.

He also was gaining a reputation for getting things done. He opened an orphanage—of course naming it St. John's—and when Bishop Francis Patrick Kenrick needed a new church, he turned to Hughes to get it done.

To the north, his old nemesis John Dubois was now bishop of New York and he was in over his head. "In November 1837," wrote Loughery, "Hughes received word that he should conclude his affairs in Philadelphia as soon as possible, as he was to be John Dubois's adjutor with right of succession and would be formally installed in that position at Saint Patrick's Cathedral on Mott Street early in the new year."

Unfortunately for Dubois, Hughes's definition of "adjutor" was not the same as Dubois's. Poor John Dubois thought Hughes "wasn't just another upstart Irishman come to make his life miserable." And you know what? He was right.

BISHOP HUGHES GOES TO NEW YORK

"He was physically imposing, attractive without being handsome," wrote Richard Shaw in his biography with a familiar title, *Dagger John: The Unquiet Life and Times of Archbishop John Hughes of New York*. "His brown, curly hair had begun to recede making his forehead more prominent. His Roman nose, sternly set mouth, and blue-gray eyes which could flash with sharp wit or equally sharp anger made him the sort of man who was often intimidating to those in his presence. The impression given was one of self-assurance and strength."[51] Hughes was confident in front of an audience, a bit of a showman who was not afraid to provoke foes. It is interesting to note that his hairline was receding, perhaps supporting the rumor that Hughes boosted his ego by wearing a toupee.

When Hughes got to New York, Dubois was incompetent and ill. In fact, two weeks after Hughes's consecration as bishop, Dubois suffered a paralytic stroke. Hughes found that the city contained fifty thousand Catholics, about 20 percent of the population of the city. He inherited a debt of three hundred thousand dollars. If he had learned one thing in Philadelphia, it was that indecision and softness didn't get things done. He would be rude if he had to be and he would give the orders—and everyone else would follow them. After surveying the situation, Hughes wrote that "conditions in New York might be worse."

THE KNOW-NOTHINGS MARCH ON PHILADELPHIA—AND DAGGER JOHN REVEALS HIS MOSCOW SOLUTION

One of the monumental events of Hughes's life occurred in Charleston, Massachusetts in 1834. Protestants' attacks on Catholics often centered around nuns and convents. The Protestants often used innuendo and rumors of sexual deviancy among the nuns to attack Catholics. Well, in Charleston the Protestants put match to word and burned a convent down. This, according to Loughery, sent Hughes "into paroxysms of rage. Like every other priest in the country, Hughes was appalled at the news from Massachusetts (and his disgust with [Lyman] Beecher and [Samuel F. B.] Morse was unmatched), but unlike some Catholic clergymen, he kept his anger about the topic at a boil all his life. Few subjects elicited more agitated outbursts from Hughes over the next thirty years than the burning of the Charlestown convent."

A decade later, burnings in Philadelphia and Hughes's response to them would be material that would help make him a legend to Catholics all over America.

But it was political actions Hughes would take that caught the attention of militant nativists. "Public-school teachers in New York City were overwhelmingly native Protestants," wrote Loughery. "Their view of their immigrant charges was often anything but enlightened. Their view of Irish Catholic immigrant children in particular could be especially dismissive or disdainful and was widely recognized as a factor in declining attendance among school-age immigrant Catholic children."

So Hughes fought to keep Catholic children out of public schools and away from the King James version of the Bible—and have the Protestants pay for it. He mounted a sophisticated political campaign and managed to get his bill through both the state assembly and senate and get his friend Governor William Seward to sign it. But it was by and large an empty victory because funding was never approved. It also served to inflame Protestants in their hatred of Catholics—especially Irish ones.

But as John Loughery keenly observed in his *Dagger John*, "John Hughes was a political creature as much as a devoutly spiritual man, and he had never been averse to working with, or jousting with, men in power, friends or opponents. He loved a good bluff, and he was rarely called on it. The belief that religious leaders should remain above politics wasn't one he entirely shared, even when he pretended it was. It would be more accurate to say that he believed religious leaders should never *appear* to be engaged in political activity."

Horace Greeley's *New York Herald*, noting Hughes's audacity, called him "the impudent priest . . . the abbot of unreason." And the now sainted and lionized Walt Whitman referred to him as "this cunning, flexible, serpent-tongued priest [who] has the insolence to appear in the political forum."

The summer of 1844 was going to be a hot one—especially in Philadelphia, Hughes's old hunting grounds where he still had many close friends. On May 6, nativists rallied near a Catholic school in the Philadelphia suburb of Kensington and ended up attacking a Sisters of Charity convent school but were fought off by Irish Catholics. This began a three-day rampage that forced many Irish Catholics to flee the city.

The convent was subsequently burned down along with several Catholic churches and businesses. Thirty homes belonging to Irish Catholics were either damaged or burned to the ground. The fight continued in early July and the end result was that thirty men were killed and another hundred—on both sides—seriously injured. This vitriol by the nativists was directed only at Irish Catholics because no German Catholic churches were torched. It was obvious who the nativists were targeting.

"Fears that the same kind of attacks might occur in New York City were widespread that spring and summer," wrote Loughery in his biography of Hughes. "This is when Hughes's most oft-quoted remark was purportedly made to New York's mayor, who asked Hughes if he were worried about his own diocese's churches. The rejoinder: no, because if a single church under my care is touched, the Protestants would need to look to their own houses of worship, as the city would be turned into a 'second Moscow.'"

Hughes was referring to 1812, when Napoleon marched on Moscow and the residents of the city decided to burn it to the ground rather than surrender it to the French emperor.

Richard Shaw in his own biography of Hughes tells a more graphic story of the Archbishop's confrontation with the mayor.

"He also called on the municipal authorities," wrote Shaw, "and bluntly warned them: 'If a single Catholic Church is burned in New York, the city will become a second Moscow.'

"The lame duck Mayor Robert Morris asked him: 'Are you afraid that some of your Churches will be burned?'

"'No sir,' Hughes countered, 'but I am afraid that some of yours will be burned. We can protect our own. I come to warn you for your own good.'"[52]

"This image," continued Loughery, maybe doubting that this confrontation actually took place, "has a wonderful, visually allusive ring to it, and one might well wish Hughes had expressed himself thus—indeed, he might have. It evokes his backbone and his manner of expression. . . . Immigrant New Yorkers loved him for the strength of his response. Men with guns patrolled the streets outside the cathedral with his permission." Not one match was struck against a Catholic Church in John Hughes's New York City.

"It was at this time," Loughery wrote, "that the first mention of the stiletto purportedly appended to his signature was raised in print. Hughes could only express astonishment that an adult of any faith could fail to distinguish a cross from a dagger, but the damage was done. 'Dagger John' entered the mythology of New York and Catholic life. The name would stick and outlive him to this day."

Another version of the sobriquet "Dagger John" is that Hughes wore a crucifix around his neck that was long and sharp like a stiletto.

Thus, a legend was born.

DAGGER JOHN BEGINS BUILDING A CATHOLIC INFRASTRUCTURE: OPENING AN ORPHANAGE WHILE BULLYING THE SISTERS OF CHARITY

After his fight over getting public funding for Catholic schools, which turned out to be an empty victory because no funds were made available and the whole effort just antagonized Protestants more than ever, Hughes turned his attention to more infrastructure. First up was a boys' orphanage, which turned into a grand fight with the Sisters of Charity.

"Thousands of boys in Manhattan, barefoot 'street Arabs,' lived an existence straight out of *Oliver Twist*," wrote Loughery, "but now five hundred of them had a chance of a better life." To give the boys a better life Hughes needed the help of the Sisters of Charity in running an orphanage.

It is ironic that he picked a fight with the Sisters of Charity because their founder, St. Elizabeth Seton, played an important part in Hughes getting into the seminary at all. Also, Hughes's sister Ellen was also a sister of Charity, going under the name of Sister Angela. The gist of the fight was that Hughes wanted the power to assign the nuns where they were most needed, either at the orphanage or in teaching positions. The good Sisters had other ideas.

In the end, some sisters left New York, thirty-three stayed, and they formed a new community called the Sisters of Charity of Saint Vincent de Paul and went to work in the orphanage. "Attacking Protestant bigots and taking on insulting journalists was one thing," wrote Loughery. "Browbeating nuns was another." Hughes probably realized the folly of his confrontation and truculence as he admitted to "a certain pungency of style."

The good works of the Sisters of Charity would continue after Hughes's death. In 1869 they would open the New York Foundling Hospital, caring for orphans. They would also be crucial in teaching in parochial schools and at one time ran St. Vincent's Hospital. Without the order that Mother Seton started, New York Catholics would have been seriously adrift.

ST. VINCENT'S HOSPITAL

St. Vincent's Hospital, located in the heart of Greenwich Village, was one of the iconic hospitals in the history of New York City. From taking on the survivors of the *Titanic* to caring for the victims of AIDS in the 1980s, it was beloved by everyone in the city, religion or no religion, until its demise in 2010.

It was the first Catholic hospital in the city, and it opened on All Saints Day, November 1, 1849, during a cholera epidemic. It was under the supervision of— surprise—Sister Angela, Archbishop Hughes's sister.

"But it is not a coincidence," wrote John Loughery,

that the first Catholic hospital in Manhattan opened with a Hughes at its head. The Sisters of Charity of New York were anything but naïve. They knew that their bishop would not allow the hospital to fail if his own sister was its director. He knew the approachable donors.

Hughes was delighted to have Ellen assume this new role, relieved that Catholic patients might no longer be forced to go to Bellevue or New York Hospital, where priests were seldom admitted without difficulty (and sacraments were never administered without opposition), and hopeful that a new model of faith-based care was being offered to the wary Irish or German immigrant. At least as important, Ellen had the same tenacity her brother exhibited when committed to a goal that she believed in. She was also, in a respectful way, willing to lock horns with her brother when she felt she had to, but he was comfortable directing philanthropically minded Catholic businessmen her way as he might not have been with a stranger.

THE NEW ST. PATRICK'S CATHEDRAL

One of the great ambitions of John Hughes's life was to build a massive Catholic Cathedral in New York. It, too, would be named in honor of St. Patrick, just as the small church on Mott Street was. Hughes decided that it would be built in the country, way up at 50th Street and Fifth Avenue on land that the archdiocese had owned since 1810. He put his architect brother-in-law William Rodrigue to work alongside a promising young architect named James Renwick, who had just built Grace Episcopal Church on Broadway and 10th Street.

From the beginning the problem was money—or more truthfully, the lack of it. Economic depressions were followed by recessions. It became apparent to Hughes that he would have to pay for the new cathedral in parts because the cost was so much. It was important to begin the project.

So the cornerstone was laid on the Feast of the Assumption, August 15, 1858. Hughes, according to Richard Shaw, addressed the big crowd at 50th Street and said, "Judging from the past, in which the clergy were at all times loyal and one minded in aiding their unworthy bishop in whatever enterprise he had engaged, so will they be in all times to come—and to them, with the powerful cooperation which they will always have their devoted flocks, I commend this great work, no matter under whose episcopal auspices it may hereafter be carried on."

Hughes had little over five more years to live and the new St. Patrick's would not be opened until nearly a quarter-century after his death, near the end of 1878. It has the features of a James Renwick church in that it looks like two Grace Churches stuck together, a handsome, stately building that would have made Archbishop Hughes proud not only for its appearance and power, but because of the vision he showed in getting the job underway.

FORDHAM UNIVERSITY—AND A FIGHT WITH THE JESUITS

On his forty-fourth birthday in June 1841, John Hughes celebrated by opening St. John's Seminary in the Bronx. The previous year he had purchased 106 acres for the project. "Hughes," wrote Richard Shaw in his Hughes biography, "who had already begun an orphanage and opened two churches, all of which he called St. John's, again showed his unbiased liking for the name and christened the new institution St. John's College. In time people would dub the school after the name of the area—not of the actual manor brought, Rose Hill—but of the larger and more ancient manor of which it was a part, Fordham."

It was the first Catholic college in the northeast. It was opened because Hughes desperately needed priests. It's first class would consist of only six students. It would fail as a seminary, but succeed as a college, now known to the world as Fordham University.

As with his mindless fight with the Sisters of Charity over assignment of nuns, Hughes would repeat the mistake again with the Jesuits, in a fight over jurisdiction of the college, including its boundary. Of all things, Hughes thought them too friendly with the Young Irelanders who were now exiled in New York. In the end, there would be an awkward settlement with the Jesuits, leaving them firmly in control of Fordham.

THE MEXICAN WAR AND THE *SAN PATRICIOS*

President James K. Polk, who was friendly with Hughes, wanted a war with Mexico, and by 1846 he would have it. Polk was very aware that the Mexicans were overwhelmingly Catholic and needed cover for his war so it would not look like an anti-Catholic hunt. So he turned to the archbishop from New York. Hughes was wary and wondered about the whole adventure, but wanted to show that his followers—the Irish—supported their new country. Polk asked Hughes to supply chaplains for the US Army's Catholics—at one point he may have suggested that Hughes go himself—many of whom were Irish. Several chaplains were finally sent, and the war was soon over without Hughes getting further involved. After all, he had enough problems in New York.

Hughes's efforts to show that his people supported their new country took a blow because of the work of the *Batallón de San Patricio*—the St. Patrick's Battalion. "No one has ever determined the exact number with any degree of accuracy," wrote Loughery, "but well over one hundred and possibly as many as two hundred U.S. soldiers had gone over to the other wide, some before war was formally declared and others after Polk's declaration of war. They fought especially valiantly in the defense of Mexico City. These men were almost all recent immigrants, a large number of them Irish Catholic, and their motives were varied. Some refused to stomach any longer the brazenly anti-Catholic attitudes and actions of their commanders, and other questions why they were being sent to kill fellow Catholics in support of the 'madness of [Polk's] plans,' as one angry deserter put it."

"The San Patricios fashioned their own green flag as an emblem to fight under," continued Loughery, "featuring one side of the Harp of Erin and a row of shamrocks and on the other Saint Patrick and the words 'Republica Mexicana.' They paid the predictable price when Mexico City fell, and they were captured. Fifty of them were hanged before assembled U.S. troops in the largest mass execution in American history. Others were tortured and branded a *D* for deserter."

It was obvious to Archbishop Hughes how deep the Protestant prejudice ran against Catholics, especially if they were Irish. The Mexican War did nothing to assuage this bigotry. But there would be other wars to fight and the Irish would get another chance.

THE NEW IRELANDERS

Written in "Poblacht Na hÉireann," the Proclamation of 1916, is: "In every generation the Irish people have asserted their right to national freedom and sovereignty; six times during the past three hundred years they have asserted it in arms." One of the times the writer, Padraig Pearse, was referring to was the New Irelander rebellion of 1848 in Ballingarry, County Tipperary. In reality, it was more of a skirmish than a rebellion.

The New Ireland movement had a mixed bag of revolutionaries, many of them Protestants like their leader William Smith O'Brien who for his troubles would be deported to Australia. Thomas Davis was also on board and today is best remembered as the composer of "A Nation Once Again." John Mitchel, a prolific journalist, is one of the great contradictions of Irish history. A stalwart for Irish freedom, he became an apologist for slavery after he settled in the United States before the Civil War. He considered slaves "an innately inferior people." He also described President Lincoln as "an ignoramus and a boor." The Catholic Thomas Francis Meagher would also get a free visit to Australia courtesy of the British and would eventually get to New York and become a general in the Union Army. And rounding out this band was a woman poet named Lady Jane Wilde, who wrote under the pseudonym "Speranza." It was a miracle she did not go to prison for her seditious actions. Later, she would have a son. His name was Oscar Wilde.

Eventually Mitchel and Meagher would land in Archbishop Hughes's New York. Hughes considered the whole Ballingarry uprising a disgrace to the Irish. "Every Irishman from Maine to Texas who has taken the slightest interest in the cause must blush and hang down his head for shame."

Meagher, according to Loughery, "became quite friendly with Hughes." As for the Protestant Mitchel, "Hughes thought him a contemptible man," which he was.

Hughes, it seems, continued to be a magnet for Ireland and her problems.

THE IRISH FAMINE HITS NEW YORK

The worst year of the Irish Famine was 1847 and thus became known as Black '47. In that fateful year, fifty-three thousand Irish refugees arrived in New York Harbor. It was double the previous year's figure. The following year brought another ninety thousand. By 1849, another 113,000 arrived in New York. In all, between 1847 and 1851, 850,000 famished Irish souls landed in America.

The arrival of the famine victims deeply moved Hughes. "My feelings, my habits, my thoughts," he said according to Loughery, "have been so much identified with all that is American that I have almost forgotten that I am a foreigner."

"The great famine," wrote Loughery, "brought him back to a consideration of his origins, and the sight of disembarking survivors of the so-called 'coffin ships' and their stories of evictions at home by 'crowbar brigades,' workhouses filled to capacity, coffin shortages, skeletal remains of relatives left unburied, and British inaction struck him 'as a great personal grief.'"

He redirected fourteen thousand dollars in funds targeted for seminary students, saying, "It is better that seminaries should be suspended than that so large a portion of our fellow-beings should be exposed to death by starvation."

The famine victims had found a friend in New York City.

SLAVERY AND THE CIVIL WAR

To say that John Hughes was ambivalent about black people is an understatement. As a young man he supervised them as a landscaper. "Whatever his exact relationship to the black men he directed—and bent and dug and mowed and planted with—in Maryland," wrote Loughery, "it is worth stopping to consider the effect a first encounter with slavery had on John Hughes. It can't have been anything other than unsettling. No abolitionist, then or ever, and no special friend of the black man, he understood the unique degradation the lash and chattel signified. He had had a taste of the attempt to enforce illiteracy and suppress political rights at home, but this was something different. Owner and owned: it was humanity at its most degraded, at both ends of the spectrum."

Yet it was at this time that the young Hughes wrote "The Slave," a poem which challenged the validity of slavery:

> Wipe from thy code Columbia, wipe this stain:
> Be free as the air, but yet be kind as free,
> And chase foul bondage from thy southern lain; if such be
> The right of man, by heaven's decree
> Oh then let Afric's sons feel what it is—to be.

"I am no friend to slavery," Hughes told the New York Courier & Inquirer when he was archbishop.

"In one sermon at Saint Patrick's Cathedral," wrote Loughery, "he referred to slavery as 'an evil' that had been revived in modern times only because of the unconscionable avarice of white men."

Yet another time he stated that "while we all know that this condition of slavery is an evil, yet it is not an absolute and unmitigated evil."

"His personal relations with black Americans were practically nil," wrote Loughery. "He had nothing to do with Pierre Toussaint, the ex-slave who had prospered in New York City and become a significant Catholic philanthropist. By the standards of our day, John Hughes was a racist man. By the standards of progressive thinkers of his own day, John Hughes was a racist man, though the charge carried less weight then, of course."

The problem for Hughes and other Irish Catholics is that the abolitionists were anti-Irish. "The question of freedom for slaves," wrote Shaw, "did not take up very much space in the priority lists of Irish Catholic immigrants. They were concerned with finding space to live in the North despite the opposition of the same Puritans who wanted to free the oppressed in the far-off South. Almost universally the native moralists who were anti-drink and antislavery were also anti-Catholic. . . . The immigrant Church could not afford the luxury of fighting for the freedom of others. It had not yet won from native Americans the acknowledgment that it had the right to exist freely itself."

With this attitude toward the slavery question it is a curiosity why Hughes was such a supporter of President Lincoln and the Union. Early in Lincoln's presidency he took a long public relations trip to Europe to defend the president and the Union among the European powers. As the war dragged on he was outspoken in his support of conscription: "Volunteers have been appealed to," said Hughes according to Richard Shaw's biography, "and they have answered the appeal; but for my own part, if I had a voice in the councils of the Nation, I would say, let volunteers continue, and the draft be made. If three hundred thousand men be not sufficient let three hundred thousand more to be called upon, so that the army, in its fulness of strength, shall always be on hand for any emergency."[53]

He was proud of the Irish from New York supporting the Union. New York had 337,800 soldiers in the Union Army and 51,206 of them were Irish born. According to Shaw, he was particularly proud of New York's Fighting 69th: "Let the Sixty-Ninth Regiment know that I shall be deeply afflicted if they should be less than brave in battle, less than humane and kind after the battle is over, and above all things, if by possibility, they should bring a tarnish upon their name, their country or their religion."

But there also seemed to be an alternate reason for his support for the Union and its army—a reason the Fenians would try to exploit come 1867. "Hughes made the Civil War into a training ground for future rebellions," wrote Shaw. "He declared: 'The Irish have, in many instances, as I have the strongest reasons for knowing, entered into this war partly to make themselves apprentices, students as it were, finishing their education in this, the first opportunity afforded them of becoming thoroughly acquainted with the implements of war.'"

THE DRAFT RIOTS

By the summer of 1863, Hughes was a very sick man. He had lacerating rheumatism in his hips, knees, and ankles. He had survived a bout of pneumonia and was suffering from Bright's Disease, a kidney disorder. It was around this time that he told his friend, Secretary of State William Seward that "I am getting old, and it is time for me to begin to gather myself up for a transition from this world to another and I hope, a better."

It was also at this time that his support for the draft would come back to haunt him and his city. One of the problems of the draft was that a rich man could buy an exemption for three hundred dollars—which was a fortune to the immigrant Irish. "The archbishop shared this sense of injustice," wrote Loughery, "yet any hint of sympathy for the Confederacy, talk of suing for peace, or direct attacks on the federal government continued to rile him from his sickbed to fits of pique."

"A further, embarrassing complication was his support the previous autumn for the institution of a draft," wrote Loughery. "He had no intention of going back on that statement. Yet he had never imagined a system that would send more Irish laborers to war while the sons of rich men—so many of whom were Protestant, so many of whom were native Americans—stayed home or went abroad. Lincoln had made a mock of his support."

It all came to a boil on July 13, 1863 when gangs of Irishmen went on a rampage, attacking black orphanages and black men, women, and children at random. "Now a tide of brute force had returned to the nativist population the evils that they themselves had sown," wrote Shaw. "Hughes said the same things now that he had said in the 1840s. The civil government had the obligation to preserve civil peace."

According to Shaw, Horace Greeley in his *New-York Tribune* blamed Hughes and "his people" for the riots. Sick or not, Hughes replied in typical Hughes fashion: "In spite of Mr. Greeley's assault upon the Irish, in the present disturbed condition of the city, I will appeal not only to them, but to all persons who love God and revere the holy Catholic religion in which they profess, to respect also the laws of man and the peace of society, to retire to their homes with as little delay as possible, and disconnect themselves from the seemingly deliberate intention to disturb the peace and social rights of the citizens of New York. If they are Catholics, I ask, for God's sake—for the sake of their holy religion—for my own sake, if they have any respect for the episcopal authority—to dissolve their bad association with reckless men, who have little regard either for divine or human laws."

Hughes invited "his people"—the majority of whom in truth did not riot—to his house at Madison Avenue and 36th Street for a talk. And a crowd of five thousand showed up. Hughes gave his talk from a balcony and spoke seated. "For myself," he began, "you know that I am a minister of God, a minister of peace, a minister who in your own trials and in years past, you know, never deserted you. With my tongue and with my pen I have stood by your fortunes always, and so shall I to the end, as long as you are right, and I hope you are never wrong. . . . If you are Irishmen, as your enemies say that the rioters are, I am an Irishman, too . . . and I am not a rioter. In this country the Constitution has made it the right of the people to make a revolution quietly every four years. Is that not so? . . . I am too old now to seek another home or another country. I want to cling by the old foundation of this, and I want the men who shall constitute the architects of the superstructure to be the right kind of men. . . . I am not a legislator. A man has a right to defend his shanty, if it be no more, or his house, or his church at the risk of his life; but the cause must be always just it must be defensive, not aggressive. . . . Look here men, the soil of Ireland was never crimsoned or moistened by a single drop of martyr's blood, and that is what no other nation can say."

"It was his last public appearance," wrote Shaw. "The effect of the riots upon his spirit only intensified what was his last illness. He suffered from Bright's disease. His rheumatism and the advent of cold weather brought the usual heaviness to his chest."

Peter Quinn, in his acclaimed novel of Irish New York in the pivotal year of 1863, *Banished Children of Eve*, wrote a paragraph that captured the thoughts of the dying Hughes after the draft riots: "All gone. Mother Seton. Dubois. Years before. What was left? Only what the mirror beheld. An image to frighten birds, not men. No red hat. Half-built church. Sickness. Old age. Now this. Undone in a week what had taken a quarter of a century to build."[54]

DEATH OF THE ARCHBISHOP

Hughes would catch a cold in the fall of 1863 and never recover. He died on January 3, 1864 and he would be eulogized by his protégé, friend, and fellow bishop, John McCloskey. Reading from St. Paul's epistle to Timothy, McCloskey said, "I have fought a good fight; I have finished my course. For the rest, there is laid up for me a crown of justice, which the Lord, the Just Judge, will render to me at that day; and not to me only, but to them also who love his coming."

McCloskey would succeed Hughes and be the first American to have the cardinal's red hat bestowed on him—something that had so eluded the old archbishop.

Archbishop Hughes would have somewhat of a resurrection fifteen years after his death. His body would be moved uptown to the new Fifth Avenue St. Patrick's Cathedral—his brainchild—which was now under the guidance of his friend, John Cardinal McCloskey.

But he would not be forgotten downtown at Old St. Patrick's on Mulberry Street. In the courtyard there is a bust of Dagger John which celebrates his remarkable life. The inscription surrounding the bust states:

Archbishop John Hughes
Old St. Patrick's
1797–1864

Immigrant
Shepherd
Patriot
Builder
Activist
Peacemaker
Advocate
Visionary
Educator
Leader

Dagger John's long winding journey, which began in County Tyrone and ended in New York with many stops in between, was finally at an end in the archbishop's crypt at his new St. Patrick's Cathedral on Fifth Avenue. New York's incorrigible Irish archbishop was home at last.

CHAPTER TWO

DOROTHY DAY

NEW YORK'S OWN "SERVANT OF GOD"

D on't call me a saint. I don't want to be dismissed so easily."

Sorry, Dorothy Day, it's too late.

Day's good works have made her into somewhat of an American Mother Teresa. She has gone from having anarchist-wobbly-socialist-communist aspirations to being a "Servant of God," step number four on the way to sainthood in the Catholic Church. Her good works on behalf of the poor and world peace have been acknowledged by the last two popes and thirty years after her death she has been dragged front and center and held up as the apotheosis of the supreme Catholic layperson.

Dorothy Day would be somewhat of an enigmatic saint. To say that Dorothy was one of the great mysteries of her epoch is an understatement. In Day's case, piety resulted in unwanted celebrity, both before and after death. Such is the story of Dorothy Day.

HOW IRISH WAS DAY?

Dorothy Day's ties to the Irish are tenuous. She was descended from Scotch-Irish Protestant stock and in her writings there doesn't seem to be much indication of her Irishness.

As with a lot of her life actions, there seemed to be a dichotomy of spirit. In her autobiography *The Long Loneliness*, she praised Jesus by declaring, "He lived in an occupied country for thirty years without starting an underground movement or trying to get out from under a foreign power"—an absolutely anti-Irish, anti-Fenian comment! Conversely, she also said, "I emphasized so much the necessity of suffering, and the glory of suffering for a cause," which is something that could have easily come out of the mouth of Irish revolutionary martyr Terence MacSwiney, who starved himself to death in the name of Irish independence, and many an Irish mother who bore their "crosses" stoically.[55]

However, because of her lifelong work among the poor in the Catholic Worker Movement, she is being propelled toward sainthood—and thus the Irish have seemed to adopt her with a vengeance.

IrishCentral.com hailed her as an "Irish American hero." CatholicIreland.net calls her "a worker for the kingdom." The New Monasticisms Ireland has her safely ensconced on their website.

Dorothy Day—like it or not—you are being claimed by your people, the Irish. God help you, Servant of God Dorothy Day.

SOWING WILD OATS IN GREENWICH VILLAGE

There is no doubting Dorothy Day's New York roots, for she was born in the independent City of Brooklyn on November 8, 1897. Her father was a newspaperman and his work took him to San Francisco in the year of the great earthquake and eventually to Chicago. Her father's quest in search of work seemed to instill in May a wanderlust that only a gypsy could appreciate. She would wander back to Chicago, to Los Angeles to work in the movie industry as a writer, and on to Mexico to live the simple life. But she would seem always, like a homing pigeon, to return to the tenements of New York or her beloved beach on Staten Island.

What makes Day's ties to the Catholic Church even more remarkable is that she started life as an Episcopalian, which many Catholics consider to be "Catholic-Lite." Although she always had an innate quest for holiness and spiritualty, her early life in Greenwich Village was marked by a raucous bohemian lifestyle. Her circle of friends circa 1918 sounded like the cast of the Warren Beatty movie *Reds*: Max Eastman, Floyd Dell, and Leon Trotsky. She was friends with John Reed, author of *Ten Days That Shook the World*. She remembered in her autobiography Reed as "a big, hearty Harvard graduate, a typical newspaperman, and very much the Richard Harding Davis reporter hero. Whenever there was excitement, whenever life was lived at high tension, there he was, writing, speaking, recording the moment, and heightening its intensity for everyone else."

According to *The Other American: The Life of Michael Harrington* by Maurice Isserman, Malcolm Cowley said in *Exile's Return:* "The gangsters admired Dorothy

Day because she could drink them under the table."[56] One of Day's favorite drinking buddies was a young playwright named Eugene O'Neill.

"It was more fun to hang around the Provincetown Playhouse," she wrote in *The Long Loneliness*, "where Eugene O'Neill and other of my friends had plays in rehearsal. After rehearsals or after performances, the usual meeting place was the back room of a saloon on the corner of Fourth Street and Sixth Avenue, nicknamed Hell Hole by its customers. Here Eugene O'Neill, Terry Karlin, an old Irish anarchist . . ., Michael Gold, and others, were my constant companions. No one ever wanted to go to bed, and no one ever wished to be alone."

"[Day] sat in the saloons for hours," wrote Louis Sheaffer in *O'Neill: Son and Playwright*, "matching the men drink for drink for drink, and knew ribald choruses of 'Frankie and Johnny' her companions had never heard of."

Although they were probably not lovers, O'Neill and Day were definitely serious drinking buddies. "He couldn't bear to be alone," she said, according to Sheaffer's biography. "Only an hour after I'd left him to go to work—I was on the *Liberator* magazine then—he'd be calling me from the Hell Hole or some other bar to come back." The Hell Hole in reality was called the Golden Swan and sat under the shadow of the Sixth Avenue Elevated railroad. Today it is remembered as the Golden Swan Garden, a lovely little park that shows no signs of its sordid past.

After all these drinking bouts Day would stagger out of the Hell Hole and although not yet a Catholic wander up Sixth Avenue to St. Joseph's Church on the corner of Washington Place for morning mass. Apparently, at that time, she took both drinking and holy mass to be equal religious experiences.

SEX BEFORE SAINTHOOD

Before her conversion to Catholicism Dorothy Day had a keen interest in sex. And her views on sex were very un-Catholic-like. While the Church has always viewed sex outside of marriage to be verboten, inside of marriage it was only for procreation. Day in her youth had a much more liberal view. "Sex was a deeper matter," she wrote in *The Long Loneliness*, "and in some obscure way had a connection with the supernatural law and God Himself. Sex and religion! It was immodest to talk of either. People were uncomfortable and embarrassed in talking about God."

Once, while she was incarcerated for protesting World War I, the only time the men and women were not segregated was at sabbath services: "Sunday was the one day in the week when they caught a glimpse of man," she wrote in *The Long Loneliness*. There were two church services during the day and for both the two balconies on either side of the auditorium were filled. Hundreds joined in the hymns. The men and women were separated, but I saw sex and felt it at its crudest and was ashamed that I should be stirred by it."

In *The Other American*, Maurice Isserman's biography of Day acolyte and social activist Michael Harrington, Isserman wrote "At the [*Catholic*] *Worker* there was a cult of Day as contemporary saint—but there was also a cult of Dorothy as former sinner. There was endless speculation among the staffers about Day's pre-Catholic past, which she tried without much success to discourage and censor. People wondered how many of, and who among, her many literary and political acquaintances had actually been her lovers. Mike's contemporary Ed Egan recalled 'everybody revered Dorothy and told terrible stories about her.'"[57]

Isserman writes about one amusing encounter between Day, Harrington, and the subject of sex. "Day was even more prudish about sex. She felt a maternal responsibility for protecting the young people in her charge from impure acts and thoughts. One evening at the *Worker*, at the dinner table, Michael was reading a psychiatric study of autoerotism. Dorothy got terribly upset. 'Michael!' she said sternly. 'We do not even *talk* about such things!'" Apparently, it was a long way from the Hell Hole.

DOROTHY DAY'S MORTAL SIN—ABORTION

Apparently, Day's morality was marked by an abortion she had around the time she was hanging around the Hell Hole. Mary O'Regan wrote on the *Catholic Herald* website that "As a 21-year-old, Day did, however, have a dalliance with another journalist, and became pregnant as a result. The fellow was a cad and pressurized her to have an abortion, and in September 1919 . . . Day made a decision that she would bitterly regret for the rest of her life. She had an illegal abortion. Afterwards, Day was weighted down with a guilt-fueled depression."

She may have been marked by guilt, but it is still amazing to note that her next relationship, which would result in the birth of her only child Tamar Teresa, was a common-law marriage to Forster Batterham. "I had known Forster a long time before we contracted our common-law relationship," she wrote, "and have always felt it was life with him that brought me natural happiness, that brought me to God."

This relationship was fraught with conflict and served several purposes as Day moved forward. First, she decided to have her daughter baptized in the Catholic Church, a pretty remarkable decision considering she was not yet a Catholic herself. It seems as if she was almost using her daughter to test out Catholicism before she took the leap herself, which she soon did. It was then that she decided that it was best that she sever the relationship with Batterham so she could concentrate on social matters.

In later life, Day was staunchly anti-abortion and pro-life. It seems like she wanted nothing to do with the lonely, frightened young girl who had an abortion in 1919.

DOROTHY DAY, JAILBIRD

Like many an Irish hero, Dorothy Day spent a goodly amount of time in prison. Her first jailing was in 1917 in Washington, DC. She was given thirty days for her protests with suffragists. She went on a hunger strike—a tactic used by Irish rebels at the time—and saw firsthand how people from the wrong side of the tracks were treated. "I would be utterly crushed by misery," she wrote in *The Long Loneliness*, "before I was released. Never would I recover from this wound, this ugly knowledge I had gained of what men were capable in their treatment of each other. It was one thing to be writing about these things, to have the theoretical knowledge of sweatshops and injustice and hunger, but it was quite another to experience it in one's own flesh."

She was next locked up by mistake in Chicago. She was staying with friends who were in the labor movement, and during the "Palmer Red Raids" following the Great War she ended up in jail, sharing cells mostly with street whores, who she found had more morals and decency than her captors. Day was catching on fast, "I gave a false name and I always had to be spoken to twice before I recognized it." During this period of incarceration she was "sharing, as I never had before, the life of the poorest of the poor, the guilty, the dispossessed."

Even in late middle age, she would continue to protest the immorality of war. In those days, New York City held civil defense drills where the streets had to be totally cleared. Today, it looks like a fool's errand against nuclear holocaust, but back then it was taken very seriously. In 1956, she was jailed for five days for protesting these inane drills. In 1957, she got thirty days. She was arrested in 1958, but let off, but rebounded in 1959 with a five-day sentence. The city soon came to its senses and abandoned the asinine drills.

It would not be her last time in the calaboose. In 1973, at the age of seventy-five, she was imprisoned for protesting with Cesar Chavez and the United Farm Workers in California.

DOROTHY DAY, POLITICIAN

The man Dorothy Day had to duel with most of her life was Archbishop of New York Francis Cardinal Spellman. Since his death, Spellman's reputation has taken a hit as his homosexual proclivities have come into the public knowledge. He had a propensity for Broadway chorus boys and his nickname among them was "Aunt Franny."

And the stories about his outrageous sexual behavior are still coming to light as proven by Lucian K. Truscott IV's article on Salon.com in 2019 called "I Was Groped by a Man Called 'Mary,'"—Mary, AKA Aunt Franny—about the time Truscott, as a West Point cadet, went to interview Spellman at his Madison Avenue residence and ended up being repeatedly felt up by the cardinal. And this all happened with a monsignor at Spellman's side who would admonish, "Now, now, eminence." Apparently, it was common knowledge what Spellman was up to.[58]

But while he was archbishop of New York he ruled with an iron fist and neither priest nor politician would cross him. Today he is known more for his real estate genius than for the ecclesiastic shepherding of his Catholic flock.

Day, for all her good works, was no fool and knew how to cover her back.

Maurice Isserman, in his Michael Harrington biography, wrote that Day "had no problem at all with acknowledging the church's authority, even as she did her best to subvert the authority of the secular state. As she once proclaimed famously, 'If the Chancery [the administrative offices of the New York diocese] ordered me to stop publishing the *Catholic Worker* tomorrow, I would.'"

According to Isserman, Harrington "would later call Day 'a real Pius XII Catholic,' and he complained that her habit of referring to arch-conservative Cardinal Spellman as 'our dear, sweet cardinal' drove him crazy."

It's amazing the rebel in Day would be so subservient to such reactionaries, but there may have been a genius guiding her acquiescence. "In March 1951," Isserman wrote, "Day was summoned by the New York Chancery office and ordered by Monsignor Edward Gaffney either to cease publication of her newspaper or drop the word 'Catholic' from its title. The paper's outspoken pacifism and its casual use of the world 'anarchism' had drawn complaints from influential conservative Catholics.

Day consulted with the staff of the paper. She recorded in her journal that Michael [Harrington], who had been at the *Worker* for only a month at that point, 'urges me to fortitude and the fighting against obscurantism in the Church.' Day smoothed over the controversy with a letter to the Chancery promising to do better in observing proprieties. Both Michael and fellow editor Bob Ludlow, to whom she showed the letter before mailing it, disapproved of her approach. They were humiliated by her submissive tone. But since the paper did not change its tone or politics noticeably in the months and years to come and continued to use the word 'Catholic' in its title, Day's tactical retreat proved the wisest course."

Day wrote in *The Long Loneliness* of her suspicions about being surveilled by the archdiocese: "In New York the Chancery office had also been informed of our activities, and when a priest came to see us in our Tenth Avenue headquarters during the seamen's strike the visit was immediately reported. This happened often enough to indicate to me that there were spies from the employers among the strikers and that the employers felt that the Church was on their side in any industrial dispute. The worker present at Mass was in the eyes of bishop and priest just like any member of Knights of Columbus or Holy Name Society, but as soon as he went on strike he became a dangerous radical, and the publicity he got linked him with saboteurs and Communists."

"In light of the archbishop's attacks against liberals, his priests were confused when Spellman failed to move against Dorothy Day," wrote John Cooney in *The American Pope: The Life and Times of Francis Cardinal Spellman.* "Spellman, however, wasn't a man who looked for trouble. He shrewdly realized that censuring Dorothy Day would create more problems than it would solve. Though her newspaper had a circulation of 150,000, the number of people active in her movement was small; their numbers and influence might increase if he focused more attention on her. Moreover, such a move wouldn't be popular in the Church. Chancellor McIntyre almost superstitiously gave money to Day's selfless cause. She was a reminder of what many priests had once intended doing with their lives. When asked why he didn't silence her, Spellman appeared momentarily startled. 'She might be a saint,' he replied."[59]

PETER MAURIN—DOROTHY DAY'S INSPIRATION AND SVENGALI

Probably the most important man in Dorothy Day's life was Peter Maurin (1877-1949), a Christian philosopher—for lack of a better description—from southern France. He was sent to her by mutual friends and she was starry-eyed from their first meeting. *The Long Loneliness* reads like a paean to Maurin. Day nearly gushes like a young girl when speaking about Maurin, who basically comes across as being a totally eccentric spiritualist. His influence was so great that they decided to start a newspaper to jump-start the movement. He wanted to call it the *Catholic Radical*, but Day prevailed with the *Catholic Worker*. The irony is that Maurin wanted the paper to be a booming voice for his philosophy—Peter Maurin and only Peter Maurin—while Day wanted it to be about the causes she cherished—injustice, poverty, the labor movement, etc. In this one instance, Day was able to win out over Maurin and the *Catholic Worker* was almost an instant success, reaching a circulation of 150,000 by 1936.

The Long Loneliness is chock full of vignettes dealing with Maurin. Here's a sampling:

"He believed in poverty and loved it and felt it a liberating force."

"He ate on the Bowery when he was in New York, at cheap restaurants of poor fare. If he had no money he went without food. He always advised people to beg if they were in need. But I know he did not like to beg himself. He preferred to go without. I used to taunt him gently with this."

"He delighted in the title of agitator."

"Peter made you feel a sense of his mission as soon as you met him."

"Peter was no dreamer but knew men as they were. That is why he spoke so much of the need for a philosophy of work."

"Peter's Christian philosophy of work was this, God is our creator. God made us in His image and likeness. Therefore we are creators."

"Peter liked to talk about the four-hour day. Four hours for work, four hours for study and discussion; but he didn't practice it." "

It seems that Peter Maurin was the man Day had sought throughout her life. The relationship was purely spiritual, but you can see the genuine trust she placed in Maurin by what she said about him in eulogy: "He was a man with a mission, a vision, an apostolate, but he had put off from himself honors, prestige, recognition. He was truly humble of heart. Never a word of detraction passed his lips and as St. James said, the man who governs his tongue is a perfect man. He was impersonal in his love in that he loved all, saw all others around him as God saw them, saw Christ in them."

DOROTHY DAY, ALL WOMAN

Day was no plaster saint. She was a woman with needs and wants. Yet it appears she shunned those needs and wants for the good of the movement. She wrote in *The Long Loneliness* that "Once a Midwest priest said to me that if I were a woman of family, the things I wrote in the *Catholic Worker* about community and personalism would have more validity. I accepted his criticism at the moment, especially since I was going through a difficult time. I was thirty-eight, wishing I were married and living the ordinary naturally happy life and had not come under the dynamic influence of Peter Maurin. Every now and then I'd look at him and groan, 'Why did you have to start all this anyway?'"

"Yet men are terrified of momism and women in turn want a shoulder to lean on. That conflict was in me. A woman does not feel whole without a man. And for a woman who had known the joys of marriage, yes, it was hard. It was years before I awakened without that longing for a face pressed against my breast, an arm about my shoulder. The sense of loss was there. It was a price I had paid. I was Abraham who had sacrificed Isaac. And yet I had Isaac. I had Tamar."

DOROTHY DAY—MOVIE STAR AND CELEBRITY

After death, Day was given the full Hollywood treatment. One of the surprising things about Warren Beatty's *Reds* is that she is not in it, because so many of her friends—Eugene O'Neill and John Reed, in particular—are prominent.

She has been celebrated in a full-length documentary *Dorothy Day: Don't Call Me a Saint* and in a book by her granddaughter Kate Hennessy, *Dorothy Day: The World Will Be Saved by Beauty.*

And although she didn't make the cut for *Reds*, she had her own movie in 1996 called *Entertaining Angels: The Dorothy Day Story* which starred Moira Kelly as Day and Martin Sheen as Peter Maurin.

It certainly was a long way from the Hell Hole, but perhaps not that far a walk from sainthood.

CHAPTER THREE
FATHER MYCHAL JUDGE

THE PADRE OF THE FDNY WAS THE REAL IRISH NEW YORK SAINT OF 9/11

As I arise on this September morn
The sun is beaming down, the streets are warm
God's in His heaven and all is well
I will go forth and do His will.
—"Mychal" by Larry Kirwan

Mychal Judge was born on May 11, 1933 and from the beginning he was unique—he beat his twin sister Dympna out of the womb by two days.

There was no one more Irish New York than Brooklyn's Father Mychal Judge, who was killed on 9/11. Both his parents were immigrants from County Leitrim, his mother Mary Ann Judge, née Fallon, was a member of Cumann na mBan during the War of Independence. He was baptized Robert Emmett after the legendary Irish revolutionary, Robert Emmet.

The young Judge was known to all as "Emmett." One of the traumatizing events of his childhood was when his father Michael died when he was six. Years later he would try to assuage this trauma by choosing "Mychal" as his new moniker. He was brought up by the stern Mary Ann. Emmett was a religious child and was devoted to the Sacred Heart. This probably surprised his mother, who although a Catholic, thought Ireland was a "priest ridden" country and was very anticlerical. "She retained an anti-clerical streak not unknown among Irish rebels," wrote Michael Daly in his biography of Judge, *The Book of Michael*. She is quoted as saying, "Too much religion is no good for anybody."[60]

It is important to remember that Mary Ann Judge was a member of the militant Cumann na mBan, the women's auxiliary of the IRA. They were one of the most radical parts of the Republican movement and voted 419–63 against Michael Collins's Treaty in early 1922. They made people like Clarke, Pearse, MacDiarmada, and Collins look like moderates. Life would not be simple for Emmett and his sisters Erin and Dympna. "Their mother was one of the Irish," wrote Daly, "who, having been 'in service,' assumed the airs of those they had served. She moved like gentry through the scruff of South Brooklyn, maintaining her own sense of class."

By age thirteen Judge knew he wanted to become a priest, to the consternation of his mother. "In his mother's experience," wrote Daly, "the priesthood led not to sanctity and grace but to sanctimony and tyranny. She was emphatic in her opposition." And Judge soon found out that Franciscan seminary life was not a summer hayride.

"Fear, fear, fear," Daly quotes Judge in his biogrpahy. "Everything is about fear. I was filled with it every hour of every day. They controlled us by fear—Never once a positive word." His seminary days were filled with study and "taking the discipline"— whipping the bare back with a small cat-o'-nine-tails. Seminarians were allowed to write only three letters home a month. Somehow he got through it all and a month after John F. Kennedy was inaugurated president in 1961, Judge, age twenty-seven, was ordained a priest.

Judge went to the beat of a different theological drummer: one penance was for a woman to do something nice for someone; he never pushed young people to go to mass: "Young people are doing it their own way. They tell me they talk to God and I believe them. . . . God's grace is always there. He'll guide them. . . . We have to leave the kids in God's hands. He has His own way of working."

RETURNING TO THE BIG APPLE

For someone who loved New York City like Judge did, it was a sacrifice for him to be assigned to the suburbs of New York and New Jersey. After nearly a quarter of a century on the job, he decided to take a sabbatical in Canterbury, England. It was during this time that Judge's ostentatious ego began to emerge. In Canterbury he had a gold earring in his left earlobe and also a rattail braid on the back of his head. When added to the green shamrock tattoo he had gotten on his butt—"I'm not sure how it got there. But I'm sure it was a good idea at the time," he said—Judge had hit his own Woodstock trifecta in middle age.

The ego was noticed by others too, like rock musician Larry Kirwan, who would often see Judge while performing at Connolly's pub. "He adored the buzz and the bright lights. . . . He had an endearingly vain side," Kirwan wrote in *Green Suede Shoes*. "In the tumult and heat of our gigs, he was always immaculate with every hair on his head plastered into place. There was almost a shine off him—not the spiritual one that's so often mentioned now—but the physical. Rarely was a man so well shaved, scrubbed, and tastefully cologned. But that was just the outside, a façade, as it were. If you looked closely enough, you could feel the inner loneliness that enabled him to empathize with the private pain he saw in everyone else."

After Canterbury he returned to the heart of New York, staying at St. Francis of Assisi on West 31st Street, which was known as "the criminal court of the Catholic Church," servicing over eight hundred thousand desperate, anonymous sinners a year.

He immediately got to work on the homeless, getting clothes for them—his stash became known as the "Brooks Brothers of the homeless"—breadlines for the homeless; and, eventually, tending to his AIDS ministry. His personality was in full bloom. His life was changing and one of the changes was Judge's decision to quit the drink. In Daly's book he described himself as "Some Mother's Son. 230 Dean St., Irish, Catholic, Democrat, priest, gay and more. . . . No one (ever) asked me!"

It was also at this time that he decided he wanted to distinguish himself from the other Michaels in the friary, so he chose "Mychal." It was to honor the long-dead father he missed so much, Michael Judge. He was asked if it was the Irish spelling and he said it was. It was not. The Irish would be either Mícheál or Míceál and would not have been pronounced Michael, but "Me-haul."

He was soon recruited by the FDNY chaplain Father Julian Deeken to help him out with his job. "It's a very simple job," his predecessor told him in the most remarkable understatement of the century. Soon, Judge was known as "the Flying Fireman."

After Judge became the FDNY chaplain replacing Deeken, his run-ins with superiors like Cardinal O'Connor became more apparent. He did not have great love for the church hierarchy, calling them BFM—Big Fat Monsignors. His unorthodox views on Catholic tradition also brought him some heat: general absolution for firefighters—giving communion to non-Catholics. "He took all those stuffy church traditions," said firefighter Liam Flaherty, "and brought them into the twenty-first century for us. Made it a lot more palatable for the regular guy."

"Word of Judge's laxity reached the archdiocese" wrote Michael Daly, "and he received a scolding letter from a young chancery official that began, 'Are you the Father Judge who gives general absolution?' Judge immediately telephoned the official and angrily declared he had never brought disrespect or embarrassment to the Church he had loved and served nearly his entire life. 'Well, don't let it happen again,' the official sputtered, stunned by the force of Judge's response. Judge hung up and laughed. 'Madness,' he later said of the incident, 'Sheer madness.'" Monsignor Brady, according to Michael Daly, his counterpart as the Brooklyn-Queens FDNY chaplain, thought him to be an ostentatious showboater.

But he was beloved within the FDNY. He served firefighters with horrific burns while caring for their families. Everyone wanted Father Mike for church events, be they funerals, baptisms, or weddings. While other clerics lectured, Judge listened. That was the big difference.

Another example of the esteem he was held in came when TWA Flight 800 crashed off the Long Island coast on July 18, 1996. Frank Carven, whose sister was lost on the flight and met Judge in a hanger at JFK International Airport, said, "He was very unassuming. I don't know how to explain it. You felt very comfortable, very safe in his presence. It was just an amazing thing with all this commotion and confusion going on around you. You felt things were going to be okay."

While comforting the victims' families, Judge ran into Cardinal O'Connor, "Ah, Father Judge," said the Cardinal, "how good of you to come."

A victim's relative said to Judge, talking about O'Connor: "Why don't you come over and meet your boss?" to which Judge replied cryptically, "He really isn't my boss."

ON BEING IRISH

Mychal Judge was proud of his Irishness, which the shamrock on his butt may have attested to. Judge had a great affinity for the FDNY Emerald Society Pipes and Drums and he spoke at the opening of the memorial to the victims of the Great Famine in lower Manhattan:

God, Father of our City, of our Nation, we stand here today a people well fed, warmly clothed and securely sheltered—We come to bless this spot where 150 years ago our ancestors came with only the strips of cloth on their backs, no house to sleep in and no potato—their staff of life—to fill their bellies. Nothing but faith, deep faith in you, faith in this blessed land you brought them to and faith in each other. And so, with faith, they built the churches, they paved the streets and dug the subways. To them today we erect and dedicate this monument, for all to see—their immigrant faith—and to renew our spirit of faith in you and each other on our immigrant journey to your heavenly kingdom. Amen.

He was involved in the peace process for Northern Ireland too: "Judge was not some diddlydee Irish American who sang the old rebel songs and romanced the modern Troubles as if it was the terrible beauty of 1916," wrote Daly. "He also was not star-struck as so many others at the gathering seemed to be. He was for all his merriment as serious about Ireland as he ultimately was about his faith. He focused on what he saw as good in [Gerry] Adams just as he did with everybody he encountered. He saw Adams as a true rebel, one who could finally bring a just peace to the North."

"You could see the expression on their faces and their eyes," said Steven McDonald in Daly's biography recalling the Adams-Judge relationship. "They were locked in on something important to both."

Adams considered Judge to be "a holy man."

SEX AND THE CELIBATE FRIAR

There's been lots of speculation about the sexuality of Father Mychal Judge. Oddly enough, he was pretty straightforward about the whole thing.

"Sexually," Judge admitted, "I am alive as I can be. The thoughts, the drives, the desires are there always."

"Judge confided," wrote Michael Daly, "that he had come away unsure whether he was gay or straight, maybe not bi but omnisexual, drawn not so much to men or to women as to all God's adult human creations. 'I didn't know what I was,' Judge said, according to [Ron] Pesci's recollection. 'I was this. I was that. I had all kinds of feelings.'"

"Sexual attraction continued to be an undeniable factor in Judge's popularity among the women of the parish," wrote Daly. "[Tom] Ferriter would recall a night shortly after Judge arrived when he attended a basketball game at the local high school wearing a gray herringbone sports coat with elbow patches rather than clerical garb. 'Every woman in that place was looking at him,' Ferriter would recall. 'A few ladies told me after a few drinks they would never cheat on their husbands, but if Michael Judge wanted to put his shoes under their bed, tell him to come over.'"

His link to homosexual behavior seems to have gone back to his days at the semi-nary. "I was the only one—so I thought," he wrote in his private journal. "We never knew, or if we did, we never discussed anything gay. I was madly in love—whatever that meant—with so many students. But I am not sure that I knew what it was all about. I did know that you were thrown out—next train—for being caught in any kind of sexual activity. I did not try it, but I had a boldness and was willing to take the chance if the chance came—Wow! How in God's name did I do 13 years of the cele-bate[sic] existence demanded of us in such a strong, straight and gay manly life? I know I am disciplined—I can do anything I put my mind to—It might be brutal—but—I'll stick to it to the end—Faithful, too."

"No one, absolutely no one lives two fuller separate lives than I do," Judge once wrote in his personal journal, apparently alluding to his gayness. "Well, I am so blessed and my life is so good. . . . Thank you Lord for all that you have given me, for all you have taken away and for all that is left."

Late in life he made a commitment to Al Alvarado, a young nurse from the island of Mindanao in the Philippines. Alvarado was young enough to be Judge's son. "Judge had long ago declared himself a servant to his God," wrote Daly, "a groom only to Christ, but Alvarado's boldness engendered a boldness in him that he remembered from his younger years. He was embarking on what would be the closest he would ever come to a long-term relationship with a man even as he was becoming ever more certain that his place as a priest was with firefighters who would almost certainly be repulsed by such a relationship. He stood before two eager and irresistible embraces that seemed to preclude each other, that seemingly could not be any less like twins."

But even Alvarado came in second to God: "He told me going into it," quoted Daly. "He told me at the beginning he could only see me so much; it could only go so far." Alvarado was realistic, "My rival was God."

Alvarado—who incidentally was not allowed to attend Judge's funeral because no one knew who he was—had an interesting observation about Judge, "I think he spent most of his life in purgatory." In the end, he was happy for the years they had together. "It was a good ten years. I would have liked another ten years, but it was a good ten years."

THE JUDGE WHO CHALLENGED "LAW AND ORDER"

Back in the 1980s the orthodoxy of the Roman Catholic Church was enforced on the East Coast of the United States by two Irishmen, Bernard Cardinal Law in Boston and John Cardinal O'Connor in New York. They soon became known as "Law and Order." They were the Polish Pope's one-two clerical punch to any who would argue against Church doctrine on homosexuality, birth control, or any other social issue that the Church chose to ignore. And it is not surprising that Mychal Judge's boss, Cardinal O'Connor, would come to loathe the friar from West 31st Street. "He couldn't stand me," stated Judge emphatically in Daly's biography.

A lot of it may have had to do with Judge's AIDS ministry.

"For several months [Judge] thought he was going to be dispatched to Japan for missionary work there," Steven McDonald recalled in his autobiography. "When Patti Ann would speak to him on the phone she'd end the conversation with, 'Sayonara, Father.' He himself said he'd been looking for some sign, some indication from God the Father as to what he should do, and that fall he'd found it. His superior at the Friary asked him to counsel AIDS victims in New York City and he'd accepted the assignment eagerly."

That ministry put him in direct opposition to O'Connor, a man often called a "hatemonger" by AIDS victims. "The reason, as every gay person knew," wrote Daly in his Judge biography,

> was that O'Connor still subscribed to official Church doctrine. The Vatican's "Halloween Letter" of October 1986 termed homosexuality a morally unacceptable "objective disorder" and barred gay groups from Church property. The same cardinal who emptied bedpans evicted the gay organization Dignity from the Manhattan church where its weekly Masses sometimes outdrew those at St. Patrick's Cathedral.
>
> O'Connor also joined his Boston counterpart, Law, in opposing a thirty-page position paper issued by the U.S. Conference of Catholic Bishops that proposed teaching in Catholic institutions that condoms could prevent AIDS. The paper emphasized that this should be done only while also teaching sexual abstinence outside of marriage, but O'Connor nonetheless told the press that

the bishops had committed a "very grave mistake." He declared that there would be no talk of condoms in his "jurisdiction."

"What others call bigotry," Daly quotes O'Connor, "we call principle. We extend our hearts to them, but we will not retreat one iota from our faith."

While O'Connor stood aloof with his holier-than-thou attitude toward AIDS victims, Judge was hands-on ministering to them. "Judge was himself on the way to being as well known among AIDS suffers as he was among the poor," wrote Daly, "and the gay community was coming to claim him as one of their own. He had said the occasional Dignity Mass, and he often spoke in the first-personal plural at AIDS funerals, though he also used 'we' at weddings and baptisms, and later would do so at fire funerals. He made no public declarations regarding his sexuality. He made no direct references to it in his private journal recording the start of his AIDS ministry."

Also, Judge's close relationship with Officer Steven McDonald, the young cop who was wounded in action and confined to a wheelchair for the rest of his life, seemed to injure O'Connor's delicate ego. "Judge was aware the cardinal had become jealous of his closeness to the McDonalds," wrote Daly. "Steven McDonald . . . was coming to see Judge more and more as Christ returned to earth in Brooklyn Irish form."

"Cardinal O'Connor would have given up his robes to be a Father Mychal," Daly reported that McDonald later said.

There is an interesting aside in Steven and Patti Ann McDonald's autobiography about the naming of their son, Conor, who many think was named after the cardinal. "If it was a girl we decided to name her Caitlin," wrote Patti Ann. "If a boy, we'd call him Conor Patrick, after the hero of Leon Uris's novel *Trinity*. The name Conor confused a number of people, who assumed I'd named him after the Cardinal."

Another sign of pettiness on O'Connor's part was that he was not happy when Judge became FDNY chaplain. "John Cardinal O'Connor was known to twitch visibly at the mention of the name Mychal Judge," wrote Daly. "The prospect of Judge replacing [FDNY Chaplain Julian] Deeken must have been particularly galling because traditionally fire chaplains are chosen by the cardinal."

Leading up to Judge's appointment as the FDNY chaplain for Manhattan, the Bronx, and Staten Island, there was a whispering campaign going on that Judge was an active homosexual and had approached a fireman for sex. Judge, according to

Daly, "suspected somebody in the cardinal's office was behind the whispering but had no proof."

While O'Connor wanted to aggressively shun Catholic homosexuals, he was not as aggressive when it came to priests molesting children in his archdiocese. Doing his best Pontius Pilate impression, O'Connor, according to Daly, said, "so many times I have wanted to cry out to say what I really feel . . . unfortunately, the archbishop of New York is a legal entity as well as being a moral and spiritual and religious leader." The fifty million dollars in lawsuits pending against the archdiocese may have had something to do with his attitude.

There was a lot of jealousy and pettiness in the way O'Connor treated Judge. When Capt. John Drennan died in a fire, O'Connor offered the Cathedral to his wife Vina for the funeral. She was delighted and declared on the phone to O'Connor himself, "And Father Judge can say the Mass!" O'Connor expected to say the mass himself.

"The cardinal didn't want [Judge] to say the Mass," Rudy Giuliani said later. Daly wrote, "the scowling cardinal was so manifestly displeased or because this happened to be his sixty-first birthday."

O'Connor died in 2000. Bernard Law had problems of his own up in Boston. Under intense pressure because of the rampant pedophilia of many of his priests and the massive cover-up orchestrated by Law himself, he resigned in 2002 and quickly took off for Rome in case he should be indicted. His plight was dramatized in the Oscar-winning film *Spotlight*. Law died in Rome in 2017.

Shakespeare wrote that "The evil that men do lives after them; The good is oft interred with their bones." Maybe for O'Connor and Law. Not so with Mychal Judge.

PRELUDE TO 9/11

On September 10, 2001, Mychal Judge's penultimate day on earth, he traveled to the Bronx. "The ancient firehouse of Engine Co. 73 and Ladder Co. 42 had been rebuilt," wrote Terry Golway in So *Others Might Live*, "like the neighborhood it served, and on September 10, a ceremony would commemorate not only the building's rehabilitation, but the revival of a borough left in ashes during the 1970s."[61]

At the ceremony, Judge would speak. "There was no mystery about Father Judge's popularity," wrote Golway. "He loved being with firefighters, and he sounded like one, with a New York accent that paid scant attention to hard *r*'s. And he was a superb speaker. He talked in complete sentences, with the cadence of a poet. Though he seemed modest, he must have taken great pride in his voice, for he was not afraid to break into song, and seemed unaware that the results were decidedly mixed."

"That's the way it is," Judge told the assembled guests, "Good days, bad days. Up days, down days. Sad days, happy days—but never a boring day on this job. You do what God has called you to do. You show up, you put one foot in front of another, you get on the rig and you do the job, which is a mystery and a surprise. You have no idea when you get on that rig, no matter how big the call, no matter how small, you have no idea what God's calling you to do.

"You love this job," he continued. "We all do. What a blessing that is. A difficult, difficult job, and God calls you to it, and he gives you love for it, so that a difficult job will be well done. Isn't He a wonderful God? Isn't He good to you, to each one of you? And to me. Turn to Him each day, put your faith and your trust and your life in His hands, and He'll take care of you, and you'll have a good life.

"You do what God has called you to do," he continued. "You show up, you put one foot in front of the other, and you do your job, which is a mystery and a surprise. You have no idea, when you get on that rig, what God is calling you to. But He needs you . . . so keep going. Love each other. Work together. You love the job. We all do. What a blessing that is."

In closing Judge recited the prayer of St. Francis of Assisi: "Where there is hatred, let me sow love. . . . Where there is darkness, light, and where there is sadness, joy."

"When Mass was over," Golway wrote, "Father Judge led the congregants in singing 'America, the Beautiful,' attacking the high notes with a bravery that matched the setting. The congregation applauded, and retired to trade small talk, handshakes and old war stories."

9/11

When the first plane hit the North Tower at 8:50 a.m. on September 11, Mychal Judge was napping at the friary on 31st Street. He immediately went across the street and took his official chaplain's car downtown. He took up his post in the lobby of the North Tower and observed as firemen rushed in and ascended by foot to fight the fires so far above.

In a video called *Saint of 9/11: The True Story of Father Mychal Judge* you can see Judge standing alone, praying as fast as he could. Lt. Mickey Kross of Engine 16 looked at Judge and got a shock. "He was kind of like praying, and he looked very troubled. That scared me. I got a chill."[62]

Later on, another firefighter told him, "You should go, Padre."

"I'm not finished," replied Judge.

By now jumpers were beginning to hit the street. Then a second plane hit the South Tower. Judge stood his ground in the North Tower. Firefighters could hear Judge praying, "Jesus, please end this right now! God, please end this!"

Although hit after the North Tower, the South Tower collapsed first, at 9:59 a.m. Judge was still on station in the lobby of the North Tower when the South Tower collapsed, sending a tornado of blinding dust into the North Tower.

It killed Mychal Judge.

And since he had no visible injuries, Daly speculated that "he may have been literally frightened to death."

NYPD uniformed officer Jose Alfonso Rodriguez came across Judge's body in the street. "There was a person laying on a corner," Rodriguez recalled on the *Saint of 9/11* DVD, "laying there and he had his jacket over his head. I see the lieutenant and he was telling me, 'Could someone go get this man a priest? It's the fire department chaplain.' I try to think of myself as a good Catholic, so I knew where there was the closest Catholic Church. I ran up to it around the corner. There was a lady there and she was ripping up linen. So I asked her, I said, 'Is there a priest here?' 'Not here. There's nobody here. They all went to help.' She told me, 'Are you Catholic?' Yeah. 'Well, in an emergency you can give last rites.' Well, I was an altar boy. I never thought I'd get promoted that fast, so I ran back. We both knelt down and we said an Our Father, I believe, A Glory Be to the Father.'"

He was eventually evacuated to St. Peter's Catholic Church and laid on the altar by firefighters—a symbol of the martyrdom suffered by three thousand New Yorkers that day.

THE SAINT OF 9/11?

"The Fire Department's general orders for September 13, 2001," wrote Terry Golway, "announced the deaths and pending funerals of Chief of Department Peter Ganci, Jr., Fire Deputy Commissioner William Feehan, and Chaplain Mychal Judge. They died, in the dry language of the department's bureaucracy, 'as [a] result of injuries sustained while operating at Manhattan Box 8087, transmitted at 0847 hours on September 11, 2001.' The funerals of all three were held on September 15. Hundreds more would follow." Judge's death certificate is listed as "Number One" of all the 9/11 deaths.

Mychal Judge's funeral was, of course, held at St. Francis of Assisi Church on West 31st Street. The rich and powerful and the poor and powerless were in attendance.

The noted Mennonite poet Ann Hostetler wrote in "Transfiguration" as if she was talking about Judge and 9/11:

> [A]s inner walls gave way, the process
> of return beginning. At the hospital entrance,
> I met the women weeping—mother, sister, niece,
> pastor—who told me the story of his last
> breath, which I imagine now

Already there is talk of making Mychal Judge a saint. In 2017, Ruth Graham wrote an article on Slate.com entitled "Could Father Mychal Judge Be the First Gay Saint?" The title of the piece brings a smile because, there being an estimated ten thousand Catholic saints, what are the statistical odds that not *one* of them was gay?

But Graham makes a good point in that the Vatican in July 2017 "expanded its criteria for sainthood, creating a new category for people who willingly sacrifice their lives for others: *oblatio vitae*, the 'offering of life.' This new category of saints does not need to have been killed directly because of their faith, and they need display only 'ordinary' virtue."[63] This new category certainly opens up a path to sainthood for Father Mike.

And Judge certainly wasn't a plaster saint by any means. Malachy McCourt recalls in *Saint of 9/11* a conversation he had with him years ago. "One of the most significant conversations I had with him was when I was going through an extremely bad time," McCourt recalled.

Everything had gone wrong in my life. My marriage was very rocky. My wife Diane and I were separated for a while. I was broke, literally broke. I was on welfare getting $270 a month and food stamps and had to go sign up for that at the age of 55 I guess I was, and I was humiliated.

I didn't know the difference between having humility and humiliation and Mychal Judge did. But talking to him one day about what I had fallen to. I had been on the peak of great success, having saloons, being on television, in films, talk shows hosts and everything else and here I am on my arse and no hope I thought. And he said to me, and I'll never forget this, he said my God he said, and you can have if you want, is all powerful, but my God has despite his power and his all-knowing and his divinity has not yet made tomorrow. So for you to worry about the future is not too good an idea because God not having made tomorrow does not know what's going to happen. God does not know what is going to happen. He has not made the future, he said, so who the fuck do you think you are?!

Larry Kirwan remembers Judge showing up at several of his performances. "Who knows if he was a saint and who cares?" Kirwan wrote in *Green Suede Shoes*. "He was the better part of us all. I barely knew the man; to me, he was another punter who came to Connolly's to let off a little steam. It was hard to ignore him, though even when he wasn't in his robes. For he was a mirror into which you looked and saw the good side of yourself. When you spoke to him, the conversation was all about you. It wasn't just that he was interested, he knew that each human has a need to be the center of attention for even a couple of minutes. He could sense the sorrow that's at the heart of us all, and he could identify its manifestation in each person. He couldn't walk away without ministering to that pain or hurt in some way."

St. Mychal. Nice ring to it.

CHAPTER FOUR
OFFICER STEVEN McDONALD

"GOD'S COP" WAS ALSO A SAINTLY, FORGIVING FENIAN

On July 12, 1986, NYPD plainclothes officer Steven McDonald was on patrol near the boathouse in Central Park when he spotted three black youths loitering. In *Why Forgive?*, McDonald described what happened next:

> While questioning them, I noticed a bulge in the pant leg of the youngest boy— it looked like he might have a gun tucked into one of his socks. I bent down to examine it. As I did, I felt someone move over me, and as I looked up, the taller of the three (he turned out to be 15) was pointing a gun at my head. Before I knew what was happening, there was a deafening explosion, the muzzle flashed, and a bullet struck me above my right eye. I remember the reddish-orange flame that jumped from the barrel, the smell of the gunpowder, and the smoke. I fell backward, and the boy shot me a second time, hitting me in the throat. Then, as I lay on the ground, he stood over me and shot me a third time. I was in pain; I was numb; I knew I was dying, and I didn't want to die. It was terrifying. My partner was yelling into his police radio: "Ten Thirteen Central! Ten Thirteen!" and when I heard that code, I knew I was in a very bad way. Then I closed my eyes.[64]

When he opened his eyes again he discovered that he was paralyzed from the neck down. Immediately, he was recognized as a hero. Steven McDonald was special, and New York City loved him as only the Big Apple can love someone. And McDonald was special in more ways than one, as the city would come to realize, because he would soon be recognized as a man who almost made the supreme sacrifice for his city, but was capable of forgiving Shavod Jones, the boy who had robbed him of a normal life.

"LIVING FORGIVENESS"

"Then," wrote McDonald in *Why Forgive?*, "about six months after I was shot, Patti Ann gave birth to a baby boy. We named him Conor. To me, Conor's birth was like a message from God that I should live, and live differently. And it was clear to me that I had to respond to that message. I prayed that I would be changed, that the person I was would be replaced by something new.

"That prayer was answered with a desire to forgive the young man who shot me. I wanted to free myself of all the negative, destructive emotions that his act of violence had unleashed in me: anger, bitterness, hatred, and other feelings. I needed to free myself of those emotions so that I could love my wife and our child and those around us."[65]

McDonald was cognizant that many in minority communities viewed police—especially Irish cops—as the enemy. "I was a badge to that kid," he wrote,

a uniform representing the government. It was the system that let landlords charge rent for squalid apartments in broken-down tenements; I was the city agency that fixed up poor neighborhoods and drove the residents out, through gentrification, regardless of whether they were law abiding solid citizens, or pushers and criminals; I was the Irish cop who showed up at a domestic dispute and left without doing anything, because no law had been broken.

To Shavod Jones, I was the enemy. He didn't see me as a person, as a man with loved ones, as husband and father-to-be. He'd bought into all the stereotypes of his community: the police are racist, they'll turn violent, so arm yourself against them. And I couldn't blame him. Society—his family, the social agencies responsible for him, the people who's made it impossible for his parents to be together—had failed him way before he had met me in Central Park.

I forgave Shavod because I believe the only thing worse than receiving a bullet in my spine would have been to nurture revenge in my heart. Such an attitude would have extended my injury to my soul, hurting my wife, my son, and others even more. It's bad enough that the physical effects are permanent, but at least I can choose to prevent spiritual injury.

McDonald reached out to Shavod Jones while he was in prison and they communicated via letter. They never really became close. Four days after being paroled in 1995, Jones was killed in a motorcycle accident.

"When I was a very young kid," McDonald recalled in *Why Forgive?*, "Dr. King came to my town in New York. My mother went to hear him speak, and she was very impressed by what she heard. I hope you can be inspired by his words too. Dr. King said that there's some good in the worst of us, and some evil in the best of us, and that when we learn this, we'll be more loving and forgiving. He also said, 'Forgiveness is not an occasional act, it's a permanent attitude.' In other words, it is something you have to work for. Just like you have to work to keep your body fit and your mind alert, you've got to work on your heart too. Forgiving is not just a one-time decision. You've got to *live* forgiveness, every day."

"WE REMEMBER OUR ROOTS, TOO"

McDonald wrote:

Irish Catholic cops, I'd always felt, were especially sensitive to the problems of minorities in New York. Black community leaders try to say white cops are racist, that they represent and defend a different class. But we remember our roots, too. My family had come to America without anything, driven from their homeland because the British had confiscated everything of value. I'd read the stories of women and children who'd died by the sides of country roads, their mouths stained with the grass they'd eaten trying to keep themselves alive. One of my great-grandmothers had been an indentured servant just a century ago, the only position she could find. And my father's family had emigrated after the First Famine, carrying almost nothing with them across the Atlantic, on the coffin ships. My family's story is that of many Irish Catholics who found a haven in the Police Department. Much of that has not changed for newly arrived Irish citizens.

THE FENIAN COP

An astute Irish novelist once wrote that "love may make the world go around, but hate gives you a reason for living!" That sentiment has driven Irish revolutionaries for three centuries in their fight against the English. Fenians are not known to have the forgiveness gene in their DNA, but Steven was a different kind of Fenian.

From his wheelchair McDonald began to take a rapid interest in the events happening in Northern Ireland in the 1980s. It began when he became an Irish citizen.

"I'd become more and more outspoken in defense of Catholics in Ulster ever since the Republic of Ireland bestowed citizenship upon me in April [1988]" he wrote in *The Steve McDonald Story* which he collaborated on with his wife Patti Ann and writer E. J. Kahn III. "That had taken an extraordinary vote of the Dáil and the Seanad, the two branches of the Irish legislature. Technically, I hadn't been eligible to become an Irish citizen; I was third-generation removed from Eire. But the Prime Minister himself, Taoiseach Charles J. Haughey, had interceded. And on August 21, he'd taken time out from a trip to the United Nations to personally confer the honor upon me. 'The Irish have made a unique contribution to this great country, the United States,' he'd said, as my family and Mayor Koch listened with pride, 'in many fields of endeavor, but I don't think there is any area in which they have made a more significant or courageous contribution than in the police service.'"[66]

The man who served as a catalyst for McDonald's Irish nationalism was Joe Doherty, who the British and American governments like to refer to as a "terrorist." Doherty was a member of the Provisional IRA who was imprisoned for killing a member of the notorious British SAS [Special Air Service], a latter-day military outfit that Irish nationalists liken to the Black and Tans of an earlier era. In 1981, Doherty made a daring escape from the Crumlin Road Jail and set out for the safety of New York City. He made a living tending bar until an informer tipped off the cops.

"The authorities then arrested him," wrote McDonald, "on fugitive charges for fleeing Northern Ireland after he and other colleagues had shot a British army captain named Wes Maycott. The Justice Department wanted to extradite him and had interred him upstate at Otisville; Cardinal O'Connor had interceded, and he'd been brought back to the city. Joe and I had begun to communicate early in the year by mail. What I was reading in these letters was not what was being released by the media in Northern Ireland, which was controlled by the British government. I had to do more. Someone had to listen to Joe. . . . If there were no DIPLOCK courts, there would be no need for the Joe Dohertys. The British don't belong there."

THE COP WHO QUOTED ROGER CASEMENT
"Any claim," wrote McDonald in his autobiography,

that the confrontations in East New York or the South Bronx are similar to the fighting on the streets of Belfast is absurd. Just absurd. We don't have a shoot-to-kill policy, like the SAS forces under the direction of the British government, or the Royal Ulster Constabulary, which represents the Protestant government. In those Irish neighborhoods, there is war. And, I believe, Irish Catholic citizens—and I can now proudly include myself—have to take stands. Joe Doherty signs his letters "Irish Republican Army Prisoner of War."

I believe that to be true.

Even before I became an Irish citizen, I'd spoken my mind . . . at a couple of Irish-American affairs I'd been invited to. At the Holy Name Society, I'd quoted Roger Casement: "Ireland has outlived the failure of all her hopes—and yet she still hopes," and then I said, "We hope for an Ireland united in the spirit of life, not divided by the spirit of death and dissension. We dream for an Ireland where civility, not barbarity, is the order of the day." When a reporter had asked me if I was speaking to the Thatcher government's support of the ruling Protestants, I'd said bluntly, "The British should get out."

When I first learned about Joe Doherty—how he'd devoted his life, since he was eighteen, to the cause of reunifying north and south Ireland—I thought of . . . the inconsistencies in my own life. I'd never done as well in high school as I might've. I'd never committed myself to cause or ideal. As a cop, I'd sometimes been lazy. But Joe Doherty had never done that. He hadn't married, hadn't had any children, and had given his whole life fighting the sins of others. And, as a result, for the past six years, he'd lived in a room half the size of my bedroom, a cubicle deliberately painted a depressing gray, without windows to see the blue sky or the stars at night.

When I first let friends and other police officers know how I felt, many were shocked. . . . [T]hey wondered how I could sympathize with a man who'd been convicted of killing a British officer. I don't pretend to understand the killing, I'd say. I think of the inconsistencies and the injustices in the legal system in the heart of Ireland where a British soldier, Private Ian Thain, convicted of murdering a Catholic citizen of the north, was released after two years and returned to active duty. I grieve for Captain Wes Maycott's widow and children. They're the innocent ones, like Patti Ann and Conor. But what happened to me and what happened to that Army officer are two separate situations. The situation in Northern Ireland is intolerable. Joe Doherty, the men he was with when Captain Wes Maycott died, and all the Catholics in Northern Ireland have the right to expect they'll be made a part of what's going on there and not be excluded by the British.

Steven also put his wheelchair where his mouth was. With his friend, Father Mychal Judge, he traveled to Northern Ireland to advance the peace process. "On August 15, 1998," wrote Michael Daly in his biography of Father Judge,

> word came from Ireland that extremists opposed to the peace process had detonated a bomb in the town of Omagh, killing twenty-six and injuring two hundred others. Judge and young Conor were at Steven McDonald's side when he held a press conference three days later to announce he was taking his message of forgiveness to Ireland in "Project Reconciliation."
>
> "First I will listen to their pain and feeling, then I will share my story," Steven told the reporters. "God has His design and He wants me to be His legs. . . . It's worth it all if I can help one person. . . . If I could change the heart and mind of one person." He and Judge then led the others in the Prayer of St. Francis. "Lord, make me an instrument of thy peace."

The prayers helped because the Good Friday Agreement stuck and has made Northern Ireland a better place to live for all parties. It also helped his friend Joe Doherty, who was released on November 6, 1998, under the terms of the Good Friday Agreement that McDonald fought hard to keep active. Doherty is now a community organizer, working with disadvantaged young people. Steven McDonald would have been proud.

"GOD'S COP"

"There's nothing easy about being paralyzed," McDonald wrote in his autobiography. "I have not been able to hold my wife in my arms for two decades. Conor is now a young man, and I've never been able to have a catch with him. It's frustrating—difficult—ugly—at times."

Even after being shot McDonald continued his career in the NYPD as an active policeman, finally achieving the rank of Detective, First Grade.

Steven McDonald died of a heart attack on January 10, 2017. The front page of the *New York Daily News* stated the obvious: GOD'S COP. But McDonald's passion for life lives on in his wife Patti Ann, who is the mayor of Malverne, Long Island, and his son, Conor, who is a sergeant on the NYPD, the fourth generation of McDonalds to serve in New York's Finest.

"When I was shot," McDonald wrote, "I asked God in a simple prayer, 'Please don't let me die.' I was found in the wilderness that's northern Central Park. I'm proof positive that God exists. . . . I know it looks bad the way I am. You might say, what's to be thankful about. But if you could see my child . . . I thank God for the gift of life."

Godspeed to God's Cop, Detective, First Grade, Steven McDonald.

PART SIX
VOTE EARLY, VOTE OFTEN
REAL *IRISH NEW YORK AND POLITICS*

T he Irish, both in Ireland and New York, know the power of the vote.

It was through Daniel O'Connell that Catholic emancipation came about in Ireland. It was through votes for Charles Stewart Parnell and the Irish Parliamentary Party that Home Rule advanced as a cause. And it was through the landslide general election of 1918 that *Dáil Éireann*, the parliament of an Irish state, came into existence.

The Irish brought this talent for politics with them to America. A prime example of an excellent New York politician was Archbishop John Hughes. He knew how to manipulate the powerful for his own means. With the massive number of Irish in New York after the Great Famine it was obvious that by the sheer force of their numbers the Irish would take control of the political apparatus in the city.

The Irish would be courted, and nurtured, by Tammany Hall. Almost all the Irish were Tammany supporters. In return for their vote, Tammany made sure you found a job and there might be shoes for the kids and a goose for Christmas. This power of the vote would not be restricted only to New York. It would go coast to coast: Boston, Philadelphia, Chicago, Kansas City, San Francisco, and Los Angeles. This power of the vote culminated in the election of John Fitzgerald Kennedy as the first Irish Catholic president in 1960. He would be assassinated three years later and nearly sixty years after his death he is still the only Catholic president in the history of the United States of America. That's one in forty-five. Geez, what are the odds, Vegas?

NO STARVING IN AMERICA

Terry Golway in his wonderful history of Tammany Hall, *Machine Made*, tells why the immigrant Irish took to politics and Tammany when they hit New York:

The Irish came to New York believing that the rules of politics were written to keep them powerless, as they had been in Ireland. When they saw the same class in New York observing the same rules, speaking the words of reform that sounded more like demands to conform, they saw no reason to turn their backs on politicians who recognized their opportunities and seized them, no reason to stand in judgment or rogues like Jimmy Walker and George Washington Plunkitt.

Once installed in power, the Irish in New York looked to government as a friend in need, a provider of last (or perhaps first) resort, as an advocate in a system constructed by others but now in their hands. They saw how power worked in Ireland. They knew that without power they might be left to starve in the name of abstract ideology. When they attained power in New York, they knew what to do with it—they made certain that they would not starve again, and that those who might allow it would be denied the power to do so.[67]

In other parts of this book we met up with Al Smith and Tammany leader "Silent" Charlie Murphy. In the early twentieth century both Smith and Murphy turned "progressive" and created important labor legislation which, along with other legislation, like Society Security, would turn into FDR's New Deal within twentieth years.

THE O'DWYERS OF COUNTY MAYO

There were many Irish politicians shaping New York politics in the twentieth century, including the O'Dwyer brothers of County Mayo. William O'Dwyer would serve his new country by becoming District Attorney of Brooklyn, prosecuting Murder, Inc., becoming a brigadier general in World War II, and finally becoming New York's hundredth mayor in 1946. He would be reelected mayor in 1949, but would resign under a cloud of corruption in 1950. Nothing was ever proved, and he was appointed ambassador to Mexico by President Truman. He died in New York in 1964.

Mayor O'Dwyer's brother Paul—younger by seventeen years—would be one of the most liberal New York politicians of the latter twentieth century. He was a proud supporter of the new Israel state and proclaimed that he was "a stakeholder for the *Haganah*," the Zionist military organization. Both O'Dwyer brothers supported Jews sending weapons to Israel in 1947 when they were harassed by the US government.

Paul also fought the United States government's harassment against Irish Americans who supported the Provisional IRA in the 1970s. Paul was one of the lawyers for the "Fort Worth Five"—New Yorkers who found themselves in a Texas jail because they would not inform for the federal government. Paul was instrumental in getting Supreme Court Associate Justice William O. Douglas to grant bail for the defendants. Paul was a perpetual candidate in New York and in 1973 he finally got elected as president of the New York City Council, where he served one term. He died in 1998 at the age of ninety-one. He remains to this day a hero to Irish New Yorkers.

In this section we will again meet up with Governor Smith and Silent Charlie because of their protégé, James J. Walker, the ninety-seventh mayor of the City of New York. Walker had a little bit of everything in him—charmer, angel, devil—which would turn him into one of New York favorite rogues, beloved, even in disgrace.

We will also take a look at how the modern political structure has changed in New York with a profile of the late James R. McManus, the Democratic boss of Hell's Kitchen.

Another grand collection of political saints and sinners in *Real* Irish New York.

CHAPTER ONE

MAYOR JAMES J. (JIMMY) WALKER

"THERE ARE THREE THINGS A MAN MUST DO ALONE. BE BORN, DIE, AND TESTIFY."

In the early 1960s Warner Bros. had a TV series on the ABC Network set in New York called *The Roaring 20's* starring the lovely Dorothy Provine as Pinky Pinkham, a nightclub entertainer who could do the Charleston and Black Bottom with a vengeance. It was based on the 1939 hit Warner movie starring James Cagney and Humphrey Bogart as battling bootleggers. The TV show opened with a video montage of speakeasies, bathtub gin, and Thompson submachine guns threatening the grand Protestant experiment called Prohibition.

Of course, the Master of Ceremonies over all this extravagant madness was the mayor, one James J. Walker, Esq.

I have to admit a weakness. I have a special fondness in my heart for rogues, especially political rogues. Like me, Jimmy Walker grew up in Greenwich Village and we walked the same parishes and streets. When I was a kid there was a bar called the Shortstop on 7th Avenue South right across the street from Greenwich House that had a huge picture of Walker in the window. And all the neighborhood kids played ball in James J. Walker Park, which was right across the street from Jimmy's home at #6 St. Luke's Place. So, even years after his death, Walker was a presence in the neighborhood.

And ghost-hunter Hans Holzer claimed that Walker's ghost, top hat and walking stick in full view, was still walking the stairs at #12 Gay Street. In *Ghosts: True Encounters with the World Beyond*, Holzer wrote, "Mayor Jimmy Walker owned the house, and used it *well*, although not *wisely*. One of his many loves is said to have been the tenant there. By a strange set of circumstances, the records of the house vanished like a ghost from the files of the Hall of Records around that time."[68] Holzer goes on to detail owner Frank Paris' encounter with the mayoral ghost. "I saw the ghost myself," Paris was quoted, "wearing evening clothes, a cape, hat, and his face somewhat obscured by the shadows of the hallway. Both Alice and I are sure he was a youngish man, and had sparkling eyes. What's more, our dog also saw the intruder. He went up to the ghost, friendly-like, as if to greet him." It seems everyone, even dogs, liked Jimmy Walker!

Bob Hope even made a movie about him (*Beau James*) that was more Hope than Walker. Jimmy would push the envelope on legality, but the man he once defeated for mayor—Fiorello La Guardia—would give him a job when he was down and out. He was tossed out by FDR, but when FDR needed his support in 1936 Walker was right behind the president.

Jimmy Walker was alternately known as "Beau James" or "New York's Night Mayor" and he was a Rogue Supreme. And like most of the Irish born in Manhattan in the late nineteenth century, his family were immigrants from Ireland and survivors of the Great Famine. His father William Henry Walker was from Castlecorner, County Kilkenny, and he first hit the streets of Greenwich Village in 1857. The elder Walker was a carpenter and builder by trade, but he soon came under Tammany influence and would eventually go to the New York State Assembly.

WILL YOU LOVE ME IN DECEMBER AS YOU DO IN MAY?

James John Walker was born on June 19, 1881, at 110 Leroy Street about two blocks from the Cunard and White Star piers that were patrolled by Irish longshoremen. He was baptized at St. Joseph's Church, the church that had once been the parish of John McCloskey, the first American cardinal. His prosperous father soon moved the family about a block away to #6 St. Luke's Place, one of the tonier streets in the Village. It appears that young Jimmy was an indifferent student and more interested in things like baseball and songwriting. He tried law school, but dropped out (he would eventually go back and get his degree).

He finally made some money writing songs. His biggest hit came in 1908 with the song "Will You Love Me in December as You Do in May?" It wasn't a bad song either:

Will you love me in December as you do in May?
Will you love me in the same old-fashioned way?

But Tammany had bigger plans for young Walker, and soon he took over his father's seat in the State Assembly. Blessed with looks, Irish charm, and wit, he soon became a favorite in the Assembly. Silent Charlie Murphy was captured by his charm, as was Al Smith. "This boy," said Smith as related by Herbert Mitgang in *Once Upon a Time in New York*, "is a greater strategist than General Sheridan and he rides twice as fast."[69]

After spending two years in the Assembly he went on to the Senate and soon made a reputation for himself by passing laws about workmen's compensation and legalizing Sunday baseball and boxing in New York State. His political career was off to a blazing start.

A CELTIC PEACOCK

Walker was always a dandy. His wardrobe was the talk of the town because all his suits—and they were innumerable—were all specially tailored to his precious measurements. Perhaps the best description of him is by Terry Golway in *Machine Made*, "And there was the mayor of New York, James J. Walker, a Celtic peacock with his movie-star looks and well-tailored suits, an immensely likable man always ready with a quip, a smile, and a handshake. Jimmy Walker was a Tammany man, too, with a fine record of support for social legislation during his years as a state lawmaker in Albany. In fact, they loved him because of his defiance of respectability, because he paid no attention to the bluenose moralists who were so quick to divide the world between good and evil, between Plymouth Rock and Ellis Island, between reformer and hack."

And Walker's suits played an important part in the image of Jimmy Walker, Mayor-About-Town. "Jimmy Walker's wardrobe," wrote Herbert Mitgang in *Once Upon a Time in New York: Jimmy Walker, Franklin Roosevelt, and the Last Great Battle of the Jazz Age*, "was very much a part of his personality and theatricality in office. He changed his outfit three times a day—twice during office hours and once again for his nighttime peregrinations. Various matching outfits were parked in different places for quick changeovers: his tailor's shop at the Ritz-Carlton, at City Hall, and wherever he slept that evening." It was widely believed that Walker spent over twenty-five thousand dollars a year on his wardrobe—more than his yearly mayoral salary.

Ed Flynn, the Democratic boss of the Bronx and a close associate of FDR, also liked the Celtic Dandy of a Peacock, according to Mitgang, "No one in New York politics was more personable or more generally liked than Jimmy Walker. No one could become really angry with him. When, as frequently happened in my relations with him, he would do something that annoyed me, I found that his manner was so boyishly disarming that my resentment usually evaporated. This was a beguiling characteristic, but one which was destined ultimately to give him much trouble. Many of the people who surrounded him were superficial and rapacious. He found it hard to believe that any of his friends were bad—or even wrong. In the end, Jimmy became the victim of some of these so-called 'friends.' "

BEAU JAMES—LADIES' MAN

Walker was also a ladies' man and didn't let little things like his marriage to Janet "Allie" Allen stand in the way. They had been married at Jimmy's church, St. Joseph's on Sixth Avenue, and, of course he was two hours late for his own marriage. "I refuse to live by the clock," he announced.

Jimmy, married man and playboy, was also a master of connubial bliss. At one time he had his house at #12 Gay Street (haunted only by his showbiz girlfriends at this time), mistress Betty Compton living not thirty yards away at 136 Waverly Place (and just around the corner from St. Joseph's Church), while Mrs. Walker lived at #6 St. Luke's Place about six blocks away, just far enough away to keep the heat down. One of his lovers according to Mitgang, French-Canadian singer and dancer Yvonne Shelton left him, saying, "This is good-bye. You're in love with a town. It's the first time I ever had to compete with that. And I'm overmatched."

Walker was also known for his pixieish sense of humor. While in Albany a Clean Books Bill was introduced. The God-fearing censors were outraged by D. H. Lawrence's dirty book, *Women in Love*. The bill didn't get very far because Walker would not support it, saying, "No girl was ever ruined by a book"—and if anyone should know, it was Jimmy Walker.

Despite all the romantic complications, Jimmy was thought highly of by Tammany and in 1925 he ran for mayor and was elected New York's ninety-seventh mayor by a grateful city. After all, it was the Roaring Twenties and New York needed a mayor like Walker. He was great at greeting celebrities like Charles Lindbergh. No one could share a car with a celebrity like Jimmy Walker. And after the parade, there was New York's thirty-two thousand speakeasies to celebrate in.

In 1929 he was up for reelection and the good-government-types had their man in Fiorello La Guardia, also a Greenwich Village boy who was born on Sullivan Street a year after Walker. "Word on the street," wrote Golway, "had it that a Republican congressman and rabble-rouser named Fiorello La Guardia would challenge him in the fall. Few gave the pudgy little man a chance—times were good in July 1929, and the people loved sharp-looking Jimmy Walker even if he spent the night hours in places few would consider respectable." Walker beat La Guardia by 865,000 to 368,000 votes. Unfortunately, a few weeks before the election the stock market crashed.

A DEVASTATING STRING OF EVENTS FOR MAYOR WALKER

Go back a year. Arnold Rothstein got shot. Rothstein was the guy who fixed the 1919 "Black Sox" World Series. He reneged on bets and was gunned down in midtown Manhattan and died on November 6, 1928. "Not since the notorious Tweed Ring was exposed in the nineteenth century," wrote Herbert Mitgang in *Once Upon a Time in New York*, "would New Yorkers become so aroused and, strangely, amused." A guy by the name of George McManus was indicted for first-degree murder, but, for some reason, by 1930 McManus had hit the streets, a free man. People wanted to know why.

Things then began to steamroll. Tammany Judge Joseph Force Crater walked out of his fine Greenwich Village apartment building at 40 Fifth Avenue and West 11th Street on August 6, 1930, and vanished into the city's ether, never to be seen again. Then there was an investigation of the Magistrates' Courts, which reeked of scandal. People—people very fond of Jimmy Walker—were looking for answers. Their prayers would be answered in the form of Judge Samuel Seabury.

"Mayor Walker's love of the city's nightlife grew stale after the stock market crashed," wrote Golway, "and the press reported fresh allegations of corruption in City Hall and in the city's judiciary. [Governor Franklin] Roosevelt had little choice but to respond to a growing public outcry against Walker, leading to his appointment of an anti-Tammany judge, Samuel Seabury—the man who couldn't bring himself to vote for Al Smith's nomination as governor in 1918—to investigate city government."

FDR had no intention of allowing Jimmy's Walker's slippery financial affairs to keep him from being elected president in 1932. Seabury was given free rein. "La Guardia and New York's Republican leaders," wrote Mitgang, "were determined to make capital out of the Rothstein murder."

BORN, DIE, TESTIFY

No one ever called Seabury "Samuel Seabury." It was always "Judge Seabury," like Judge was his first name. "Seabury was a Tammany foe from central casting," wrote Golway. "He had the austere bearing of a cleric—perhaps not surprising, given that he was the descendant of an Anglican bishop—and he was utterly convinced of his own moral purity. And he was not wrong about Tammany's failings in the post-[Silent Charlie] Murphy era."

"On the surface," Mitgang wrote, "Seabury appeared to be the patrician lawyer and Walker the man of the people. In their private law practice, the opposite was true. Walker's minor legal career had not been devoted to aiding society's underprivileged. As a state senator, he brought some clout to his clients because of his name and visibility. Occasionally, he served as a court-appointed attorney in homicide cases. The law was a place for him to hang his hat and pick up some extra money, but he devoted his main energies in his political career and his personal wanderings. . . . But they inhabited two different worlds, and fate would make them rancorous enemies. Jimmy Walker's father was a carpenter who became commissioner of public buildings in New York City at a time when Irish Catholics ruled Tammany Hall. Seabury's father, a professor of canon law at the General Theological Seminary, named his son after their ancestor, the first Episcopal bishop in the United States."

But Seabury also had his own personal agenda. "Unknown to all but his closest friends and family," Mitgang admitted, "he harbored a grudge against Tammany for not helping him to become governor [in 1916]."

Seabury, it seemed, was a quixotic narcissist, fantasizing of a White House in his future. "Judge Seabury dreamed," wrote Mitgang, "that the national attention he gained from what became known as the Seabury investigations would make lightning strike—and even lead to his nomination for president at the 1932 Democratic convention."

Seabury dragged Walker down to Foley Square in early May 1932 to answer questions about his affairs. Before Walker walked in he quipped, "There are three things a man must do alone. Be born, die, and testify."

Before Walker took the stand Seabury had been dragging all kinds of Tammany types in and most of them admitted that on small salaries they had amassed fortunes, all tucked away in Little Tin Boxes.

Seabury pressed Walker on a ten thousand dollar letter of credit Equitable Coach had obtained for him to pay for his recent European trip. Mitgang observed that "there had been a second application from Service Bus, a competing company, to sell the city surface transportation. Walker favored Equitable, which owned no buses, over Service, which had a large fleet." Walker had no sensible answer.

Another point of contention was the $246,000 Paul Block, a newspaper publisher and wealthy investor, had given to Walker over a two-year period in a brokerage account. Walker claimed the gift was innocuous with no quid pro quo. However it was during this time period that both the 6th and 8th Avenue subway lines were under construction. Block had an investment in a tile company that made subway tiles. They were going to need a *lot* of subway tiles. Maybe that had something to do with the quarter of a million bucks Block had given Walker.

Walker finally got away from Seabury, but he was bloodied. "This fellow Seabury would convict the Twelve Apostles if he could," exclaimed Walker after getting off the stand. Walker had met his Inspector Javert. The ball was now in FDR's court.

FDR VS. SEABURY

Seabury's Walker hearings were over in May. In June, the Democratic National Convention opened in Chicago. Roosevelt quashed any hopes that Al Smith might have had for a comeback and became the nominee against President Hoover in 1932. Before beating Hoover, FDR would have to take on Walker and Seabury.

Roosevelt had known Walker since their days in the New York State Senate together and FDR liked Jimmy as much as he distrusted Seabury. "This fellow Seabury is merely trying to perpetrate another political play to embarrass me," wrote the governor in a private letter to Edward House, one of his political advisers. "His conduct has been a deep disappointment to people who honestly seek better government in New York City by stressing the fundamentals and eliminating political innuendoes."

Back at the convention, Roosevelt had had a sniff that Seabury was after his nomination. "There was another way to which Roosevelt's bluntness was meant to be a subliminal message to Judge Seabury," wrote Herbert Mitgang in *Once Upon a Time in New York*. "Roosevelt's closest political aide, Louis Howe, had discovered a startling piece of news. He told Roosevelt that Seabury was making moves behind the scenes to capture the Democratic nomination for himself. Howe said that Seabury's friends had approached people on Capitol Hill to sound them out about his own candidacy in case the convention was deadlocked. Roosevelt and his operatives knew that despite Seabury's newborn fame, he had no delegates and didn't stand a chance of obtaining the nomination."

In early August Walker and Seabury gathered before Roosevelt in Albany—in this case he was judge and jury—and Seabury presented his evidence to FDR. "My only desire is that the matter may be dealt with solely upon its merits," said Seabury. "In my judgment, the evidence presents matters of the gravest moment to the people of the City of New York. I therefore present it to Your Excellency [FDR], who alone, under the Constitution and the laws, is empowered to act."

Walker came out swinging against Seabury, mocking his lack of electability when he ran for governor. "Mr. Seabury," began Walker, "would set up his opinion of my fitness for the office of Mayor as against the decision of 867,522 citizens who did me the honor of voting for me in the last City election, representing a plurality victory of 499,847 votes. Judge Seabury's own repudiation at the polls in 1916, when a candidate for Governor, probably explains his loss of confidence in popular elections. This distrust that he manifests for popular government he wants you to assume and, in spite of the votes of the people who supported me, to remove me from office."

Walker's needling of Seabury didn't help him when Paul Block's $246,000 brokerage account was brought up. The tale of the tile company and the new subway system left FDR almost speechless. "It's the most extraordinary business proposition I ever heard of," was all he could say.

"I think Roosevelt is going to remove me," Walker confided to a friend, according to Mitgang. "Papa made me eat my spinach."

As the world watched, the president-to-be was trying to decide if he should remove Walker—which Seabury wanted but FDR, at heart, didn't—Al Smith stepped in and told Walker, "Jim, you're through. You must resign for the good of the party."

And like that it was over.

On September 1, 1932 at 10:40 p.m. Walker notified the City Clerk of New York, "I hereby resign as Mayor of New York, the said resignation to take effect immediately."

On September 10, Walker sailed for Europe to meet up with girlfriend Betty Compton. His threat to run for election as mayor in the special election sailed with him. He telegraphed the nominating convention, "I request that my name be withheld from the convention." Jimmy Walker's elective political life was over. He was succeeded by a Tammany hack named John P. O'Brien who when asked who his new police commissioner would be, retorted with one of the great lines in New York City political history—"I don't know—they [Tammany] haven't told me yet."

RESURRECTION AFTER DISGRACE

"A few months after settling in Nice," Mitgang wrote, "Walker telephoned his wife in Florida to say he wanted her to file for divorce. With regret, Allie complied, charging that Jimmy had deserted her in 1928. They never saw or spoke to each other again. Allie ended her days running a religious bookstore at St. Patrick's Roman Catholic Church in Miami Beach."

Walker, fifty-one, was married to Betty Compton, twenty-eight, on April 19, 1933 in Cannes, France. Of course, the mayor of Cannes performed the ceremony at City Hall.

Walker was in Europe because he was waiting to see if the United States government was going to bring charges against him as they looked at his tangled finances. His base was outside of London, but he made many junkets to the continent. Money never seemed to be a problem. He suggested he was living off Betty, who had invested her money in gold which was really worth its weight during the Depression. Jimmy Walker had begun his resurrection.

When he met the ex–King George of Greece he was quick to quip: "Your Majesty, you and I made one terrible mistake—we both neglected to take out unemployment insurance."

And Walker was smart enough to keep up old friendships, especially with FDR's Postmaster General Jim Farley. They met up in Paris, much to the chagrin of the stale Judge Seabury. Gene Fowler in his laudatory biography of Walker, *Beau James: The Life and Times of Jimmy Walker*, recalled the verbal duel, "Of the Farley-Walker reunion Seabury said, 'It was not an edifying sight to see the Postmaster General of the United States making a pilgrimage to meet Mr. Walker, and to hear that he eulogized him in Paris. Take this as you like it. I think it was a disgusting spectacle.' In reply Farley observed, "Walker and I have been personal friends, as everyone knows, for twenty years. Perhaps Judge Seabury can't understand what it really means to love a friend.' "

Farley also confided to Walker in 1935 that FDR was keeping an eye out for him. "He [FDR] frequently asks for you," wrote Farley, "and no matter what is said to the contrary, Jim, he always has a friendly feeling toward you."

After two investigations into his finances, Walker was cleared, and he and Betty returned to New York just in time for FDR to run for reelection in 1936.

BEAU JAMES IS ADMIRED AGAIN

By 1936, Al Smith had turned into the thing he hated most all his life—a right-winger who hated progressives. Of course, the progressive Smith hated the most was FDR, who somehow was sitting in the White House while Smith was stuck in New York running the Empire State Building—or the "Empty State Building" as it was called because of its large vacancy rate. Smith had gone full reactionary as a member of the Liberty League.

Who would come to FDR's defense against his old colleague?

Beau James!

"When in 1936 Smith made his 'taking a walk' speech at Carnegie Hall," wrote Fowler, "Walker delivered what he called his first and last political speech of the campaign. It was at the dedication of the new Democratic Club in his own Assembly district early in October of 1936. Jim stepped to the microphone and assailed Smith severely, although not by name, and made a political declaration for Roosevelt. There was great applause, although several pro-Smith Tammany leaders were present."

"But even if my wounds were now as fresh and painful as they were at that time," Walker later told Joel Slonim of *The Day*, a Jewish newspaper, according to Fowler "I would still regard it as my duty to combat the Liberty League and Al Smith. It is not the personality of Franklin Roosevelt that is the issue in this campaign; the ideas which he represents are important. President Roosevelt has become the symbol of liberalism as opposed to reaction. Reaction goes hand in hand with racial and religious bigotry and with anti-Semitism. I shall always be on the side of the masses against their oppressors."

And he was getting around town again, being a toastmaster in demand. In 1937 he finally got a job as assistant counsel of the State Transit Commission at twelve thousand dollar a year. Of course he was immediately attacked by Seabury as the "Captain of the Tin-Box Brigade."

In May 1938, Betty and Walker met FDR at the White House: "The President and Walker visited alone for ten minutes," wrote Fowler. "Mr. Roosevelt did not mention the hearings of 1932, but spoke warmly of the old days at Albany and of old friends. He was most cordial and asked that Betty be shown in from an anteroom where she had been waiting."

Next was a meeting with the Little Flower at City Hall. "We were trying to find out if Diogenes was on the level!" Walker joked. And soon after he called La Guardia "the greatest mayor New York ever had."

Not surprisingly, a year later La Guardia appointed Walker as "czar" of labor relations in the women's coat-and-suit industry at a salary of twenty thousand dollars plus five thousand in expenses. Seabury went bombastic, saying that La Guardia had "stepped down from his position of political leadership among those who are striving for decent municipal government in the United States."

"Next day Mayor La Guardia said that he was 'pained' to learn of this adverse criticism," wrote Fowler, "then added: 'Judge Seabury is motivated by an obsessed hatred for President Roosevelt.' "

About his new job in the garment industry Walker would joke, "They are always buttonholing me."

There would also be a rapprochement with Al Smith. On a chance meeting with Al Smith he said, "Al, we've been apart too long."

"Much too long, Jim," Smith said.

"It's important to me, Al, that it never happen again."

"It never really happened, Jim."

It seemed that no one could stay mad at Jimmy Walker for very long.

DIVORCE RESULTS IN A VERY STRANGE DOMESTIC ARRANGEMENT

In the beginning things went well with Betty. They adopted two children, and it seemed that they loved New York again and New York loved them too.

Jimmy was once again the toast of the town—out speaking every night or going to the fights with friends. He was in big demand once again—and it began to take its toll on Betty.

"Jim was unaware that his frequent absences from Betty were re-creating in her mind the old-time feeling of loneliness," wrote Gene Fowler in *Beau James*. "Betty's loneliness," Fowler continued, "was not the only matter which now plagued her. She became increasingly aware that Jim longed to return to the Church but could not do so while married in violation of Roman Catholic rules. Walker said but little to Betty, or to anyone else, in respect to his desire to regain religious peace. She divined, however, that he had been undergoing a spiritual conflict for considerable time."

Betty went to be psychoanalyzed and soon after informed Jimmy that "I'm going to get a divorce," stunning Walker, who replied, "I can only give you back to yourself." Walker did not contest the Florida divorce and they were to share in the custody of their two children, Mary Ann and James Jr.

Then Betty changed her mind.

"Soon after the divorce Betty became dissatisfied with her new freedom," Fowler wrote, "and asked Jim 'to take her back.' He replied, 'Monk [his nickname for Betty], I simply never can go back to a personal situation once I have gone away. And this time it is you who have gone away, and I think it best for you not to try to come back." It was a unique divorce that only Jimmy Walker could be involved in. "[H]e was seen with Betty at the theatre, cafés, and elsewhere in public," Fowler recalled. "He seemed most attentive, and obviously still loved the beautiful woman who had divorced him."

On a South American cruise, Betty met consulting engineer Theodore Knappen. And things were about to get stranger. "Knappen proposed marriage. Betty replied that she would 'have to ask Jim,'" Fowler wrote. "Knappen's calm deportment as she recited the story of her life with Walker, Knappen's courtesy, his seeming strength of character, deeply impressed Betty. . . . 'All right, Betty. We'll ask Jim. I think I'm going to like him.'"

When presented with the proposal, Walker said, "Ted, I think you'll be good for Betty." Knappen and Betty were married in Jersey City on May 11, 1942. Walker, wrote Fowler, "managed the official details, procured the licence, then persuaded the clerk not to notify the newspapers until the ceremony had been concluded and the newlyweds gone." About the only thing Walker didn't do was give the bride away.

Betty and Knappen had a child of their own, fulfilling one of Betty's biggest dreams. But it was during her pregnancy that Betty discovered that she had breast cancer. She resisted her physician's call for an abortion and gave birth to a baby boy in January 1944. As she lay dying, she made one more request of Walker. "I want all the three children, Mary Ann and Jim Jim and the baby, to be raised together. . . . I want them all under one roof and never to know the difference between adoption and being born to any special parent. Never. I want you and Ted to live together after I go."

"I agree, Monk," responded Walker, "We'll take care of all three kids together. Sure we will."

On July 12, 1944, Betty passed away. She was survived by two husbands and three children.

MAY IN DECEMBER

Knappen and Walker did indeed live together with the three kids on both Long Island and in a New York apartment. The agreement lasted about a year and a half before Knappen departed and Walker's sister Nan and her two sons moved into Jimmy's New York apartment.

Walker resigned his garment industry job and became the president of Majestic Records. He was still quick with a quip, according to Fowler, "I used to press suits and now I'm pressing records."

As Betty suspected, Walker continued his slow walk back to the Church. "Never once," Walker maintained, "did I deny my faith to square it with my actions. It is true that I acted against my faith and my Church, but I always believed in and felt with the Faith of my Fathers and the Church of my God. The glamour of other days I have found to be worthless tinsel, and all the allure of the world just so much seduction and deception. I now have found in religion and repentance the happiness and joy that I sought elsewhere in vain."

Walker's demise would be relatively quick. He was having dizzy spells and the doctors thought that he might have a blood clot on the brain. It all ended for Jimmy Walker on November 18, 1946. For a guy who was supposed to be a big crook, he left a small estate of fifteen thousand dollars and no life insurance.

Jimmy finally got the answer to his song when thirty thousand New Yorkers solemnly walked by his casket.

"Will you love me in December as you do in May?"

The answer was yes, Beau James. They would.

CHAPTER TWO

JAMES R. McMANUS

THE GREAT-NEPHEW OF "THE McMANUS" GUIDED HELL'S KITCHEN DEMOCRATIC POLITICS INTO THE TWENTY-FIRST CENTURY

They're all gone now, the Boss Tweeds, the likes of George Washington Plunkitt, *The* McManus, Big Tim Sullivan, Silent Charlie Murphy, even the ones who weren't Irish, like Carmine DeSapio. They have gone to that great caucus in the sky where political bosses probably try to rig the odds of getting into heaven—if not hell.

The last one who passed in 2019, Jim McManus—a self-admitted "street-pickled New Yorker"—was a much more benevolent boss. Helping the new immigrants who were inundating his Hell's Kitchen neighborhood—Hispanics, Chinese, Sri Lankans, and even the occasional new Irish—he helped them apply for citizenship and explained the American way of life to them. He was the great-nephew of "*The* McManus," one of the legendary Democratic bosses, and he didn't fall far from the family political tree.

THE RESULT, NOT THE PROCESS

The Democratic Clubhouse back in the day would often be the centerpiece of both social and political life in the neighborhood. In his book, *Machine Made*, Terry Golway revealed how the clubhouse worked. "Some reformers," wrote Golway, "could not help but notice how Tammany figures—not just [Silent Charlie] Smith and [Robert F.] Wagner but also more complicated characters such as Bowery's Big Tim Sullivan and West Side leader Thomas McManus—did more than simply advocate for the poor and downtrodden. They were their problems, in part because so many Tammany figures were not far removed from the experience of tenement life, the catastrophic loss of a parent (usually a father), and the sense of powerlessness that was partner to poverty."

Golway tells a revealing story about *The* McManus and how FDR's future secretary of Labor, Frances Perkins, came to appreciate how *their* system worked. "Perkins," wrote Golway,

> recalled hearing about the work of the local Tammany leader, Thomas McManus, and his clubhouse, which was nearby on Ninth Avenue. Unannounced and unknown to McManus, Perkins showed up at the clubhouse one day, to the surprise of some low-level Tammany operatives gathered in the club's main room, talking politics. Clouds of tobacco smoke clung to the ceilings, and every now and then one of the McManus team made use of one of the spittoons scattered around the room. When Perkins asked to see McManus, she was ushered into the boss's office without hesitation or even a question.
>
> McManus was known not by his first name but as *The* McManus. Everybody, including the newspapers, referred to him that way. The title was a testament to the resiliency of Gaelic culture in the streets of New York, for in preconquest Ireland, the chieftains of great tribes were known as 'The O'Neill' or 'The O'Donnell,' or, in this case, 'The McManus.' Thomas McManus, a plain-speaking, middle-aged man with a receding hairline and a dashing Van Dyke beard, became a power in Tammany Hall in the early twentieth century. Perkins found him surrounded by petitioners, but he put aside his other business when this earnest young woman entered his office. She told him she was there on behalf of a boy who was in trouble. McManus asked whether he lived in the district (the 15th Assembly district). He did. He asked whether Perkins lived in the district. She did. McManus took down the boy's name and told Perkins to return to the club the following afternoon.
>
> She did. The boy, McManus told her, would be released from the Tombs prison at six o'clock that evening.
>
> "I don't know how he did it," Perkins later said of *The* McManus's actions. "I'm sure it was irregular." But she concluded that the result, not the process, was what mattered.

ET TU, MCMANUS!

The clubhouse of old was certainly corrupt. The district leader in the same Hell's Kitchen neighborhood that Jim McManus would represent, George Washington Plunkitt, famously was in favor of "honest graft."

"Everybody is talkin' these days about Tammany men growin' rich on graft," Plunkitt once said, "but nobody thinks of drawin' the distinction between honest graft and dishonest graft."[70]

"There's an honest graft," he went on, "and I'm an example of how it works. I might sum up the whole thing by sayin': 'I seen my opportunities and I took 'em.'"

That was until he ran into Thomas McManus who beat him for district leader in 1905. "Caesar had his Brutus. . . . I've got *The* McManus!" *Et tu,* McManus!

The McManus's great-nephew, James R. McManus, was born in Hell's Kitchen in 1934. He attended Power Memorial Academy not far from home and then graduated from Iona College. In 1941 his father, Eugene McManus, became district leader. "McManus says that when his father died in 1963," wrote journalist Dennis Duggan in *The Irish in America* edited by Michael Coffey with text by Terry Golway, "he acted quickly to replace him as club president, relying on his father's sage deathbed advice to 'move quickly after I'm gone because they'll be planning your demise at my wake.' And so he did, stopping in to get the votes of several Manhattan Democratic county leaders on the way back from seeing his father's body into the grave." The late Senator Daniel Patrick Moynihan, also a product of Hell's Kitchen, in reference to The McManus culture, called the current McManus dynasty the "McMani."[71]

THE TIMES THEY ARE A CHANGIN'

Since his election to the district leadership in 1963, times changed under his regime. "Like his father," wrote Sam Roberts in McManus's obituary in the *New York Times,* "grandfather and great-uncle, Jim McManus was an elected district leader, a relatively minor functionary in the great scheme of political office but a major neighborhood figure in the days when the clubhouses were cogs of well-greased machine politics, when a well-connected local party boss could find a loyal constituent a job, an apartment or a key to getting out of jail."

Of course the times changed as the old Irish longshoremen moved out and the yuppies moved in. The real estate industry started calling Hell's Kitchen "Clinton" as if they were trying to eradicate a colorful neighborhood's past. "In the old days, you could get people jobs, take care of their problems, help with their daily life," McManus told the *Times* in 2017. "But you just can't help anybody anymore. You can't even take care of a jury notice."

"There isn't much James McManus doesn't know about the city and especially about Hell's Kitchen," wrote Dennis Duggan. "He may be an artifact, a leftover from the era of daylong picnics, of torchlight marches through the city's streets, and of hands-on control of the election machinery, but McManus can still do favors for people, can still call in chits, and can do 'contracts with politicians who need his help.'"

Duggan's description of the McManus Midtown Democratic Association brings back memories of days gone by. "There is a feeling of bonhomie and well-being here," Duggan wrote, "of people looking for help and people trying to offer it. The club-house features a giant American flag and a real voting machine on which first-timers are taught to vote. For McManus, there is nothing as precious as the right to vote."

McManus clearly lamented the changing times, but change with the times he did. "He also remained nimble," wrote Roberts, "partly by reaching accommodation, if sometimes grudgingly, with real or potential rivals when faced with defeat." He even supported George McGovern in the 1972 presidential election, which made some people happy and others unhappy. "You make a deal with a reform leader and the next year he's got a judgeship and there's someone new who doesn't know anything about past promises," he told the *Times* in 1972, suggesting that lawyers be disqualified from district leaderships. "You're much better sticking with a saloonkeeper or an undertaker like me, who couldn't become a judge even if he wanted to."

Hell's Kitchen is famous for its collection of Westie Irish gangsters. "We didn't interfere with the mob on the docks, and they didn't interfere with our politics," Mr. McManus explained in 1992. "Once, they brought an old man into the club who needed a place to live. I said, 'What was your profession?' He said: 'Pickpocket, but I can't work anymore because my eyes are going. But I never robbed a working guy in my life.' I got the guy an apartment."

But how is the system still "greased?"

"He concedes," wrote Duggan, "that corruption flourished in some of the club-houses, but he insists that 'the savings and loan scandals make those people look like pikers. The rascals are still here, only they work for the white-shoe law firms and the banks. The bottom line,' he says, 'is that these people don't want the little people to have any power. But I have great faith in human greed. These rascals don't know when to stop.'"

"I wouldn't do anything for money that I wouldn't do for nothing," he said. "What I mean is, a little old lady comes in and wants a favor. I do it. A big law firm wants a favor. I say, buy 50 tickets for my cocktail party. They're not bribing me. They're just supporting me."

VOTING THE FUNERAL PARLOR

While as leader of the McManus Midtown Democratic Association (now run by his nephew Thomas McManus), he helped people with their everyday needs, and he also helped many transport to the next world. Since 1963 when his father suddenly and unexpectedly died, he ran the McManus & Ahern Funeral Home which his father founded in the 1930s.

"I got involved with the business after my father died," he told the New York Post in 2008. "Since I was a child I'd hung out with him and helped him run the home, but I never thought I'd become as involved as I did when I did. He was only 51, and I thought he'd be around for a long time."[72]

He had some interesting moments as a funeral director. "I'm here for the family," he told the Post. "I once had a wake uptown, and I rented a room from a home owned by a corporation. The family wanted it up there. So the home's manager came in at the stroke of 9 and yelled at a room full of mourners, 'It is now 9 p.m., please leave.' I pushed him against the wall and said, 'If you ever do that again at one of my funerals, I will throw you out the window.' To him it was just a job. To me it was about helping a family deal with losing a loved one."

In times of grief people sometimes do bizarre things. McManus recalled a few. "You make sure people don't do anything foolish while they're grieving. I had a woman whose husband was shot dead in a local bar, and she wanted to spend all his insurance money on the funeral. I wouldn't let her. I told her we'd give him a good burial that wouldn't embarrass her, but you have three kids you have to raise, and you'll need some of the money for that."

In another episode reminiscent of the funeral scene in The Last Hurrah by Edwin O'Connor, McManus had to think fast when no one showed up. "I once did a funeral for the husband of a very rich woman. She picked out a bronze casket and spent a lot of money. The home was set up with beautiful floral arrangements, but no one showed up. It was just me and her sitting there. I did my best to console her, but it was still very sad. So I made a call to the club, and 15 or 20 people showed up. She asked who they were, and I just told her they were friends of her husband."

"In the old days, we used to vote the graveyards," Lawrence Mandelker, Mr. McManus's election lawyer, told the *Times'* Sam Roberts. "Jim is a reformer. He votes the funeral parlor."

And Jim McManus was a man who planned ahead. "I have my own funeral already planned. It will be here, and my family has had a plot for 110 years in Calvary Cemetery out in Queens. It's a plot for 48 people, so there's still plenty of room for me."

PRO BONO FOR THE POOR AND DISENFRANCHISED

"'People ask me what do we do,' says McManus, wearing his trademark suspenders, a white shirt and a tie, and a neatly pressed suit, 'and I tell them that this club is like a law firm that does pro bono work for the poor and the disenfranchised,'" he told Duggan, "McManus makes it clear in conversations at his club and at Gallagher's, a nearby steak house he frequents, that politics was taken away from the clubs by reformers because 'no one wants the people to have a say in things that affect them.'"

"'My dad never pushed me into politics,' he told Duggan, 'and it has been a good life for me. I am able to do things for people who can't help themselves. I am a good politician because I am just an average guy. I know how people feel and what they need. I know how to deal with the bureaucrats, too. The bureaucracy is like the army. You should always get to know the corporals, not the generals, because the generals are too busy trying to look and sound like generals to listen to anyone.'"

PART SEVEN

TOUGH IRISH WOMEN

IF YOU WANT SOMETHING DONE, GET AN IRISH WOMAN TO DO IT

In these pages we have already visited with five Irish women who made their mark on New York City—Nora Connolly, Maeve Brennan, Marianne Moore, Dorothy Day, and Rosemary Mahoney's grandmother, Julia Fraher.

In this chapter we will deal with another two—Margaret Sanger, who basically invented birth control in America, and a woman who was the antithesis of Sanger, the infamous Mary Mallon, AKA, Typhoid Mary.

Margaret Sanger, née Higgins, reminds me so much of her Irish contemporaries, the women of the War of Independence. She had the fierce determination and one-dimensional outlook as such revolutionary women as Mary MacSwiney, Kathleen Clarke, Countess Markievicz, and writer Dorothy Macardle. She also had the toughness of her American contemporary, Bronx labor agitator Elizabeth Gurley Flynn, a close friend of both James Connolly and James Larkin.

Mary Mallon, of course, was tough, but misguided. In a strange way she was an indirect serial killer of three, and infected many more. Her failure to isolate herself was indeed criminal. But there was something about her that was admirable too. An Irish immigrant in New York City, she fought for her good name and would not go easily. She was tough as nails and even pulled a kitchen carving fork on her main nemesis who was harassing her. She was treated unkindly by society—not unlike the first AIDS suffers of another time—and even the *New York Times* mocked her in a tiny obituary. In the end she is the direct opposite of Margaret Sanger, who is thought of today as a pioneer while Mallon is only associated with disease and death. But in their own way both were very tough Irish women, making their imprint on *Real* Irish New York.

CHAPTER ONE

MAGGIE HIGGINS, AKA MARGARET SANGER

THE FOUNDER OF PLANNED PARENTHOOD WAS AN IRISH-CATHOLIC REBEL WITH A BIRTH CONTROL CAUSE

his may come as a shock to all those religious fanatics who think that birth control and abortion are sins against God, but I'm sure they'd be totally shocked to realize that the woman behind the birth control movement was a little Irish Catholic girl named Maggie Higgins. Today she is known by her married name, Margaret Sanger, but she went to bat for birth control with the same Irish zeal with which Michael Collins shot British spies. It is obvious that, like Collins, the blood of "Rebel Cork" flowed through their veins.

Both her parents, Anne Purcell Higgins and Michael Hennessy Higgins, were born in County Cork during the Great Famine and escaped as children to the Americas, her father coming through Canada. Maggie was born in 1879 Corning, New York, where her father worked as a stonemason, mostly cutting gravestones. In *Margaret Sanger: A Life of Passion*, author Jean H. Baker commented that, "These Catholic-born parents never considered the number of their offspring, for they believed it was the purpose of marriage and the nature of sex for women to bear children."[73]

The number of Higgins children and pregnancies is staggering. Anne Higgins, according to Baker, had "eleven children in twenty-two years and suffered seven miscarriages. She had been pregnant eighteen times in thirty years of marriage." It is thus not surprising that Anne died from tuberculosis (TB) at the age of forty-eight. Her husband Michael lived to be eighty. That fact was not lost on Maggie Higgins.

Maggie inherited a lot of her rebel instincts from her father who was anticlerical and held many socialist views. Because of his anticlerical views, Maggie was not baptized in the Catholic Church until she was fourteen. Her father's bias against the Church once had a priest calling her "a child of the Devil."

"Corning," wrote Baker in her biography, "had taught her about class divisions and the arrogance of the Catholic Church. Her conflicts with the church, begun when she was the loyal daughter of a nonbeliever, would forever spur her endeavors." By the time she was in her middle teens, Maggie's instinct was to get the hell out of Corning.

"Very early in my childhood," she said according to Baker, "I associated poverty, toil, unemployment, drunkenness, cruelty, quarreling, fighting, debts, and jails with large families."

She found a haven for a while at Claverack College, but was forced to leave because of financial problems. But she kept pushing, eventually going to nursing school at White Plains Hospital. There she became expert in the field of obstetrics and gynecology. It was here that she discovered that she, like her mother, had TB. But it was not the TB of the lungs that had killed her mother, but TB of her tonsils and lymph glands which she might have gotten by drinking unpasteurized milk. It would dog her for the next twenty years until an operation finally took care of the problem.

ENTER WILLIAM SANGER

At a dance at the New York Eye and Ear Infirmary she met a German-Jewish immigrant named William Sanger. He was a draftsman at McKim, Mead and White, one of the leading architectural firms in the country. By this time Maggie was known as "Peg," and Sanger's persistence finally stole her heart. In 1902 Sanger took her out of her job at the hospital, drove her to get a license, and she returned twenty minutes later a married woman.

"Meanwhile," wrote Baker, "doctors saw birth control not as an opportunity to improve women's health, but rather as a hazard threatening their professional practices. Overwhelmingly, they opposed any forms of artificial contraception for women, although exceptions were made for men, who were encouraged to use condoms to prevent venereal infection when they visited prostitutes."

As a nurse Sanger delivered babies by herself and also informed her patients of the two cheapest means of contraception, condoms and coitus interruptus. She was also a fan of the pessary, an early form of IUD. "It's the rich that knows the tricks," she told her poor patients on the Lower East Side, "while we have all the kids."

In quick succession she had three children herself—Peggy, Grant, and Stuart. However, family would always come second to her. By the spring of 1911, she had ditched nursing to become a fifteen dollars-a-week organizer for the New York Woman's Committee for Propaganda for Socialism and Suffrage. Along with her contemporaries Emma Goldman and Elizabeth Gurley Flynn, she was all in for the working man and woman. "The little nurse from New York," as she was known in labor circles, went to support striking silk workers in Hazelton, Pennsylvania, where she was arrested for loitering and given five days in jail. A cop referred to her as "a New York bowery bum."

These labor strikes educated her in the "uses of subversive publicity" and she soon left the Socialist Party, just as she had left nursing. But what she had learned along the way would now go into her campaign for what she called "birth control." "Margaret Sanger's early radicalism," wrote Jean H. Baker, "had led directly to observation on the plight of the female poor, and from there to a birth control agenda grounded in feminism."

CONFRONTING THE COMSTOCK LAWS

It was after she left the Socialist Party that she started drifting apart from her husband and began to take on lovers. Mabel Dodge, Jack Reed's lover, ran a salon in Greenwich Village and Sanger was the star attraction. "It was she who introduced to us all the idea of birth control," wrote Dodge, "and it along with related ideas about sex, became her passion. . . . Margaret Sanger was the first person I ever knew who set out to rehabilitate sex and [she] was openly an ardent propagandist for the joys of the flesh. . . . Margaret Sanger was an advocate of the flesh who set out to make it a scientific, wholly dignified and proper part of life." From Sanger's various affairs it was obvious, as Dodge noted, that Sanger knew "how to heighten pleasure and prolong it [until] the whole body was sexualized."[74]

"Margaret Sanger enacted her personal convictions about monogamy's stifling effect on erotic love and the necessity of women's sexual independence," wrote Baker. "Sex had become something she could study through practice."

She was about to confront the obscenity laws, especially the Comstock laws which were passed during the Grant Administration in 1873. The law's official name was the

"Suppression of Trade in, and Circulation of, Obscene Literature and Articles of Immoral Use." It was named after Anthony Comstock who ran a one-man campaign against "lust—the boon companion to all other crimes." Looking back at him today he comes across as the Inspector Clouseau of Sex. But the punishment was no laughing matter—five thousand dollars and imprisonment for five years.

Sanger took on the Comstock Law with her new publication, *The Woman Rebel*. The first issue had an article called "The Prevention of Conception." She caught the attention of the law.

The US Post Office declared *The Woman Rebel* "obscene and unmailable." A postal official, according to Baker, added "that bitch that edits it, named Margaret Sanger . . . has been trying to fool us by mailing it wrapped up in respectable newspapers and magazines. Don't let any get through." Sanger was charged with four counts of violating the Comstock laws. If found guilty she could have gotten up to forty years in prison.

It was at this time that Emma Goldman—who would be deported in the anarchist scare of the 1920s—said that "they would not believe me when I told them that you were a little, delicate woman, refined and shrinking, but that you did believe in the daring and courage of woman in her struggle for freedom."

"A WOMAN'S BODY BELONGS TO HERSELF ALONE"
It was at this time that Sanger made one of her most powerful statements about a woman's body, a statement that is as powerful today as it was in 1914. "A woman's body," she wrote in *The Woman Rebel*, "belongs to herself alone. It does not belong to the United States of America or any other government on the face of the earth. . . . Enforced motherhood is the most complete denial of a woman's right to life and liberty."

"If I must go to jail," she said, "I will give them something to send me in on. Everyone has crawled under cover in denying their support of me with an 'I-told-you-so.' . . . Fortunately it is good to stand alone, so with sleeves up in true Irish fashion, I'm in the fight to win."

While awaiting trial Sanger suddenly disappeared. Under the alias Bertha Watson, she fled to England via Canada on November 2, 1914 for a self-imposed exile that lasted a year. In London she waited on tables in a tearoom to support herself. She met sexologist Havelock Ellis and they became fast friends, but not lovers. She took on another lover, Lorenzo Portet, a Spanish anarchist in exile. Meanwhile her estranged husband back in New York was convicted under the Comstock laws and his sentence was a fine or a month in jail. He chose jail. A month later, in what could be described as poetic justice, Anthony Comstock died.

TRAGEDY STRIKES

Margaret Sanger returned to New York in October 1915 to face trial. A month later tragedy struck when daughter Peggy died of pneumonia on November 6, 1915. It was at this point that Sanger showed an interest in mysticism and, perhaps, the occult.

"Peggy's death," wrote Baker, "awoke feelings of mysticism in Sanger, a woman who had always credited her Celtic origins for her childhood premonitions and extra-terrestrial visitations. As Sanger described the death scene: 'Peggy was sleeping. Her pulse was so soft and slow. I was unable to realize that the end was near and had my fingers on her ankle to get the pulse when before my eyes arose another Peggy horizontally sleeping [who] rose about a foot or more—fluttering and quivering a moment as if taking leave of its bondage and slowly and majestically [she] soared and floated across the bed and out through the iron closed door. . . . Peggy had left for the great unknown and beyond.' Her mother spent the rest of her life searching, and often finding, this ethereal, levitating daughter in the spirit world."

For a woman of science she certainly had an interest in parapsychology. During the 1920s on a visit to Ireland she also did something odd when, according to Baker, "she searched for her grave from a previous life. 'You remember,' she explained to her friend Juliet Rublee, 'that my quabal [a form of medium] said I was Queen Seotia. Well, there was such a person, the daughter of Pharoa supposed to be long before history began.'"

THE GOVERNMENT BLINKS

Sanger was actually looking forward to the trial. "It is not so much Margaret Sanger who goes on trial," she said, "but rather [for women] it is your inherent right to own and control your bodies."

She was getting lots of publicity and the government, for a change, was feeling the heat. The government dropped the case when the US attorney in New York—over the objection of his boss, the attorney general—refused to make Sanger a martyr and dropped the charges. The *New York Sun* wryly remarked that "the anomaly of a prosecutor who was loath to prosecute and a defendant who was anxious to be tried." Sanger immediately went on a lecture tour and told her followers to "agitate, educate, organize and legislate."

Sanger was on a roll now and opened the first birth control clinic in Brownsville, Brooklyn, on October 16, 1916 with the motto, "Do not kill, do not take life, but prevent."

"To make birth control the measurable, scientific subject she intended," Jean H. Baker wrote in her biography, "the clients paid a voluntary ten-cent registration fee, signed a slip certifying that they were married, gave information about their family, childbearing history, and their husbands' wages, and agreed that the information about birth control they received was for their personal use."

But the government was not finished with Sanger, according to Baker's biography. In a sting, a policewoman arrested Sanger at her clinic and Sanger let her have it: "You dirty thing. You are not a woman. You are a dog." The policewoman told her to "tell that to the judge in the morning." Sanger went right back at her: "No I'll tell it to you now. You dog, and you have two ears to hear me too." Within weeks she opened another clinic in Brooklyn and was arrested again. She took on Jonah J. Goldstein as both her lawyer and lover. In the verdict, she received a sentence of five thousand dollars or thirty days in jail. She took the jail time.

She got out of jail on March 7, 1917. One month later, the United States joined the war effort on the side of the Allies. She opposed the war, but the government, in one of the great hypocritical actions, adopted many of her birth control methods that she was jailed for espousing. This became necessary because the government discovered that 15 percent of draftees had venereal disease. The military was soon paraphrasing her pamphlets on sex education. Secretary of the Navy Josephus Daniels, apparently without irony, said, "Men must live straight lives if they would shoot straight."

BATTLING THE CATHOLIC CHURCH

All the notoriety of jail time only brought more attention to Sanger and her cause. Always looking for new ways to publicize birth control she even made her own silent film called *Birth Control*. Of course, the theater was closed down by the city.

Besides the government, her biggest antagonist was the Catholic Church. "For Sanger," wrote Baker, "lifetime celibacy, rather than any text, explained the Catholic clergy's crabbed notions of sexuality, and she used the pages of her new monthly magazine, *The Birth Control Review*, for ridicule. How could priests, needing to elevate their personal sacrifice and knowing nothing about sex, make rules about behavior that they understood only vicariously and often lasciviously? After a priest termed her birth control movement 'a cult,' she called on the faith's women to defy such ignorance and abandon their clubs, societies, and even membership in the Catholic-sponsored White Cross nurses. Sanger never failed to report the number of Catholic women, usually around a third of her clients, who defied the church's dictates."

Sanger would not be silenced. "In the *Review*," Baker wrote, "Sanger also criticized the Catholic Church for its intrusions into civil rights and its violations of the free speech of American citizens. She provided personal examples—the church's efforts to force theater owners to close down when Sanger came to town, the unofficial sub rosa instructions to Catholic police officers to arrest birth control advocates selling the *Review*, the threatening phone calls by prominent members of the Knights of Columbus to mayors and councilmen to pass special ordinances targeting her literature, the picketing and disruption of her speeches, and the intimidating threats by prominent Catholics to boycott vendors who sold her magazine."

One of her biggest foes was Archbishop Patrick Hayes of the New York diocese. She was scheduled to address a meeting at Town Hall when Hayes persuaded the NYPD to break up the proceedings. "Here was a ridiculous thing," Sanger later wrote in her autobiography according to Baker, "the Catholic Church held such power in its hand that it could issue orders to the police, dissolve an important gathering of adult and intelligent men and women and . . . then not feel called upon to give any accounting."

Citing federal obscenity laws, Hayes retorted that "the law of God and man, science, public policy, human experience are all condemnatory of birth control as preached by a few irresponsible individuals. . . . of the reasons for the lack of genius in our day is that we are not getting to the end of families."

"Sanger," wrote Baker, "found hers not just in capitalism but in what she held as its institutional coconspirator, the American church, especially its repressive Roman Catholic version, whose dogmas about the will of God were delivered to submissive women by a 'debauched priesthood.'"

SANGER AND EUGENICS—"A CALCULATED, PRAGMATIC TACTIC"

The Random House College Dictionary defines eugenics as: "the science of improving the quality of a breed or species, esp. the human race, by the careful selection of parents."

Eugenics one hundred years ago, unlike today, was a very popular concept. One of its most vigorous proponents—and foe of Sanger—was ex-President Theodore Roosevelt, who was a supporter of "positive eugenics." TR was in favor of four children per family "from old native stock or self-respecting daughters and sons of immigrants." Paul Popenoe was also a supporter of eugenics and made the statement—sometimes erroneously credited to Sanger—"More children from the fit, less from the unfit."

"Tentatively in these years and then wholeheartedly in the 1920s," wrote Baker, "Margaret Sanger became a fellow traveler and then a promoter of the eugenics movement. For the most part her acceptance of the movement was a calculated, pragmatic tactic. She needed allies, and eugenics—the expert qualifications of its proponents, the scientific trappings of its evidence, its expanding networks of journals and associations, its general acceptance among Americans, and even its international connections—represented an opportunity to find friends and join a popular movement."

"Neither mating of healthy couples," wrote Sanger in a paper entitled "Birth Control and Racial Betterment", "nor the sterilization of certain recognizable types touches the great problem of the unlimited reproduction of those whose housing, clothing and food is inadequate."

What hurt Sanger's reputation is that the popular "positive eugenics" of the 1920s became the "negative eugenics" of Nazi Germany. But in both positive and negative eugenics there is a huge racist ingredient that cannot be ignored. Sanger, daughter of Irish immigrants, somehow overlooked this element of the eugenics movement.

"Today its atrocities have no justification," wrote Baker, "though Sanger's acceptance must be put into the context of her times. . . . Sanger's support of eugenics, the latter largely unchallenged in the United States during these years, ultimately cost her some of her reputation, while at the same time it revealed her passion for the cause of birth control, along with her pragmatism."

THE BIRTH CONTROL TIDE TURNS

Sanger spent a lot of time in the 1920s traveling to the Far East and especially England, where she had a lot of admirers and lovers. (It should be noted that even one of

Sanger's grandchildren, according to Baker, thought her to be a "nymphomaniac.") In 1922 in London she took on another husband, James Noah Slee, a conservative Republican and Episcopalian. Baker in her biography called him "a sexual naïf." This marriage, too, had its oddities. They lived in separate although adjoining apartments near Gramercy Park. She, of course, kept her stable of lovers.

The birth control movement continued to flourish under her guidance. Cracks in the Comstock Laws began to appear when Judge Frederick Crane of the New York Court of Appeals ruled that doctors were excepted from the laws. Sanger organized the American Birth Control League (ABCL) and published and edited *The Birth Control Review* and continued to lecture from Yale to Harlem. She was also banned in Boston by Mayor James Michael Curley, a good Irish Catholic, who referred to her movement as "child murder propaganda."

In 1923, she decided to open a dispensary called the Birth Control Clinical Research Bureau (BCCRB). Because of Judge Crane's decision, she needed a doctor to work at the clinic. She struck out with the first woman doctor, Dorothy Bocker, but she struck gold with the next, Dr. Hannah Stone. In 1925 she had 1,655 patients visit the clinic. By 1929 that number rose to 9,737. The number of clinics was also growing across the United States—twenty in 1925 rose to fifty-five by 1930.

WINDING DOWN

By 1930, Sanger had resigned from both the American Birth Control League and as editor of *The Birth Control Review*. By that time, the BCCRB was flourishing. "By 1931," Baker wrote, "sixteen doctors, five trained nurses, four social workers, and several researchers served a growing annual population of over 18,000 clients who still must be called patients. By 1934 the clinic had records on 49,798 women."

Despite Judge Crane's decision, there was still harassment from police. In another undercover sting, a policewoman named Mrs. McNamara sought information then closed down the clinic citing the Comstock laws. Ironically, Mrs. McNamara had gynecological problems of her own and later returned to the clinic for advice. The case was eventually thrown out by the judge.

As the Depression deepened, Sanger was disappointed by FDR, who, she claimed to Havelock Ellis, had "an adolescent mind." Another opponent was the bigoted Detroit radio priest, Father Charles Coughlin. Sanger retorted by announcing that a full one-third of her patients were Catholics.

A lot of her time was spent on getting the word out by lecturing and making sure that birth control was given prominent publicity. She was named the honorary chair of the Birth Control Federation of America, which was soon renamed the Planned Parenthood Federation of America over her opposition. She opposed the rebranding because it took two words—birth control—out of the equation.

In old age, Sanger suffered from leukemia and senility and battles with her son, Grant, who had put her in an old-age home over her objections. She died on September 6, 1966, days before her eighty-seventh birthday. There was even controversy in death over her age because she had cut five years off the real year of her birth.

Her last triumph was that she lived to see the Comstock laws overturned by the United States Supreme Court in 1965 in the landmark decision *Griswold v. Connecticut*, which found it was unconstitutional to interfere with birth control because it was a violation of a person's right to privacy.

Upon her death, the *New York Times*—a critic of Sanger's when the birth control movement was in its infancy—wrote, "The birth control movement grew out of one woman's outrage at the suffering she saw among the poor. It grew into a view of family planning accepted and practiced in a majority of American homes, a cause wisely promoted throughout the world and an international consensus that population control is necessary to human welfare and global peace."[75]

And never forget that the birth control movement came about because a little Irish girl from Corning, New York, Maggie Higgins, decided that women should have the right *not* to be permanently pregnant.

CHAPTER TWO

MARY MALLON, AKA TYPHOID MARY

MARY MALLON OF COUNTY TYRONE REMAINS ONE OF THE MOST NOTORIOUS IRISH IMMIGRANTS IN NEW YORK CITY HISTORY

Typhoid Mary.

Like Jack the Ripper, it is a nickname that will go down in history as a deadly sobriquet.

Typhoid Mary's real name was Mary Mallon, and she was born on September 23, 1869, in Cookstown, County Tyrone. At the tender age of fourteen, she immigrated to New York, where she lived with an aunt and uncle. Perhaps taking inspiration from the town of her birth, she became a cook, working for well-to-do families all over the city. By all indications, she was a fine cook and was treasured by the families she worked for.

PANIC IN OYSTER BAY

Oyster Bay, Long Island, was the location of President Theodore Roosevelt's Summer White House. It was also a tony place for well-to-do New Yorkers to vacation away from the stifling heat of the city. In August 1906, a typhoid epidemic hit the Warren family as they were vacationing. George Thompson, the owner of the house, was concerned that a stigma would be attached to the house and he would be unable to rent it out the following summer. To get to the bottom of the outbreak, he hired a freelance "sanitary engineer," Dr. George Soper, who was not a medical doctor.

Depending on your point of view, Soper is either a hero or a dope. Soper comes across as a mixture of Louis Pasteur, Inspector Javert, and Inspector Clouseau. He was a balding middle-aged man who sported a mustache and smoked a pipe. He could have easily played Dr. Watson in a Sherlock Holmes movie.

With things like contaminated water and sanitary conditions already ruled out, Soper decided to work backward. He knew the incubation period for typhoid was ten to fourteen days. He decided to check into everyone connected with the Warren family in the month of August. According to celebrity chef Anthony Bourdain in his cheeky book, *Typhoid Mary: An Urban Historical*, Soper admitted that he first "went to the employment agency where I was given the missing cook's former places of employment and the different people who had furnished her with references. Working from agency to agency I came in possession of little fragments of her history for ten years. What do you suppose I found out? That in every household in which she had worked in the last ten years there had been an outbreak of typhoid fever. Mind you, there wasn't a single exception."[76]

Soper would not be deterred. "Following her trail backward to cases in 1904," he revealed, "I found she had worked at the home of Henry Gilsey at Sands Point, Long Island, where four of seven servants suddenly got the disease. Going back still further, I found that five weeks after Mary had gone to cook at the summer home of J. Coleman Drayton at Dark Harbor, Maine, in 1902, seven out of nine persons in the house contracted typhoid, and so did a trained nurse and a woman who came to the house to work by the day. There had been an outbreak of the disease in New York in 1901, and I had reason to believe that Mary was behind this. In 1904, Tuxedo Park, the fashionable summer resort, was stricken . . . and (I) discovered she had cooked there in that time."

In *Typhoid Mary*, Bourdain stared down Soper and his tactics. "He [Soper] was going to make his bones with this case," wrote Bourdain. "He foresaw himself as the poster boy for epidemiologists and health professionals, an honored and much-sought-after speaker at all the medical societies, a hero to the afflicted, a newspaper personality, idol to generations of aspiring engineers."

Bourdain's book is sympathetic to Mary. "That he [Soper]," wrote Bourdain, "might have been racist, sexist, and far too influenced by the prejudices of his class— as has been suggested by revisionist accounts—a flawed, ambitious fellow who looked for the first likely Irish woman he could clap the manacles on."

CONFRONTING MARY—OR, HAVE CARVING FORK, WILL TRAVEL

Soper finally tracked Mary to a family on Park Avenue. "Imagine my surprise and my utter joy," he gushed, "when I found the famous germ-carrier working as a cook in that household."

Their first meeting did not go well.

"I had my first talk with Mary in the kitchen of (the) house," he wrote. "I suppose it was an unusual kind of interview, particularly when the place is taken into consideration. I was as diplomatic as possible, but I had to say I suspected her of making people sick and that I wanted specimens of her urine, feces, and blood."

Imagine if a stranger with no legal authority came into your workplace and demanded that you turn over your urine, feces, and blood to him. What would you do? Well, Mallon came after him with a carving fork, scaring the feces out of Soper.

It's almost comical the way Soper describes his confrontation: "She seized a carving fork and advanced in my direction. I passed rapidly down the long, narrow hall, through the tall iron gate, out through the area, and so to the sidewalk. I felt rather lucky to escape. I confessed to myself that I had made a bad start. Apparently Mary did not understand that I wanted to help her."

Soper was obviously frightened by Mary's truculence. It should be remembered that Mary was not a delicate little thing. She has been described by many as being one hell of a big woman, weighing up to two hundred pounds. Soper himself described her as "athletic [with] a good figure . . . at the height of her physical and mental faculties . . . [a woman who] prided herself on her strength and endurance and at that time, and for many years after, never spared herself the exercise of it."

According to Bourdain, Dr. William H. Park said Mary was "a large, healthy-looking woman" and Emma Goldberg Sherman remarked that "her hands were tremendous. She was a big woman."

Mary had Soper just where she wanted him: "She upbraided me for connecting her with outbreaks of typhoid fever in every household she had worked in. . . . The circumstances connected with the case were most pathetic. In the face of all this, Mary refused to submit herself to an examination and would not divulge a single fact about her past life, her relatives, her friends, in fact, she refused to say a thing to assist me."

Since Mallon wouldn't talk to him, Soper decided to follow her after work. He discovered that she lived at 33rd Street and Third Avenue, under the shadow of the

Third Avenue El. "She was spending her evenings with a disreputable looking man who had a room on the top floor and to whom she was taking food," Soper said. "His headquarters during the day was in a saloon on the corner." Soper started supplying Mallon's man, named Breihof, with drink to learn about Mary.

"We know nothing of her early experiences with men," wrote Bourdain, "or with love, or even her feelings about men in general. Though she was a church-going Irish Catholic woman living in less-than-enlightened times, she seems to have been living comfortably in sin with the unimpressive Mr. Breihof."

Since he was getting nowhere with Mary and was probably physically afraid of her, Soper went to the commissioner of the New York City Health Department with his case. According to Bourdain, a Dr. Josephine Baker was dispatched to get samples from Mary at her workplace. What occurred was something out of a Keystone Cops one-reeler. When confronted by Dr. Baker, Mary bolted and could not be found. When discovered, she leapt out a window and disappeared. She was finally cornered in a backyard water closet. Dr. Baker described the whole scene: "She fought and struggled and cursed. I tried to explain to her that I only wanted the specimens and that then she could go back home. She again refused and I told the policemen to pick her up and put her in the ambulance. This we did, and the ride down to the hospital was quite a wild one." Dr. Baker added that she "sat on her all the way to the hospital." The result of tests found a "pure culture of typhoid."

"When we hear of Mary vaulting fences," Bourdain wrote, "smacking around cops, shacking up in a one-room tenement apartment with an alcoholic gentleman to whom she was not married, it's helpful to put that seemingly unique assertiveness in its proper perspective. If there were 'new women,' really, in 1907, then you could hardly find a better example than Mary Mallon, a single, childless, domestic laborer pinned to the floor of a careening Health Department ambulance."

ROUND UP THE USUAL IRISH SUSPECTS

One wonders if Mary was targeted because she was poor, Irish, and female. Remember, in the early twentieth century there were still plenty of "No Irish Need Apply" signs hanging in the windows of businesses in New York City. If Soper had discovered that the WASP mistress in the Park Avenue house where Mallon worked was the carrier, do you think he would have demanded samples of her urine, feces, and blood?

In 1922, while Mary was confined to North Brother Island, a man named Tony Labella caused two outbreaks of typhoid that resulted in a hundred illnesses and five deaths (as compared to Mallon's fifty-one people infected, three dead). Yet you never hear anything about a "Typhoid Tony."

"Mary Mallon was one of *these* new women," wrote Bourdain. "Formed out of poverty and abuse, newly arrived in a strange land, where the Irish were, for some time, considered only slightly elevated from apes. They were 'white niggers,' without a pot to piss in, and as women even less likely to raise themselves from their circumstances. Without family or husbands, they learned to hustle, to negotiate, to endure. They acquired marketable skills and demanded to be paid for them. It was from the early practices of avoiding marriage, working for themselves, saving money, learning, that Irish women began moving into professions like teaching and nursing. At a time when most professions were considered unsuitable for women, many began to break through."

"If Mary was part of anything," Bourdain wrote, "she was part of a very different movement, one forged in hunger, dislocation and social upheaval, a sea-change which pushed millions of women out of their homeland and away from their traditional roles, across the sea and into the lonely business of domestic servitude."

WELCOME TO NORTH BROTHER ISLAND

North Brother Island is a piece of rock sticking out of the East River just west of the Bronx and within view of Rikers Island. (Yes, there is a South Brother Island.) Today it is abandoned, used only as a bird sanctuary.

Without being indicted, tried, or convicted of anything, Mary Mallon was sent to Riverview Hospital on North Brother. There it was discovered that Mary was the first American to be an asymptomatic carrier of the bacillus called *salmonella typhi*. "She denied ever having been sick with the disease," wrote Judith Walzer Leavitt in her book *Typhoid Mary: Captive to the Public's Health*, "and it is likely she never knew she had it, suffering only a mild flu-like episode."

Pretty soon, Mary got sick and tired of North Brother Island. "I am not segregated with the typhoid patients," she wrote to the court, "there is nobody on this island that has typhoid. . . . There was never any effort by the Board authorities to do anything for me excepting to cash [sic] me on the island and keep me a prisoner without being sick nor needing medical treatment . . . when I first came here . . . they took two blood cultures and feces . . . [then] three times a week say Monday Wednesday and Friday respectfully until the latter part of June . . . after that they only got the feces once a week which was on Wednesday . . . now they have given me a record for nearly a year for three times a week (!!)"

Frustrated, she found a lawyer, one George Francis O'Neill, who filed a claim of habeas corpus on her behalf. It is believed that newspaper magnate William Randolph Hearst, always looking for a good story, was behind the hiring of O'Neill. "He [Hearst] was sympathetic to the Irish, certainly," wrote Bourdain. "This was both tactically wise and seemingly heartfelt. Any imagined constituency would be largely Irish working class and have to, by necessity, include and appeal to the large numbers of public servants, politicians, Irish organization members, eating clubs and ward-heelers who made the day-to-day of New York politics run smoothly and profitably. An editorial in the *Journal-American* on St. Patrick's Day reveals a near-militant admiration for the cause of Irish republicanism and goes on to excoriate Americans for their relative gutlessness and compliance in the face of adversity and inequity."

While Mary was at North Brother, Soper again showed up, offering to write a book about her if she would tell him her story. He promised to turn over all royalties to her. Mary told him where he could shove his book and royalties. She received a marriage invitation from a deranged fan in Michigan. And she was urged to have her gallbladder removed, as if it was a miracle cure. "I said no," said Mary, "no knife will be put on me . . . I've nothing the matter with my gall bladder."

Unfortunately for Mary, the law was against her: Section 1170 of the Charter of Greater New York: "Said board may remove or cause to be removed to proper place . . . any person sick with any contagious, pestilential or infectious disease: shall have exclusive control of the hospital for the treatment of such cases."

Section 24, Chapter 383 of the Laws of 1903: "It shall require the isolation of all persons and things exposed to such diseases. . . . It shall prohibit and prevent all intercourse and communication with or use of infected premises, places and things."

Bourdain cited the precedent of *Seavey vs. Preble*: "persons may be seized and restrained of their liberty and ordered to leave the state."[77]

Thus, Justice Erlanger ruled on July 16, 1909: "The risk of discharging the inmate of the Riverside Hospital is too great to be assumed by the Court. The injury which may be done to innocent persons . . . are incalculable. . . . While the court deeply sympathizes with this unfortunate woman, it must protect the community against a recurrence of spreading the disease."

And Erlanger truly sympathized with Mallon: "Every opportunity should . . . be afforded this unfortunate woman to establish, if she can, that she has been fully cured. And she may, after further examination of her . . . renew the application, or, if the petitioner prefers, the matter may be sent to a referee . . . to take testimony and report to the court with his opinion. . . . This will allow her the opportunity to cross examine witnesses called against her and to offer her own medical experts to sustain her claim."

Mary contested the whole thing. "The contention that I am a perpetual menace in the spread of typhoid germs is not true," she said. "My own doctors say I have no typhoid. I am an innocent human being. I have committed no crime and I am treated like an outcast—a criminal. It is unjust, outrageous, uncivilized. It seems incredible that in a Christian community a defenseless woman can be treated in this manner."

Then Mary hit the nail on its head. "There were two kinds of justice in America," she said. "All the water in the world wouldn't clear me from this charge, in the eyes of the Health Department. They want to make a showing; they want to get credit for protecting the rich, and I am the victim."

Finally, New York Health Commissioner Ernst J. Lederle, PhD, came to the rescue: According to Bourdain he said, "She has promised to report to me regularly and not to take another position as a cook. I am going to do all I can to help her. . . . For Heaven's sake, can't the poor creature be given a chance in life?! An opportunity to make her living and have her past forgotten? She is to blame for nothing—and look at the life she has led!"

All of a sudden, Mary Mallon was free and unleashed on New York once again.

A NEW OUTBREAK CATCHES MARY RED-HANDED

"For five years," Soper wrote, "Mary traveled about New York and its vicinity without restraint and without her identity being discovered by the authorities. I was not asked to find her again, but I think I could have done so."

She promised not to work as a cook and took jobs beneath her as a laundress and ran a rooming house. But alarm bells went off again when there was a new outbreak in March 1915 at Sloan Hospital for Women and it was discovered that Mallon was working in the kitchen as a cook.

"It's a measure of how little she cared about herself or anybody else," wrote Bourdain, "that she would risk infecting pregnant women and newborn children with typhoid. It was . . . well . . . indefensibile. . . . [It] speaks volumes about how far she had fallen and how little she cared."

She was, of course, returned to North Brother Island, where she would remain until her death twenty-three years later. People get the impression that Mary was locked up and isolated. This was not the case at all. She had a job on the island and lots of freedom. She was allowed to leave the island on a day pass. "Mary Mallon," Bourdain noted, "during the worst years of the Great Depression, had her own home, a paying job, and the freedom, at least, to visit friends, shop, sightsee as she wished."

In December 1932, she suffered a paralyzing stroke and was bedridden for the rest of her life.

At her death she left cash gifts to friends and St. Luke's Church in the Bronx where her funeral would take place. She also left four thousand dollars to her friend Adelaide Offspring. She paid for her own gravestone, which simply said:

Mary Mallon
Died on November 11, 1938
JESUS MERCY

In death she was not treated kindly, especially by the *New York Times* in their obituary, which appeared on November 13, 1938 and read:

TYPHOID MARY BURIED

NINE PERSONS ATTEND MASS FOR HER AT CHURCH IN THE BRONX

Nine persons attended a requiem mass at St. Luke's Roman Catholic Church . . . yesterday morning for Mary Mallon, the first known typhoid bacilli carrier in America, who died on Friday in Riverside Hospital on North Brother Island. The woman, known as Typhoid Mary, died of a paralytic stroke. Those present, including three women, three men and three small girls, would not identify themselves. The Rev. Vincent S. McCambley was the celebrant. Typhoid Mary had lived on the island since 1907, with the exception of a five-year period from 1910 to 1915, and had received frequent visits from the priests at St. Luke's. Burial was in St. Raymond's Cemetery, the Bronx.

The obit was tiny, just over a hundred words, and referred to her as "Typhoid Mary" and not by her given name. Imagine the uproar if in Richard Nixon's obituary the *Times* referred to him as "Tricky Dick."

Even in death, Mary Mallon could not shake the stigma of being Irish, a woman, and alone in a foreign land.

PART EIGHT

THE SACRED IRISH NEW YORK SALOON, THE LION'S HEAD

WHAT THE PUB IS TO DUBLIN, THE SALOON IS TO NEW YORK

On the first page of *Managing Mailer*, his chronicle of the Mailer-Breslin mayoral campaign of 1969, Joe Flaherty wrote: "The warmth of the room appealed to my Irish heart; it seemed like a blend of wood and whiskey, combining the best aspects of the womb and coffin."

He was talking about a room in Norman Mailer's Brooklyn Heights home, but he could have easily been speaking of the *Real* Irish New York saloon, a stopping point for Irishmen and women between "womb and coffin."

In Ireland the pub can be the center of social intercourse. In the country, it brings a chance for neighbors with distance between them to get together. (I remember sitting in a pub in County Louth one summer evening when the local *Garda* [cop] came by at 11:30 p.m. warning us to move along. A half-hour later he joined us for the rest of the night.) In Dublin City it is not only a place of conversation, but history as well. At the Brazen Head down by the River Liffey, the ghost of Robert Emmet is still in the house plotting revolution. Just off Dame Street at the Stag's Head you can sit in the same snug as Michael Collins did in 1917 when his office was just up the street at #10 Exchequer Street. And, of course, with James Joyce you have a plethora of pubs to visit where he drank, from the Brian Boru in Phibsboro to Davy Byrnes on Duke Street.

THE PUB BECOMES THE SALOON

When the Irish came to New York they brought this love of pubs with them. Only in New York the pub became the "saloon." There have always been neighborhood Irish saloons. And there have been chains also, like the Blarney Stone or the Blarney Rose where cheap beer and whiskey went hand in hand with a thick corned beef sandwich. Scattered around New York there are still some exceptional Irish joints. The Landmark Tavern in the middle of Hell's Kitchen on 11th Avenue has gone from serving Irish longshoremen to a much tonier crowd. P.J. Clarke's has been freed from under the Third Avenue El and *The Lost Weekend* to become a must-see tourist attraction.

Downtown, some of the best drink and grub can be found at Molly's Shebeen on Third Avenue and 22nd Street. (A *"shebeen,"* by the way, is an Irish speakeasy.) A few blocks away on East 18th Street there is the Old Town, which has been doing business at this location since 1892. It started out as a German restaurant (there were a lot of Germans in the Union Square area in the day, with Luchow's famous German restaurant operating on East 14th Street). But today the Old Town is firmly controlled by the Irish, being run by the Meagher family. It was popular with both Seamus Heaney and Frank McCourt back in the day.

You can go all the way to the Battery and have a Guinness at the bustling Dead Rabbit on Water Street, about two blocks from the Staten Island Ferry. Bouncing back uptown you can search for the ghost of Dylan Thomas at his favorite Irish bar, the White Horse. It's been there since 1880 and has gone from longshoremen to yuppies. In the 1950s, the Clancy Brothers and Tommy Makem got their start in the back room.

CHAPTER ONE

THE LION'S HEAD—THE GREAT GOOD PLACE

The Irish bar I spent a lot of my life in is no more. It has been mentioned numerous times in this book, because it was the home base of Frank McCourt, Pete Hamill, and Joe Flaherty. It was located at 59 Christopher Street, and it was called the Lion's Head. It was owned by Wes Joice, an ex-cop, and a Jew from Boston named Al Koblin. It was filled with writers and rogues and it was the best place I've ever drank in. Koblin once keenly observed that it was a place where "the Irish thought like Jews and the Jews drank like Irish."

Maybe the best description of it was from *A Drinking Life* by Pete Hamill, who for years was a regular:

In the beginning, the Head had a square three-sided bar, with dart boards on several walls and no jukebox. The location, a few steps from the Sheridan Square station of the Seventh Avenue IRT, was perfect for newspapermen from the *Post*, the *Times*, and the *Herald Tribune*; the *Village Voice* was then cramped into a few tight rooms upstairs; and within a few weeks of its opening, the joint was a roaring success.

I don't think many New York bars ever had such a glorious mixture of newspapermen, painters, musicians, seamen, ex-communists, priests and nuns, athletes, stockbrokers, politicians, and folksingers, bound together in the leveling democracy of drink. On any given night, the Clancy Brothers would take over the large round table in the back room and the place would be loud with 'The Leaving of Liverpool' and 'Eileen Aroon'; and 'The West's Awake.' Everybody joined in the singing, drinking waterfalls of beer, emptying bottles of whiskey, full of laughter and noise and a sense that I can only describe as joy.

It was as if we'd all been looking for the same Great Good Place and created it here. Not in some foreign land but in the West Village. I was soon one of the regulars, there every night, and sometimes every day. In the growing chaos of the Sixties, the Head became one of the metronomes of my life, as regulating as the deadlines for my column. It was also the place in which everything was forgiven. Lose your job? Betrayed by your wife? Throw up on your shoes? Great: have a drink on us.

WORLD-CLASS BATHROOM GRAFFITI

What do you get when you put a bunch of drunken writers in the bathroom of a saloon like the Lion's Head? How about some of the best, most erudite graffiti in the world.

The Head was many things to many people, but the head at the Head was an everyman's tabloid. Everyone was fodder, be they newspaper icon, presidential candidate, or your average Joe at the bar.

Legend says that on a cold March night in 1968 Bobby Kennedy and his entourage (probably including Head regulars Pete Hamill and Jack Newfield) made their way to the Lion's Head to talk over Kennedy's prospects in the 1968 presidential race. When word of the senator's imminent arrival was made known, it is said that all available hands were sent to paint the door to the men's room and scrub the walls above the urinal of their salacious scribblings.

The Head regulars took their graffiti seriously. Cartoonist Bill Lee recalls that owner Al Koblin once had the bathroom painted and was accused of "book burning!"

The Head has been dead now for nearly a quarter of a century, and the bathroom—the same one—at the Kettle of Fish doesn't have the same buoyancy. As Pete Hamill noted to me on the Head's sacred graffiti, "All buried now, under coats of puritanical paint, awaiting the arrival of some urban archaeologist."

Here's a sampling:

"It's no coincidence that Son of Sam is writing to Jimmy Breslin." And "Profanity is the crutch of the inarticulate motherfucker." Also, "Edith Head gives good wardrobe." —observed Bill Lee

Over the urinal, in two different handwritings:
"Save Soviet Jewry"
"Win Valuable Prizes"—seen by Dermot McEvoy

This graffiti is from the Lion's Head Ladies—you should pardon the appellation!
—Room:

"Fighting for peace is like fucking for chastity!" —Tania Grossinger, author, observed

In one handwriting: "My mother made me a homosexual," and below that, in different handwriting: "If I give her yarn, will she make me one, too?" —Claude Scales glimpsed

The only graffiti I know for certain was in the ladies' jacks was the one that said, "George Kimball is the best fuck in the Lion's Head." I know because when it vanished in one refurbishment I had to put it back on the wall again. —George Kimball, author and sportswriter for the *Boston Herald*

"George Kimball is a great lay!" This appears to be a wonderful advertisement for George until we found out that it was written by George himself. —Al Koblin

"I like grils"
Different handwriting: "You mean girls"
Different handwriting: "What about us grils?" —Raynor Smith ogled

My favorite piece of graffiti. In one script: "I'd like to suck what you have in your hand." Reply, in different script: "You'd suck a wrench? I'm the PLUMBER!" —Pete Hamill surveyed

One of the first things I remember was the graffiti in the ladies' room which read, "Make love, not Irishmen." —Mary Gallagher remembered

"The Clancy Brothers sing like rabbits, drink like birds, and fuck like fish." —Al Koblin recalled

Sartre: to be is to do
Camus: to do is to be
Sinatra: do be do be doooo—Clark Whelton recollected

NO FIGHTING ON THE PEACE BUS

To say that the Lion's Head was a lefty-leaning bar is an understatement. It was populated with former members of the Abraham Lincoln Brigade left over from the Spanish Civil War, labor organizers, Adlai Stevenson Democrats, Robert F. Kennedy partisans (like regulars Pete Hamill and Jack Newfield), and even a few members of the Village Independent Democrats from across the street (among whom was Edward I. Koch, future mayor of New York, who was famous for throwing his dime tips around like they were manhole covers). There were also a lot of World War II and Korea vets weaned on the GI Bill of Rights who knew the folly of war—especially wars ten thousand miles away.

Come November 1969, the patrons from the Head and the 55 Bar next door decided to hire a "Peace Bus" and join the protest festivities down in DC. Now the clientele from the 55 was made up of a lot of 86ers—guys barred for life—from the Lion's Head. As Koblin noted to me, "Mixing Lion's Head and 55 regulars together was like mixing Shiites & Sunnis in the same mosque. A fight was bound to ensue." So, not unlike the scene in *Dr. Strangelove* ("Gentlemen. You can't fight in here. This is the war room!"), guess what happened on the Lion's Head Peace Bus? Yep, a fight broke out, and fifty years later several regulars still nostalgically remember it:

AL KOBLIN, THEN A BARTENDER AT THE HEAD: "Yeah, I was on that peace-march bus. It was all organized by Tony Heyes and had people on it from the Head and from the 55. The bus left Sheridan Square around 2 a.m., so we were all shitfaced. Naturally, a fight broke out. [Newspaperman Dennis] Duggan had been catcalling a lot and finally he got into it with Eddie Callahan, a big guy from the 55. I was sitting near the front and I remember Doug Ireland waddling down the aisle to tell me that someone was beating up on Dennis. I said he probably deserved it, and tried to get back to sleep. The bus was from NJ somewhere and the driver was a tough-looking Jersey guy. He made one announcement before we left: "No smoking dope until we're on the other side of the Chesapeake Bay Bridge.""

GEORGE KIMBALL, A ONE-EYED ROGUE WHO WOULD GO ON TO A NOTABLE SPORTSWRITING CAREER AT THE

BOSTON PHOENIX AND THE BOSTON HERALD: In 1969, I think it was, the Lion's Head chartered a bus to one of the big antiwar demonstrations in Washington. It loaded up outside the bar at the 4 a.m. closing time on Friday night and came back on Sunday. Wes [Joice] contributed a case of whiskey for the journey, and I think several people brought their own. Somewhere in New Jersey there was a fight on the Peace Bus—Dennis Duggan and somebody I didn't know got into a pretty ineffectual fistfight that was quickly broken up but for safety's sake the combatants were banished to different parts of the bus, with Dennis riding up front and his antagonist in the rear.

Further fisticuffs were discouraged when the driver, named Tom, informed the passengers that he was moonlighting and that in his day job he was a New Jersey state trooper. Al Koblin and I were riding in the two front seats and had some interesting conversations with Tom en route. Then as we were approaching the Delaware Memorial Bridge I asked Tom if he still had arrest powers once we were out of his jurisdiction, and he said that there were some circumstances, like if he were in hot pursuit of a speeder, in which he might, but that basically the answer was no.

"Good," I said, so the moment we crossed the Delaware line in the middle of the river I lit a joint. Tom just laughed.

JACK DEACY, FUTURE COLUMNIST FOR THE NEW YORK DAILY NEWS AND PR MAN FOR THE CITY: Unfortunately, I was not on the peace bus because I didn't book early enough. But I was there waving goodbye at 4 a.m. in front of the Lions Head when they pulled away. It was Duggan and Eddie Callahan in the fight, and it might have been Doug Ireland who exclaimed: "No fighting on the peace bus." Doug was very quick. I took the train down and back and went to the Lion's Head where the peace busers had gathered. A few of them, Doug Ireland and John Bergin, got tear gassed by the DC police and that was good for another week's storytelling.

DICK WALTON, AUTHOR OF A DOZEN BOOKS: I was on that bus and remember my amusement, shared by many, that fisticuffs should break out on a peace bus. But it was a bit after the bars closed and a few of the patrons might have been a bit tiddly. It was an extraordinary bus ride. Thousands, maybe tens of thousands, of buses were converging on D.C. and the rest stops were a madhouse. Hundreds of buses and endless lines at the johns, often long lines of women . . . at the men's rooms. And the crowd on the mall was immense: hundreds of thousands. I think some estimates were as high as two million. I can't remember the performers, but there were lots of them, very famous ones. I do remember Peter, Paul & Mary.

CHAPTER TWO
ARCHIE MULLIGAN

THE ENSIGN PULVER OF THE LION'S HEAD AND THE LEGEND OF THE PURPLE PAPAL PAPER

The thing that made "the Head," as the regulars called it, were the bartenders. There was Mike Reardon, Tommy Butler, Tom Dillon, Archie Mulligan, Al Moran, Liam Keaveney, George Wrage, stuttering Shelley Rich, a handsome Greek named Tom Athans, a bearded anthropologist with a doctorate named Richie Schmertzing, a token Englishman, handsome Philip Cain (the Irish Head got its revenge on Cain when he married a tough Republican and equally beautiful person named Sinead from Derry), and a lone Jew named Paul Schiffman who could drink the lot of them under the bar. You might be noticing somewhat of an Irish pattern here. And yet, I think the two that stand out to me after all these years are Archie Mulligan and Tommy Butler.

The first time I came into the Lion's Head in the daytime it was 1973 and Archie Mulligan was behind the stick. (The second time I came into the Head, Don Schlenker, all beard and hair, was behind the bar and I thought, "My God, it's Rasputin!") Everyone called Mulligan "Archie" because he was a dead ringer for the cartoon character. His real name was Paul and his trade—no one in those days working in the bar business in the Village was ever really working in the bar business—was "actor." And, according to Archie, he performed the best Ensign Pulver of all time on stage in the play *Mister Roberts*—Hank Fonda had told him so personally!

Archie may have been a failed actor, but he was one of the great performers of all time. Archie's shift began at noon and by 12:30 you could be sure that he had cracked his first scotch and soda of the day. (The rack scotch was "B&L" and Archie assured me by the second or third you couldn't tell the difference between it and the top-shelf stuff). To say that Archie was a bad bartender is an understatement. (Although I remember him singing his own lyrics to the Platters "The Great Pretender": "Oh, yes, I'm the great bartender," Archie used to sing.) I remember restaurateur Nick Pinto desperately trying to get a drink from him one day and finally pronouncing, "Archie, you couldn't be a bartender if you were a method actor!" And God forbid that the joint should get really busy. One Friday night, the bar was four deep, and I'm begging for a drink. I finally catch Archie's eye. I was hopeful, but Archie reached into the rack and grabbed a B&L for himself, "Bite the bullet!" he admonished.

Archie Mulligan told me that Marilyn Monroe once came on to him and demanded sex. But Archie wouldn't do it. Why not? "I respected Joe DiMaggio too much!" Or was it Arthur Miller?

But maybe my favorite Archie story involves Archie, me, and Al Koblin, the Head's owner. Archie was late for work so many times that I heard Al tell Archie that if he was late one more time it was curtains for him. So one Sunday I come into the bar just after the noon opening. The staff, waitresses, and kitchen help are standing around. "Where's Archie?" I asked. Everyone shook their heads. I told them to cover for him and I'd go over to Cornelia Street and get Archie. I banged on his door and yelled, "Archie!"

"Yo!" returned from the other side of the door.

"Archie, it's 12:30."

"Oh, shit!"

Well, I went back to the Head and at one o'clock Archie came marching in dressed in this old raincoat that Columbo wouldn't stoop to wear. He hung up his coat and got behind the bar. Not two minutes later Al Koblin walked in. "How's it going, Arch?"

"Tip top, Al. Tip Top!"

THE PURPLE PAPAL PAPER

But Archie's tallest tale was that of the Purple Papal Paper. Frederick Exley, author of the acclaimed *A Fan's Notes*, was also a regular when he was in town. Exley, in a piece about the Head that appeared in *GQ Magazine* in January 1991, recalled the infamous PPP:

During that summer [1969] Schlenk and I became friends as indeed I also befriended another of the bartenders, the now-legendary fiery redheaded little pugilist Archie Mulligan, who claimed to have sparred with Ali—not bad for a dude who didn't top the scale at 130. If Schlenk was for a time mysterious about his place in artistic realms, Archie wasn't in the least so, having, he claimed, been granted a Purple Papal Paper. Archie said that once you died, were given last rites and were brought back to life—as Archie had been, not once, not twice, but *three times, mind you*—the archdiocese of New York convened bishops to establish the validity of your claim. If established, no less than Francis Cardinal Spellman laid the Purple Papal Paper on you. According to novelist and regular Lucien K. (*Dress Gray*) Truscott IV, Archie never produced the purple parchment, which didn't deter Wes Joice . . . from grilling Archie on his three deaths and resurrections, trying to catch him in a contradiction. If Wes ever succeeded, Truscott did not record it.[78]

Other regulars at the Head had their own Archie stories. "One night," lawyer Claude Scales told me, "I was sitting next to Arch, who was off duty and thoroughly in his cups. He told me a long, disjointed story, the gist of which seemed to be that, on some occasion, all that stood between him and suicide was a tuna fish sandwich."

"I once got a Temperance lecture from Archie," Bill Lee told me. "It took him twenty minutes and seven shots of Scotch from start to finish."

"You talk about how you had to sit at the kitchen end of the bar to get a drink from Archie," Al Koblin told me. "From an owner's perspective, that was only half the battle. The other half was to get Mulligan to collect for it. One good way to get a free drink was to sit at one end of the bar and have a friend sit at the other end. You order a whiskey. Just as Archie brings it to you, your buddy at the other end yells, 'Hey Arch, gimme a beer.' By the time he pours it and serves it, Archie has forgotten to collect for your whiskey."

And Pete Hamill remembers how Archie served as traffic cop for Head regulars during the Stonewall riot in 1969. "The cops put wooden horses on the sidewalk just before the Head (and the Stonewall)," Hamill told me. "Nobody could get past them from the 7th Avenue end, not even the Lion's Head customers. But Archie negotiated with the cops. He was then stationed at the wooden horse barrier. Saying, 'Okay, Lion's Head guy' or 'She's with us.' And so the bar at the Head ended up full, and mainly laughing, while tumult ruled in the street! Ah, stately unplump Archie."

Archie had some acting jobs, such as on the soap opera *Ryan's Hope*, playing a sanitation worker who drank at the Irish bar. Archie's big break came in 1980 when he moved to California and his brother Jim Mulligan became the executive producer for the sitcom *Flo*, which was a spin-off from the popular *Alice* sitcom starring Linda Lavin. *Flo* starred Polly ("Kiss mah grits!") Holliday and Geoffrey Lewis, and Archie appeared in one episode. We didn't hear much from Archie after that, but he—and the Purple Papal Paper—is still remembered fondly by the surviving Head clientele.

CHAPTER THREE
TOMMY "SUGAR" BUTLER
THE HEAD'S LOVABLE TOUGH GUY
BEHIND THE STICK

The Three Amigos at the Head were Joe Flaherty, Paul Schiffman, and Tommy Butler. They shared a love of the ponies, Irish whiskey, good writing, and laughter. All three were great storytellers, and Butler could certainly hold his own.

Tommy was the son of an IRA man who had to flee County Roscommon during the War of Independence to protect his own health from the Black and Tans. He eventually landed in Washington Heights, where he ran the River Shannon bar. Tommy and his family lived above the bar and he could see the lights of the Polo Grounds from his room. His love for the New York Giants made his bond with Flaherty absolute. Although Flaherty grew up in Brooklyn, he inherited a love for the Giants through his father because John J. McGraw was their manager, proving that the Irish tribal blood is thicker than water.

Tommy was a character out of Shakespeare or O'Casey—bigger than life with a gift of the words, a natural raconteur. He went to Cardinal Hayes High School for a few years before dropping out (not unlike Flaherty) and ended up in the army at Fort Hood, Texas. And that's where some of his funniest stories began. He claimed that once he was in a bar there and all the Texans were bragging about how great Texas was. The New Yorker in Butler was piqued. "If there was a back door to the Alamo," he announced to one and all, "Texas would still be part of Mexico!" Needless to say, a riot broke out with Tommy holding his own.

The reason he could hold his own was because of his massive frame. He was about six feet tall and in his prime probably weighed about 230 pounds. For a man his size, he had the quickness and punch of a middle linebacker, with tremendously quick feet. It was no surprise that he was also a fantastic dancer.

Another of his army stories is just as funny. He was the driver returning to a base in the South with a couple of buddies in a car with New York plates. For some reason, in the middle of Georgia, they were pulled over by a state trooper. "Boys," said the trooper, "no one goes this fast through Georgia." From the back seat came the wise-guy New York reply—"yeah, no one except General Fucking Sherman." Tommy and his pals got to live rent free for the next few days courtesy of the state of Georgia.

THE HOUSE BOOKIE

Tommy not only followed the horses, but made book on them too. Janelle Hardin Morton's family owned two horses, White Star Line and Mrs. Warren, and soon she and Butler became fast friends. "I started placing bets because Tommy was a bookie," she told me. "I don't know if he was a 'real' bookie or if he was just fooling with me. But he loved the track, and he did know the horses. My family had some fillies in those days, doing well at the track. I'd ask Sugar to put twenty dollars across the board on Mrs. Warren in 1977, and he'd do it, and voilà. It would give us a return. My family had a couple of other fillies also, so it was pretty easy for me. I just bet on my own horses, and it was fun for Tommy, because our horses were winning at that time. I do remember that he was thrilled when White Star Line won the Kentucky Oaks, which is the fillies' equivalent to the Derby, and is run the day before. He was thrilled because he won money, too. Sugar had a heart as big as gold, and he was a magnanimous, hearty man."

Tommy was also busy on a Sunday during the football season taking bets on the NFL. He once told me that he got his sobriquet "Sugar" from the guy he was making book with. It may also have had something to do with his girth.

The late George Kimball of the *Boston Herald* told me a funny story about Tommy and his recently acquired Cadillac: "He explained that he'd gotten a great deal on the Caddy, which had been the property of some recently deceased low-level mobster. Either the guy was a friend of Tommy's or maybe owed him money and maybe both, but Tommy ended up with the car at an irresistible price. Only problem was, he said, that everybody in Brooklyn knew the car had belonged to the bookie. 'I drive it through my neighborhood,' Butler said, 'and people come up and start tossing policy slips through the window.'"

LAW AND ORDER AT THE LION'S HEAD

Drinking manners were demanded at the Head. Someone once stated that it was the only bar in New York which had a "preempted strike policy." The dean of discipline was, of course, Tommy Butler. I remember once I was in my cups drinking whiskey silently when this kid next to me yells at Butler. "I want a drink and I want it now! And you have ten seconds to get it to me. One-thousand-one! One-thousand-two!" He didn't make it to "One-thousand-three." All I saw was a blur behind the bar as Butler grabbed the kid by the neck, slammed his head under the bar, then opened the door and threw the perpetrator into the street.

George Kimball recalled a time to me when a customer pulled a knife on him. "With an agility that was absolutely astonishing," Kimball said, "he vaulted straight over the bar, all three hundred pounds of him, jumped right on top of the guy, and started banging his head off the floor. 'You FUCK! You bring a fucking KNIFE in here to use on ME! I oughta stick it up your ass, You FUCK!' I thought he was going to kill the guy. I'm not sure he even actually hit him, but he banged his head off the floor so many times he was like a rag doll by the time Tommy dragged him up he steps and flung him out into the street."

Lawyer and regular Bob Poulson related to me another incident. "Talk about Tommy Sugar moving like a linebacker. One night while he was bartending Tom saw some kid lift a wallet out of a purse slung over a barstool and bolt through the door. Tom took off after him and either Mike Reardon or Wes Joice and I followed sprinting up 7th Avenue. After a couple of blocks Mike, Wes, and I were finished sprinting, but Tom and the kid carried on for a few more blocks. Finally we caught up with them and Sugar had the kid pinned against the wall pleading for his life. Actually Tom never hit him. Just recovered the wallet and scared the kid out of ever showing up at the Head again."

Tommy was also a great supporter of immigrants, perhaps remembering the travails of his immigrant father. Around midnight, several of the South American immigrant dishwashers around the Village would descend on the Head to have a few beers. One of the regulars, a Village bartender, a man not a bigot but trying to make a joke, commented that "they look like they all come from the same side of the mountain."

Tommy immediately came down and snapped, "these kids are trying to support their families back home. Shut the fuck up." Lesson learned.

Angela Derecas was a waitress in Tommy's time. She told me: "But as much as Tommy Sugar could be a linebacker, he was also a graceful soft-shoe, quite the dancer to those swinging jazz standards. And he could also rock-and-roll! I can see him now sa-shaying and be-bopping down the length of the bar to the sounds of 'Electric Avenue.' Remember that juke box tune? 'We're gonna rock down to . . . Electric Avenue . . .

and then I'll take you higher.' That song and dance number was the cue for me and Raya and Sha to meet him at the service bar, coyly smiling, probably needing a bit of the hair of the dog to get us through the shift. We'd present him with a dozen fresh limes, and he would gleefully squeeze them singing and dancing the whole time pouring out those 'fresh-but-for-the-waitresses-only' margaritas! 'And then he took us higher.'"

BELOVED

Tommy was a total gentleman and beloved by men and women alike and capable of great acts of kindness. Writer Maureen O'Brien told me how he found her an apartment. "I first came to the Lion's Head during the Christmas holiday season of 1990. I was then a young editor/reporter at *Publishers Weekly* magazine, in a miserable marriage, and desperate to find an apartment that I could afford on my own, which, on my annual salary of twenty-four thousand, was a tough nut to crack. During my lunch break, I walked down to Bleecker Street to check out an apartment. It was horrible and I was in tears. On my way back to the magazine, I stopped into the Lion's Head for the first time, having read about it in the *Voice* when I was growing up in Detroit. The place was empty, except for Tommy Butler He noticed that I was crying. He was so kind to me. After bending his ear for about thirty minutes, I headed back to work armed with a phone number that Tommy had given to me of a 'super' he knew who had a nice little studio apartment for rent in my price range on nearby Jones Street. My life changed forever. So grateful."

The late Tania Grossinger, author of *Growing Up at Grossinger's*, told me how Tommy saved her from a predator:

I've only recently become a 'fixture' at the Lions Head, a privilege which entitled me to one free drink for every two I pay for. This particular evening Tommy Butler, whose largesse includes both his body and his heart, is behind the bar. The man on my right starts a conversation. He is a physician, he says, and lives around the corner. He has seen me here before. He would like to buy me a drink. I see no reason to refuse and we start a pleasant conversation. Before long he invites me to dinner at Jack Delaney's, a steakhouse across the way. Tommy immediately places his large frame in front of us. "No, she can't." He gives me a stern look. "She's having dinner with me when I finish my shift."

Without as much as an "excuse me," my new friend puts some money on the bar and leaves. Tommy doesn't even wait to be asked for an explanation. "That asshole gave that same I'm a doctor, I live around the corner, I've seen you here before, let's get a bite to another girl last night. She crawled back just before we closed, her face a bloody pulp. Someone took her to St. Vincent's, but she didn't want to press charges. Just now Al [Koblin] alerted me that he was the same guy. Sorry to have to screw up your evening." It was the first, but thankfully, not my last time at the Lion's Head.

Tommy's daughter Laura told me how her father introduced her to Judy Collins. "'Send in the Clowns' reminds me of when my father brought me to see Judy Collins at the Garden State Arts Center sometime in the early 70s. It's now the PNC Bank Center if you've never been, it's an amphitheater and small enough to be intimate. My father was always bragging about Judy Collins and I fell in love with her in the 70s. . . . Who didn't! She's beautiful with those big eyes and that *voice*!! He said he knew her and as a teen, I, of course, rolled my eyes at one of his far-fetched stories. But when he said she gave him tickets and to come backstage after the concert I knew it wasn't another story. I got to meet Judy Collins and she gave me a guitar pick and a signed picture. I was star-struck."

SUGAR MEETS HIS END

Tommy died on a weekend in the early fall of 1994. We knew something was wrong when several friends couldn't reach him to bet on the NFL games. Sometime before that he had called me up and asked to borrow $175. I didn't have it, so I had to take it off one of my credit cards.

In those days, the Head had a pool for Monday Night Football. I was sitting home one Tuesday afternoon when the phone rang. It was Tommy's friend and fellow barman Paul Schiffman. "Why don't you come on down?" he asked me.

"I'm broke," I told him.

"No, you're not. You won the football pool."

I headed down to the Head in high spirits. Shifty gave me the envelope. In it was exactly $175.

Thanks, Sugar. I still miss you.

EPILOGUE

A WORLD-FAMOUS AUTHOR WALL

The Head became famous for its wall full of framed book jackets. The first jacket I remember was Fred Exley's *Pages from A Cold Island*, his follow-up to *A Fan's Notes*, one of the great works of the 1960s. It hung alone, scotch-taped to the wall.

Soon it was joined by others and Al Koblin decided to buy picture frames at Lamston's and do a proper job of it. Over the years, the jackets went up: Pete Hamill's *The Gift*, Martin Cruz Smith's *Gorky Park*, Vince Patrick's *The Pope of Greenwich Village*, *Report from Engine Company 82* by Dennis Smith, Tania Grossinger's great piece of Americana, *Growing Up at Grossinger's*, *Air Time* by Gary Paul Gates, and Max Gordon's wonderful *Live at the Village Vanguard*. There were so many more it's hard to keep track: Denis Hamill, Quentin Crisp, Vic Ziegel, David Bradley, Malcolm Braly, David Markson, Joe Flaherty, Bob Drury, Donald Westlake, and Alice Denham, just to name a few.

The last jacket to go up, just before the Head closed in 1996, was Frank McCourt's *Angela's Ashes*. "He was indeed very proud to have *Angela's Ashes* go up on the wall," Frank's widow, Ellen, told me. "Mike Reardon called him down to the bar and didn't tell him why. They had a drink together and Mike said, 'turn around' and there was the framed jacket on the wall. He nearly wept."

I don't think Lanford Wilson ever had a jacket up on the wall because he was a playwright, but he was a delight. During the 1970s and '80s Lanford had a string of successful plays on Broadway. He had a devoted following of suburban ladies who read that he drank at the Head and they would often descend on the bar en masse after a Saturday matinee. I remember several Saturdays when they bravely marched into the Head in the middle of the baseball season when the raucousness was at its zenith. They spied Lanford, engulfed him, and Lanford, ever the gentleman, gave them his time and bought them drinks until they left.

It was often said that writers went to Elaine's uptown to be seen and that they came to the Head after working all day at their craft. There aren't many bars that could boast of having two Pulitzer Prize–winning authors on their daily roster: Lanford Wilson for *Talley's Folly* and Frank McCourt for *Angela's Ashes*. It appears that genius does, sometimes, come out of a bottle.

OUR REVELS NOW ARE ENDED

The Lion's Head closed on October 12, 1996—I often point out it died on Columbus Day, not on St. Patrick's Day—and a way of drinking and thinking had ended in New York. There were many reasons for its demise, from high rents to a change in the way people thought and acted. Today, for some reason, people would rather squawk on their cell phones or social media than talk face-to-face. Back then it was mouth-to-mouth combat. The gentrification of Greenwich Village did not help. Young people, because of high rents, could not come to Greenwich Village anymore. They would head to places like Williamsburg to chase their dreams—until the grim reaper known as gentrification followed. A lot of people with money came to the Village for the color provided by the locals. What they discovered was that they evicted the people out of the Village that they wanted to drink with.

"We were in Germany when the bar closed," Ellen McCourt told me, "and Frank received a call in our hotel room from the *New York Times* asking for a comment. He waxed lyrical about the great times he had had there and groused about how, as a teacher, he couldn't hang out all night like all the writers who didn't have to get up and stand in front of thirty-five pimply-faced teenagers."

You won't see any more Joe Flahertys, Frank McCourts, Tania Grossingers, Archie Mulligans, Paul Schiffmans, or Tommy Butlers in the Village because they just can't afford it. Rogues with rent-controlled apartments have been replaced by trust-fund babies in co-ops. But for one shining moment they were all there. A lot of the Head regulars are dead. Apparently, time doesn't stand still for anything, including the regulars of the sacred saloon.

Sometimes when I return to the Head—now the Kettle of Fish, the foremost Green Bay Packer Bar in New York City, run by an Irishman from Milwaukee, Patrick Daley—I can still feel my friends and I swear I can hear Flaherty making people roar with laughter and Nick Pinto shouting out "Good gracious said Sister Ignatius, I'm shocked that the Bishop has piles" and Archie telling one of his outrageous stories. Their ghosts are still there, but these are happy ghosts, full of life and mirth.

I think the best epitaph of the Lion's Head was written by Tom Paxton with his wonderful song, "Comedians and Angels," which sums up the legacy of the Head:

Comedians and angels, I miss my friends tonight

And like Tom Paxton, I, too, miss my friends tonight.

ENDNOTES

1. https://en.wikisource.org/wiki/Speech_fro m_the_Dock_(Emmet).
2. Conor O'Clery, *Daring Diplomacy: Clintons Secret Search for Peace in Ireland* (Boulder: Roberts Rinehart Publishers, 1997), 198.
3. George Carlin, *Last Words: A Memoir* (New York: Free Press/Simon & Schuster, 2009), 27.
4. American Masters, *Augustus Saint-Gaudens: Master of American Sculpture*. First aired on PBS on June 23, 1986.
5. Brian Maye, "An Irishman's Diary," *The Irish Times*, Tue, Aug 9, 2011, https://www.irish-times.com/opinion/an-irishman-s-diary-1.593341.
6. The Clancy Brothers and Tommy Makem with a foreword by Pete Hamill, *The Irish Songbook* (New York: Collier Books, 1971), iv.
7. Liam Clancy, *The Mountain of the Women: Memoirs of an Irish Troubadour* (New York: Doubleday, 2002), 279.
8. Bruce Weber, "Liam Clancy, Last of the Folk Group, Dies at 74," obituary of Liam Clancy, *New York Times*, December 5, 2009: https://www.nytimes.com/2009/12/05/arts/music/05clancy.html?searchResultPosition=1
9. Larry Kirwan, *Green Suede Shoes: An Irish-American Odyssey* (New York: Thunder Mouth Press/Avalon, 2005), 5.
10. Terry Golway, *So Others Might Live: A History of New York's Bravest, The FDNY from 1700 to the Present* (New York: Basic Books, 2002), 171.
11. Terry Golway, *Machine Made: Tammany Hall and the Creation of Modern American Politics* (New York: Liveright Publishing/W.W. Norton, 2014), 194.
12. David Von Drehle, *Triangle: The Fire That Changed America* (New York: Atlantic Monthly Press, 2003), 28.
13. Emmet O'Connor, *James Larkin* (Radical Irish Lives Series: Cork University Press, 2002), 5.
14. O'Connor, *James Larkin*, 12.
15. David Krause, *Sean O'Casey and His World* (London: Thames and Hudson Ltd, 1976), 12.
16. O'Connor, *James Larkin*, 51.
17. Terry Golway, *Irish Rebel: John Devoy and America's Fight for Ireland's Freedom* (New York: St. Martin's Press, 1998), 209.
18. O'Connor, *James Larkin*, 56.
19. Lorcan Collins, *16 Lives: James Connolly* (Dublin: The O'Brien Press, 2012), 64.
20. Collins, *16 Lives: James Connolly*, 157.
21. O'Connor, *James Larkin*, 12.
22. O'Connor, *James Larkin*, 199–200.
23. O'Connor, *James Larkin*, 221.
24. Helen Litton, *16 Lives: Thomas Clark* (Dublin: The O'Brien Press, 2014), 144.
25. Lorcan Collins, *16 Lives: James Connolly*, 266.
26. Shirley Quill, *Mike Quill: Himself* (Greenwich: Devin-Adair, Publishers, 1985), 27.
27. Quill, *Mike Quill: Himself*, 307.

28. Mike Quill Editorial, *New York Times*, January 29, 1965: https://timesmachine.nytimes
    .com/timesmachine/1966/01/29/79294736.html?pageNumber=26

29. Angela Bourke, *Maeve Brennan: Homesick at The New Yorker* (New York: Counterpoint/
    Perseus, 2004), 131.

30. Barney Rosset, *My Life in Publishing and How I Fought Censorship* (New York: OR
    Books, 2016), 13.

31. Richard Seaver, *The Tender Hour of Twilight: Paris in the '50s, New York in the '60s: A
    Memoir of Publishing's Golden Age* (New York: Farrar, Straus and Giroux, 2012), 323.

32. J. B. Lyons, *Oliver St. John Gogarty: The Man of Many Talents: A Biography* (Dublin:
    Blackwater, 1980), 283.

33. Ulick O'Connor, *The Times I've Seen: Oliver St. John Gogarty: A Biography* (New York:
    Ivan Obolensky, Inc., 1963), 321.

34. Deirdre Bair, *Samuel Beckett: A Biography* (New York: Summit Books/Simon & Schus-
    ter, 1978), 266.

35. Brendan Behan, *Brendan Behan's New York with drawings by Paul Hogarth.* (Boston:
    Little, Brown and Company, 1964), 12, 42.

36. Rae Jeffs, *Brendan Behan: Man and Showman* (London: Corgi, 1968), 144.

37. "Brendan Behan Dies in Dublin," obituary of Brendan Behan, *New York Times*, March
    21, 1964: https://www.nytimes.com/1964/03/21/brendan-behan-dies-in-dublin.
    html?- searchResultPosition=1

38. Linda Leavell, *Holding on Upside Down: The Life and Work of Marianne Moore* (New
    York: Farrar, Straus and Giroux, 2013), 13.

39. Jimmy Breslin, *Can't Anybody Here Play This Game?* (Chicago: Ivan R. Dee, Publisher,
    2003), 117.

40. Jimmy Breslin, *How the Good Guys Finally Won: Notes from an Impeachment Summer*
    (New York: Viking Press, 1975), 1.

41. John Hockenberry, "Did 'Son of Sam' Really Act Alone?", NBC News, July 2, 2004:
    http://www.nbcnews.com/id/5351509/ns/dateline_nbc-newsmakers/t/did-son-sam-really
    -act-alone/

42. Jimmy Breslin, *The World According to Jimmy Breslin* (New York: Ticknor & Fields,
    1984), "Por Unas Horas," 51.

43. Joe Flaherty, *Chez Joey: The World of Joe Flaherty* (New York: Coward, McCann &
    Geoghegan, Inc., 1974), xiii.

44. George Washington Plunkitt on New York City as a state, Libquotes: https://libquotes
    .com/george-washington-plunkitt/quotes/city

45. Christopher Lehman-Haupt, "The Last Hurrah? Did Somebody Whisper 'Hurrah'?"
    review of *Managing Mailer* by Joe Flaherty, *New York Times*, May 20, 1970.

46. Joe Flaherty, *Chez Joey: The World of Joe Flaherty* (New York: Coward, McCann &
    Geoghegan, Inc., 1974).

47. Flaherty, *Chez Joey*, 205.

48. Frank McCourt, *Angela's Ashes* (Simon & Schuster, 1996), 11.

49. Jim Dwyer, "A Marriage that Made a Masterpiece Appear," *New York Times*, July 25,
    2009: https://www.nytimes.com/2009/07/26/nyregion/26about.html.

50. John Loughery, *Dagger John: Archbishop John Hughes and the Making of Irish America*
    (Ithaca: Cornell University Press, 2018), 31.

51. Richard Shaw, *Dagger John: The Unquiet Life and Times of Archbishop John Hughes of
    New York* (New York: Paulist Press, 1977), 123.

52. Shaw, *Dagger John*, 197.

53. Shaw, *Dagger John*, 365.

54. Peter Quinn, *Banished Children of Eve: A Novel of Civil War in New York* (New York: Overlook Press, 1994), 564.

55. Dorothy Day: *The Long Loneliness* (New York: Harper & Row, 1952), 205.

56. Maurice Isserman: *The Other American: The Life of Michael Harrington* (New York: Public Affairs, 2000), 83.

57. Isserman, *The Other American*, 83.

58. Lucian K. Truscott IV: "I Was Groped by a Man Called 'Mary' " Salon, February 9, 2019: https://www.salon.com/2019/02/09/i-was-groped-by-a-man-called-mary-the-world -changes-but-not-the-catholic-church/

59. John Cooney: *The American Pope: The Life and Times of Francis Cardinal Spellman* (New York: Times Books, 1984, 90.

60. Michael Daly: *The Book of Mychal: The Surprising Life and Heroic Death of Father Mychal Judge* (New York: Thomas Dunne Books/St. Martin's Press, 2008), 11.

61. Golway, *So Others Might Live*, 1.

62. *Saint of 9/11: The True Story of Father Mychal Judge* (Hart Sharp Video, 2006)

63. Ruth Graham: "Could Father Mychal Judge be the First Gay Saint?", September 11, 2017 (https://slate.com/news-and-politics/2017/09/father-mychal-judge-was-a-9-11 -hero-could-he-also-become-the-first-gay-saint.html)

64. Johann Christoph Arnold, Foreword by Steven McDonald, *Why* Forgive? (Walden, NY: Plough Publishing House, 2010)? 175.

65. Arnold, *Why Forgive?*, 176.

66. Steven McDonald and Patti Ann McDonald with E. J. Kahn III, *The Steven McDonald Story* (New York: Donald I. Fine, Inc. 1989), 225.

67. Terry Golway, *Machine Made*, 306.

68. Hans Holzer, *Ghosts: True Encounters with the World Beyond* (New York: Black Dog & Leventhal Publishers, 1997), 456-7.

69. Herbert Mitgang, *Once Upon a Time in New York: Jimmy Walker, Franklin Roosevelt, and the Last Great Battle of the Jazz Age* (New York: Cooper Square Press, 2003), 61.

70. George Washington Plunkitt on New York City as a state: https://libquotes.com/ george-washington-plunkitt/quotes/city

71. Dennis Duggan, contributor: *The Irish in America*, edited by Michael Coffey with text by Terry Golway (New York: Hyperion/Disney, 1997), 126.

72. C. J. Sullivan, "Family Man," *New York Post*, January 21, 2008: https://nypost. com/2008/01/21/family-man/

73. Jean H. Baker, *Margaret Sanger: A Life of Passion* (Hill & Wang/Farrar, Straus and Giroux, 2011), 9.

74. Baker, *Margaret Sanger*, 62.

75. "Margaret Sanger Is Dead at 82," Margaret Sanger obituary, *New York Times*, September 7, 1966: https://www.nytimes.com/1966/09/07/archives/margaret-sanger-is-dead-at -82-led-campaign-for-birth-control-mrs.html

76. Anthony Bourdain, *Typhoid Mary: An Urban Historical* (New York: Bloomsbury, 2001), 17.

77. Bourdain *Typhoid Mary*, 107–108.

78. Frederick Exley, "The Last Great Saloon," *GQ Magazine*, December 1990, 291–332.